Parallel Programming with Microsoft® Visual Studio® 2010 Step by Step

Donis Marshall

Published with the authorization of Microsoft Corporation by:
O'Reilly Media, Inc.
1005 Gravenstein Highway North
Sebastopol, California 95472

ISBN: 978-0-7356-4060-3

1 2 3 4 5 6 7 8 9 QG 6 5 4 3 2 1

Printed and bound in the United States of America.

Microsoft Press books are available through booksellers and distributors worldwide. If you need support related to this book, email Microsoft Press Book Support at mspinput@microsoft.com. Please tell us what you think of this book at http://www.microsoft.com/learning/booksurvey.

Acquisitions and Developmental Editors: Russell Jones and Devon Musgrave
Production Editor: Holly Bauer
Editorial Production: Online Training Solutions, Inc.
Technical Reviewer: Ashish Ghoda
Copyeditor: Kathy Krause, Online Training Solutions, Inc.
Proofreader: Jaime Odell, Online Training Solutions, Inc.
Indexer: Fred Brown
Cover Design: Twist Creative • Seattle
Cover Composition: Karen Montgomery
Illustrator: Jeanne Craver, Online Training Solutions, Inc.

This book is dedicated to my mother, who is extremely proud that I am a published author.
She even gives my books to friends at her church—even though none of them are programmers.
But that does not matter. Thanks, Mom!

Contents at a Glance

Table of Contents

What do you think of this book? We want to hear from you!

Microsoft is interested in hearing your feedback so we can continually improve our
books and learning resources for you. To participate in a brief online survey, please visit:

microsoft.com/learning/booksurvey

What do you think of this book? We want to hear from you!

Microsoft is interested in hearing your feedback so we can continually improve our books and learning resources for you. To participate in a brief online survey, please visit:

microsoft.com/learning/booksurvey

Foreword

It started with the hardware, tubes, and wires that didn't do anything overtly exciting. Then software gave hardware the capability to do things—exciting, wonderful, confounding things. My first software program was written to wait in queue for a moment of attention from *the* one computer in school, after it finished the payroll, scheduling, and grading for the entire school system. That same year, personal computing was born, putting affordable computational capabilities—previously the purview of academia, banks, and governments—in businesses and homes. A whole new world, and later a career, was revealed to me one delicious line of code at a time, no waiting required. As soon as a program was written, I could celebrate the outcome. So another program was written, then another, and another.

We learn linear solutions to math problems early in life, so the sequencing concept of "do this, then that" is the zeitgeist of programmers worldwide. Because computers no longer share the same computational bias of the human brain, bridging the gap between linear, sequential programming to a design that leverages parallel processing requires new approaches. In order to produce fast, secure, reliable, world-ready software, programmers need new tools to supplement their current approach. To that end, *Parallel Programming with Microsoft Visual Studio 2010 Step by Step* was written.

Donis Marshall has put together his expertise with a narrative format that provides a mix of foundational knowledge and practical decision-making criteria for unleashing the capabilities of parallel programming. Building on the backdrop of six previous programming titles, real-world experience in a wide range of industries, and the authorship of dozens of programming courses, Donis provides foundational knowledge to developers new to parallel programming concepts. The *Step by Step* format, combined with Donis's information-dissemination style, provides continual value to readers as they grow in experience and capability.

The world of parallel programming is being brought to the desktop of every developer who has the desire to more fully utilize the architectures of modern computers (in all forms). Standing on the shoulders of giants, the Microsoft .NET Framework 4 continues its tradition of systematically providing new capabilities to developers and system engineers. These new tools provide great capabilities and a great challenge for how and where to best use them. *Parallel Programming with Microsoft Visual Studio 2010 Step by Step* ensures that programmers worldwide can effectively add parallel programming to their design portfolios.

Tracy Monteith

Introduction

Parallel programming truly redefines the programming model for multicore architecture, which has become commonplace. For this reason, parallel programming has been elevated to a core technology in the Microsoft .NET Framework 4. In this version of the .NET Framework, the Task Parallel Library (TPL) and the *System.Threading.Tasks* namespace contain the parallel programming implementation. Microsoft Visual Studio 2010 has also been enhanced and now includes several features to aid in creating and maintaining parallel applications. If you are a Microsoft developer looking to decompose your application into parallel tasks that execute over separate processor cores, then Visual Studio 2010 and the TPL are the tools you need.

Parallel Programming with Microsoft Visual Studio 2010 Step by Step provides an organized walkthrough of using Visual Studio 2010 to create parallel applications. It discusses the TPL and parallel programming concepts in considerable detail; however, this book is still introductory—it covers the basics of each realm of parallel programming, such as task and data parallelism. Although the book does not provide exhaustive coverage of every parallel programming topic, it does offer essential guidance in using the concepts of parallel programming.

In addition to its coverage of core parallel programming concepts, the book discusses concurrent collections and thread synchronization, and it guides you in maintaining and debugging parallel applications by using Visual Studio. Beyond the explanatory content, most chapters include step-by-step examples and downloadable sample projects that you can explore for yourself.

Who Should Read This Book

This book exists to help Microsoft Visual Basic and Microsoft Visual C# developers understand the core concepts of parallel programming and related technologies. It is especially useful for programmers looking to take advantage of multicore architecture, which is the current trend in the industry. Readers should have a basic familiarity with the .NET Framework but do not have to have any prior experience with parallel programming. The book is also useful for those already familiar with the basics of parallel programming who are interested in the newest features of the TPL.

Who Should Not Read This Book

Not every book is aimed at every possible audience. Authors must make assumptions about the knowledge level of the audience to avoid either boring more advanced readers or losing less advanced readers.

Assumptions

This book expects that you have at least a minimal understanding of .NET development and object-oriented programming concepts. Although the TPL is available to most, if not all, .NET Framework 4 language platforms, this book includes examples only in C#. However, the examples should be portable to Visual Basic .NET with minimal changes. If you have not yet picked up either of these languages, consider reading John Sharp's *Microsoft Visual C# 2010 Step by Step* (Microsoft Press, 2010) or Michael Halvorson's *Microsoft Visual Basic 2010 Step by Step* (Microsoft Press, 2010).

With a heavy focus on concurrent programming concepts, this book also assumes that you have a basic understanding of threads and thread synchronization concepts. To go beyond this book and expand your knowledge of threading, consider reading Jeffrey Richter's *CLR via C#* (Microsoft Press, 2010).

Organization of This Book

This book is divided into seven chapters, each of which focuses on a different aspect or technology related to parallel programming.

- Chapter 1, "Introduction to Parallel Programming," introduces the fundamental concepts of parallel programming.

- Chapter 2, "Task Parallelism," focuses on creating parallel iterations and refactoring sequential loops into parallel tasks.

- Chapter 3, "Data Parallelism," focuses on creating parallel tasks from separate operations.

- Chapter 4, "PLINQ," is an overview of parallel programming using Language-Integrated Query (LINQ).

- Chapter 5, "Concurrent Collections," explains how to use concurrent collections, such as *ConcurrentBag* and *ConcurrentQueue*.

- Chapter 6, "Customization," demonstrates techniques for customizing the TPL.

- Chapter 7, "Reports and Debugging," shows how to debug and maintain parallel applications and rounds out the full discussion of parallel programming.

Finding Your Best Starting Point in This Book

The different sections of *Parallel Programming with Microsoft Visual Studio 2010 Step by Step* cover a wide range of technologies and concepts associated with parallel programming in the .NET Framework. Depending on your needs and your current level of familiarity with parallel programming in the .NET Framework 4, you might want to focus on specific areas of the book. Use the following table to determine how best to proceed through the book.

If you are	Follow these steps
Knowledgeable about the concepts of parallel programming	Start with Chapter 2 and read the remainder of the book.
Familiar with parallel extensions in the .NET Framework 3.5	Read Chapter 1 if you need a refresher on the core concepts.
	Skim Chapters 2 and 3 for the basics of Task and Data Parallelism.
	Read Chapters 3 through 7 to explore the details of the TPL.
Interested in LINQ data providers	Read Chapter 4 on PLINQ and Chapter 7.
Interested in customizing the TPL	Read Chapter 6 on customization.

Most of the book's chapters include hands-on samples that let you try out the concepts just learned. No matter which sections you choose to focus on, be sure to download and install the sample applications on your system.

Conventions and Features in This Book

This book presents information using conventions designed to make the information readable and easy to follow.

- Each exercise consists of a series of tasks, presented as numbered steps listing each action you must take to complete the exercise.

- Most exercise results are shown in a console window so you can compare your results to the expected results.

- Complete code for each exercise appears at the end of each exercise. Most of the code is also available in downloadable form. (See "Code Samples" later in this Introduction for instructions on finding and downloading the code.)

- Keywords, such as *System.Threading.Tasks*, are italicized throughout the book.

- Each chapter also concludes with a Quick Reference section reviewing the important details of the chapter and a Summary overview of the chapter contents.

System Requirements

You will need the following hardware and software to complete the practice exercises in this book:

- One of the following: Windows XP with Service Pack 3, Windows Server 2003 with Service Pack 2, Windows Vista with Service Pack 1 or later, Windows Server 2008, Windows Server 2008 R2, Windows 7, or Windows 7 SP1.

- Visual Studio 2010, any edition. (Multiple downloads might be required if you are using Express Edition products.)

- A computer with a 1.6-GHz or faster processor (2 GHz recommended).

- 1 GB (32-bit) or 2 GB (64-bit) RAM (Add 1 GB if running in a virtual machine).

- 3.5 GB of available hard disk space.

- A 5400-RPM hard disk drive.

- A DVD-ROM drive (if installing Visual Studio from DVD).

- An Internet connection to download the code for the exercises.

Depending on your Windows configuration, you might require Local Administrator rights to install or configure Visual Studio 2010.

Code Samples

Most of the chapters in this book include exercises that let you interactively try out new material learned in the main text. All the example projects, in both their pre-exercise and post-exercise formats, are available for download from the web:

http://go.microsoft.com/FWLink/?Linkid=222678

Click the Examples link on that page. When a list of files appears, locate and download the Parallel_Programming_Sample_Code.zip file.

 Note In addition to the code samples, your system should have Visual Studio 2010 installed.

Installing the Code Samples

Follow these steps to install the code samples on your computer so that you can use them with the exercises in this book.

1. Unzip the Parallel_Programming_Sample_Code.zip file that you downloaded from the book's website.

2. If prompted, review the displayed end user license agreement. If you accept the terms, select the Accept option, and then click Next.

 Note If the license agreement doesn't appear, you can access it from the same webpage from which you downloaded the Parallel_Programming_Sample_Code.zip file.

How to Access Your Online Edition Hosted by Safari

The voucher bound in to the back of this book gives you access to an online edition of the book. (You can also download the online edition of the book to your own computer; see the next section.)

To access your online edition, do the following:

1. Locate your voucher inside the back cover, and scratch off the metallic foil to reveal your access code.

2. Go to *http://microsoftpress.oreilly.com/safarienabled*.

3. Enter your 24-character access code in the Coupon Code field under Step 1.

(Please note that the access code in this image is for illustration purposes only.)

4. Click the CONFIRM COUPON button.

   A message will appear to let you know that the code was entered correctly. If the code was not entered correctly, you will be prompted to re-enter the code.

5. In this step, you'll be asked whether you're a new or existing user of Safari Books Online. Proceed either with Step 5A or Step 5B.

   5A. If you already have a Safari account, click the EXISTING USER – SIGN IN button under Step 2.

   5B. If you are a new user, click the NEW USER – FREE ACCOUNT button under Step 2.

   - You'll be taken to the "Register a New Account" page.

   - This will require filling out a registration form and accepting an End User Agreement.

   - When complete, click the CONTINUE button.

6. On the Coupon Confirmation page, click the My Safari button.

7. On the My Safari page, look at the Bookshelf area and click the title of the book you want to access.

How to Download the Online Edition to Your Computer

In addition to reading the online edition of this book, you can also download it to your computer. First, follow the steps in the preceding section. After Step 7, do the following:

1. On the page that appears after Step 7 in the previous section, click the Extras tab.

2. Find "Download the complete PDF of this book," and click the book title.

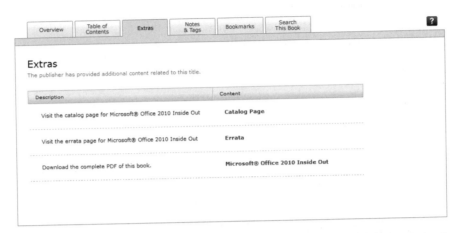

A new browser window or tab will open, followed by the File Download dialog box.

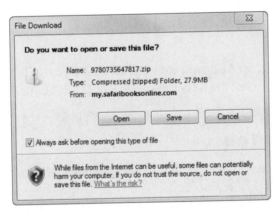

3. Click Save.

4. Choose Desktop and click Save.

5. Locate the .zip file on your desktop. Right-click the file, click Extract All, and then follow the instructions.

Note If you have a problem with your voucher or access code, please contact *mspbooksupport@ oreilly.com*, or call 800-889-8969, where you'll reach O'Reilly Media, the distributor of Microsoft Press books.

Acknowledgments

I'd like to thank the following people: Russell Jones, for his infinite patience. Ben Ryan, for yet another wonderful opportunity to write for Microsoft Press. Devon Musgrave, for his initial guidance. The support of my friends: Paul, Lynn, Cynthia, Cindy, and others. Adam, Kristen, and Jason, who are the bright stars in the universe.

Errata and Book Support

We've made every effort to ensure the accuracy of this book and its companion content. Any errors that have been reported since this book was published are listed on our Microsoft Press site at oreilly.com:

http://go.microsoft.com/FWLink/?Linkid=223769

If you find an error that is not already listed, you can report it to us through the same page.

If you need additional support, email Microsoft Press Book Support at *mspinput@microsoft .com*.

Please note that product support for Microsoft software is not offered through the addresses above.

We Want to Hear from You

At Microsoft Press, your satisfaction is our top priority, and your feedback our most valuable asset. Please tell us what you think of this book at:

http://www.microsoft.com/learning/booksurvey

The survey is short, and we read every one of your comments and ideas. Thanks in advance for your input!

Stay in Touch

Let's keep the conversation going! We're on Twitter: *http://twitter.com/MicrosoftPress*

Chapter 1
Introduction to Parallel Programming

After completing this chapter, you will be able to

- Explain parallel programming goals, various hardware architectures, and basic concepts of concurrent and parallel programming.

- Define the relationship between parallelism and performance.

- Calculate speedup with Amdahl's Law.

- Calculate speedup with Gustafson's Law.

- Recognize and apply parallel development design patterns.

Parallel programming will change the computing universe for personal computers. That is a grandiose statement! However, it reflects the potential impact as parallel computing moves from the halls of academia, science labs, and larger systems to your desktop. The goal of parallel programming is to improve performance by optimizing the use of the available processor cores with parallel execution of cores. This goal becomes increasingly important as the trend of constantly increasing processor speed slows.

Moore's Law predicted the doubling of transistor capacity per square inch of integrated circuit every two years. Gordon Moore made this proclamation in the mid-1960s and predicted that the trend would continue at least 10 years, but Moore's Law has actually held true for nearly 50 years. Moore's prediction is often interpreted to mean that processor speed would double every couple of years. However, cracks were beginning to appear in the foundation of Moore's Law. Developers now have to find other means of satisfying customer demands for quicker applications, additional features, and greater scope. Parallel programming is one solution. In this way, Moore's Law will continue into the indefinite future.

Microsoft recognizes the vital role of parallel programming for the future. That is the reason parallel programming was promoted from an extension to a core component of the common language runtime (CLR). New features have been added to the Microsoft .NET Framework 4 and Microsoft Visual Studio 2010 in support of parallel programming. This is in recognition of the fact that parallel programming is quickly becoming mainstream technology with the increased availability of multicore processors in personal computers.

Parallel code is undoubtedly more complicated than the sequential version of the same application or new application development. New debugging windows were added to Visual Studio 2010 specifically to help maintain and debug parallel applications. Both the

Parallel Tasks and Parallel Stacks windows help you interpret an application from the context of a parallel execution and tasks. For performance tuning, the Visual Studio Profiler and Concurrency Visualizer work together to analyze a parallel application and present graphs and reports to help developers isolate potential problems.

Parallel programming is a broad technology domain. Some software engineers have spent their careers researching and implementing parallel code. Fortunately, the .NET Framework 4 abstracts much of this detail, allowing you to focus on writing a parallel application for a business or personal requirement while abstracting much of the internal details. However, it can be quite helpful to understand the goals, constraints, and underlying motivations of parallel programming.

Multicore Computing

In the past, software developers benefitted from the continual performance gains of new hardware in single-core computers. If your application was slow, just wait—it would soon run faster because of advances in hardware performance. Your application simply rode the wave of better performance. However, you can no longer depend on consistent hardware advancements to assure better-performing applications!

As performance improvement in new generations of processor cores has slowed, you now benefit from the availability of multicore architecture. This allows developers to continue to realize increases in performance and to harness that speed in their applications. However, it does require somewhat of a paradigm shift in programming, which is the purpose of this book.

At the moment, dual-core and quad-core machines are the de facto standard. In North America and other regions, you probably cannot (and would not want to) purchase a single-core desktop computer at a local computer store today.

Single-core computers have constraints that prevent the continuation of the performance gains that were possible in the past. The primary constraint is the correlation of processor speed and heat. As processor speed increases, heat increases disproportionally. This places a practical threshold on processor speed. Solutions have not been found to significantly increase computing power without the heat penalty. Multicore architecture is an alternative, where multiple processor cores share a chip die. The additional cores provide more computing power without the heat problem. In a parallel application, you can leverage the multicore architecture for potential performance gains without a corresponding heat penalty.

Multicore personal computers have changed the computing landscape. Until recently, single-core computers have been the most prevalent architecture for personal computers. But that is changing rapidly and represents nothing short of the next evolutionary step in computer architecture for personal computers. The combination of multicore architecture and parallel programming will propagate Moore's Law into the foreseeable future.

With the advent of techniques such as Hyper-Threading Technology from Intel, each physical core becomes two or potentially more virtual cores. For example, a machine with four physical cores appears to have eight logical cores. The distinction between physical and logical cores is transparent to developers and users. In the next 10 years, you can expect the number of both physical and virtual processor cores in a standard personal computer to increase significantly.

Multiple Instruction Streams/Multiple Data Streams

In 1966, Michael Flynn proposed a taxonomy to describe the relationship between concurrent instruction and data streams for various hardware architectures. This taxonomy, which became known as Flynn's taxonomy, has these categories:

- **SISD (Single Instruction Stream/Single Data Stream)**   This model has a single instruction stream and data stream and describes the architecture of a computer with a single-core processor.

- **SIMD (Single Instruction Stream/Multiple Data Streams)**   This model has a single instruction stream and multiple data streams. The model applies the instruction stream to each of the data streams. Instances of the same instruction stream can run in parallel on multiple processor cores, servicing different data streams. For example, SIMD is helpful when applying the same algorithm to multiple input values.

- **MISD (Multiple Instruction Streams/Single Data Stream)**   This model has multiple instruction streams and a single data stream and can apply multiple parallel operations to a single data source. For example, this model could be used for running various decryption routines on a single data source.

- **MIMD (Multiple Instruction Streams/Multiple Data Streams)**   This model has both multiple instruction streams and multiple data streams. On a multicore computer, each instruction stream runs on a separate processor with independent data. This is the current model for multicore personal computers.

The MIMD model can be refined further as either Multiple Program/Multiple Data (MPMD) or Single Program/Multiple Data (SPMD). Within the MPMD subcategory, a different process executes independently on each processor. For SPMD, the process is decomposed into separate tasks, each of which represents a different location in the program. The tasks execute on separate processor cores. This is the prevailing architecture for multicore personal computers today.

The following table plots Flynn's taxonomy.

Flynn's Taxonomy	Single Data Stream	Multiple Data Streams
Single Instruction Stream	SISD	SIMD
Multiple Instruction Streams	MISD	MIMD

Additional information about Flynn's taxonomy is available at Wikipedia: *http://en.wikipedia.org/wiki/Flynn%27s_taxonomy*.

Multithreading

Threads represent actions in your program. A process itself does nothing; instead, it hosts the resources consumed by the running application, such as the heap and the stack. A thread is one possible path of execution in the application. Threads can perform independent tasks or cooperate on an operation with related tasks.

Parallel applications are also concurrent. However, not all concurrent applications are parallel. Concurrent applications can run on a single core, whereas parallel execution requires multiple cores. The reason behind this distinction is called *interleaving*. When multiple threads run concurrently on a single-processor computer, the Windows operating system interleaves the threads in a round-robin fashion, based on thread priority and other factors. In this manner, the processor is shared between several threads. You can consider this as *logical parallelism*. With physical parallelism, there are multiple cores where work is decomposed into tasks and executed in parallel on separate processor cores.

Threads are preempted when interrupted for another thread. At that time, the running thread yields execution to the next thread. In this manner, threads are interleaved on a single pro-cessor. When a thread is preempted, the operating system preserves the state of the running thread and loads the state of the next thread, which is then able to execute. Exchanging run-ning threads on a processor triggers a *context switch* and a transition between kernel and user mode. Context switches are expensive, so reducing the number of context switches is important to improving performance.

Threads are preempted for several reasons:

- A higher priority thread needs to run.
- Execution time exceeds a quantum.
- An input-output request is received.
- The thread voluntarily yields the processor.
- The thread is blocked on a synchronization object.

Even on a single-processor machine, there are advantages to concurrent execution:

- Multitasking
- A responsive user interface
- Asynchronous input-output
- Improved graphics rendering

Parallel execution requires multiple cores so that threads can execute in parallel without interleaving. Ideally, you want to have one thread for each available processor. However, that is not always possible. *Oversubscription* occurs when the number of threads exceeds the number of available processors. When this happens, interleaving occurs for the threads sharing a processor. Conversely, *undersubscription* occurs when there are fewer threads than available processors. When this happens, you have idle processors and less-than-optimum CPU utilization. Of course, the goal is maximum CPU utilization while balancing the potential performance degradation of oversubscription or undersubscription.

As mentioned earlier, context switches adversely affect performance. However, some context switches are more expensive than others; one of the more expensive ones is a cross-core context switch. A thread can run on a dedicated processor or across processors. Threads serviced by a single processor have *processor affinity*, which is more efficient. Preempting and scheduling a thread on another processor core causes cache misses, access to local memory as the result of cache misses, and excess context switches. In aggregate, this is called a *cross-core context switch*.

Synchronization

Multithreading involves more than creating multiple threads. The steps required to start a thread are relatively simple. Managing those threads for a thread-safe application is more of a challenge. Synchronization is the most common tool used to create a thread-safe environment. Even single-threaded applications use synchronization on occasion. For example, a single-threaded application might synchronize on kernel-mode resources, which are shareable across processes. However, synchronization is more common in multithreaded applications where both kernel-mode and user-mode resources might experience contention. Shared data is a second reason for contention between multiple threads and the requirement for synchronization.

Most synchronization is accomplished with synchronization objects. There are dedicated synchronization objects, such as mutexes, semaphores, and events. General-purpose objects that are also available for synchronization include processes, threads, and registry keys. For example, you can synchronize on whether a thread has finished executing. Most synchronization objects are kernel objects, and their use requires a context switch. Lightweight synchronization objects, such as critical sections, are user-mode objects that avoid expensive context switches. In the .NET Framework, the *lock* statement and the *Monitor* type are wrappers for native critical sections.

Contention occurs when a thread cannot obtain a synchronization object or access shared data for some period of time. The thread typically blocks until the entity is available. When contention is short, the associated overhead for synchronization is relatively costly. If short contention is the pattern, such overhead can become nontrivial. In this scenario, an alternative to blocking is *spinning*. Applications have the option to spin in user mode, consuming

CPU cycles but avoiding a kernel-mode switch. After a short while, the thread can reattempt to acquire the shared resource. If the contention is short, you can successfully acquire the resource on the second attempt to avoid blocking and a related context switch. Spinning for synchronization is considered lightweight synchronization, and Microsoft has added types such as the *SpinWait* structure to the .NET Framework for this purpose. For example, spinning constructs are used in many of the concurrent collections in the *System.Collections.Concurrent* namespace to create thread-safe and lock-free collections.

Most parallel applications rely on some degree of synchronization. Developers often consider synchronization a necessary evil. Overuse of synchronization is unfortunate, because most parallel programs perform best when running in *parallel* with no impediments. Serializing a parallel application through synchronization is contrary to the overall goal. In fact, the speed improvement potential of a parallel application is limited by the proportion of the application that runs sequentially. For example, when 40 percent of an application executes sequentially, the maximum possible speed improvement in theory is 60 percent. Most parallel applications start with minimal synchronization. However, synchronization is often the preferred resolution to any problem. In this way, synchronization spreads—like moss on a tree—quickly. In extreme circumstances, the result is a complex sequential application that for some reason has multiple threads. In your own programs, make an effort to keep parallel applications parallel.

Speedup

Speedup is the expected performance benefit from running an application on a multicore versus a single-core machine. When speedup is measured, single-core machine performance is the baseline. For example, assume that the duration of an application on a single-core machine is six hours. The duration is reduced to three hours when the application runs on a quad machine. The speedup is 2—(6/3)—in other words, the application is twice as fast.

You might expect that an application running on a single-core machine would run twice as quickly on a dual-core machine, and that a quad-core machine would run the application four times as fast. But that's not exactly correct. With some notable exceptions, such as super linear speedup, linear speedup is not possible even if the *entire* application ran in parallel. That's because there is always some overhead from parallelizing an application, such as scheduling threads onto separate processors. Therefore, linear speedup is not obtainable.

Here are some of the limitations to linear speedup of parallel code:

- Serial code
- Overhead from parallelization
- Synchronization
- Sequential input/output

Predicting speedup is important in designing, benchmarking, and testing your parallel application. Fortunately, there are formulas for calculating speedup. One such formula is Amdahl's Law. Gene Amdahl created Amdahl's Law in 1967 to calculate maximum speedup for parallel applications.

Amdahl's Law

Amdahl's Law calculates the speedup of parallel code based on three variables:

- Duration of running the application on a single-core machine
- The percentage of the application that is parallel
- The number of processor cores

Here is the formula, which returns the ratio of single-core versus multicore performance.

$$Speedup = \frac{1}{1 - P + (P/N)}$$

This formula uses the duration of the application on a single-core machine as the benchmark. The numerator of the equation represents that base duration, which is always one. The dynamic portion of the calculation is in the denominator. The variable P is the percent of the application that runs in parallel, and N is the number of processor cores.

As an example scenario, suppose you have an application that is 75 percent parallel and runs on a machine with three processor cores. The first iteration to calculate Amdahl's Law is shown below. In the formula, P is .75 (the parallel portion) and N is 3 (the number of cores).

$$Speedup = \frac{1}{(1 - .75) + (.75 / 3)}$$

You can reduce that as follows:

$$Speedup = \frac{1}{25 + 25}$$

The final result is a speedup of two. Your application will run twice as fast on a three-processor-core machine.

$$Speedup = 2$$

Visualizing speedup can help you interpret the meaning of Amdahl's Law. In the following diagram, the evaluation of speedup is presented as a graph. Duration is represented as units of equal length. On a single-core machine, application duration is four units. One of those units contains code that must execute sequentially. This means that 75 percent of the application can run in parallel. Again, in this scenario, there are three available processor cores. Therefore, the three parallel units can be run in parallel and coalesced into a single unit of duration. As a result, both the sequential and parallel portions of the application require one unit of duration. So you have a total of two units of duration—down from the original four—which is a speedup of two. Therefore, your application runs twice as fast. This confirms the previous calculation that used Amdahl's Law.

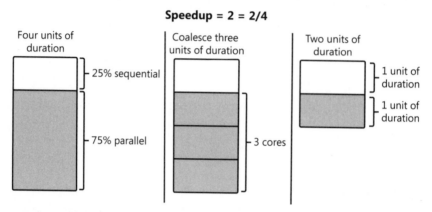

You can find additional information on Amdahl's Law at Wikipedia: *http://en.wikipedia.org /wiki/Amdahl%27s_Law.*

Gustafson's Law

John Gustafson and Edward Barsis introduced Gustafson's Law in 1988 as a competing principle to Amdahl's Law. As demonstrated, Amdahl's Law predicts performance as processors are added to the computing environment. This is called the *speedup*, and it represents the performance dividend. In the real world, that performance dividend is sometimes repurposed. The need for money and computing power share a common attribute. Both tend to expand to consume the available resources. For example, an application completes a particular operation in a fixed duration. The performance dividend could be used to complete the work more quickly, but it is just as likely that the performance dividend is simply used to complete more work within the same fixed duration. When this occurs, the performance dividend is not passed along to the user. However, the application accomplishes more work or offers additional features. In this way, you still receive a significant benefit from a parallel application running in a multicore environment.

Amdahl's Law does not take these real-world considerations into account. Instead, it assumes a fixed relationship between the parallel and serial portions of the application. You may have an application that's split consistently into a sequential and parallel portion. Amdahl's Law maintains these proportions as additional processors are added. The serial and parallel portions each remain half of the program. But in the real world, as computing power increases, more work gets completed, so the relative duration of the sequential portion is reduced. In addition, Amdahl's Law does not account for the overhead required to schedule, manage, and execute parallel tasks. Gustafson's Law takes both of these additional factors into account.

Here is the formula to calculate speedup by using Gustafson's Law.

$$\text{Speedup} = \frac{S + N (1 - S)}{S + (1 - S)} - O_n$$

In the above formula, S is the percentage of the serial code in the application, N is the number of processor cores, and O_n is the overhead from parallelization.

Software Patterns

Parallel programming is not a new concept; it has been around for some time, although mostly on large or distributed systems. Parallel computing has more recently been available on personal computers with Threading Building Blocks (TBB), OpenMP, and other parallel solutions. So although parallel computing might seem new, the concepts are actually mature. For example, design patterns have been developed to help programmers design, architect, and implement a robust, correct, and scalable parallel application. The book *Patterns for Parallel Programming* by Timothy G. Mattson, Beverly A. Sanders, and Berna L. Massingill (Addison-Wesley Professional, 2004) provides a comprehensive study on parallel patterns, along with a detailed explanation of the available design patterns and best practices for parallel programming. Another book, *Parallel Programming with Microsoft .NET: Design Patterns for Decomposition and Coordination on Multicore Architectures* by Colin Campbell et al. (Microsoft Press, 2010) is an important resource for patterns and best practices that target the .NET Framework and TPL.

Developers on average do not write much unique code. Most code concepts have been written somewhere before. Software pattern engineers research this universal code base to isolate standard patterns and solutions for common problems in a domain space. You can use these patterns as the building blocks that form the foundation of a stable application. Around these core components, you add the unique code for your application, as illustrated in the following diagram. This approach not only results in a stable application but is also a highly efficient way to develop an application.

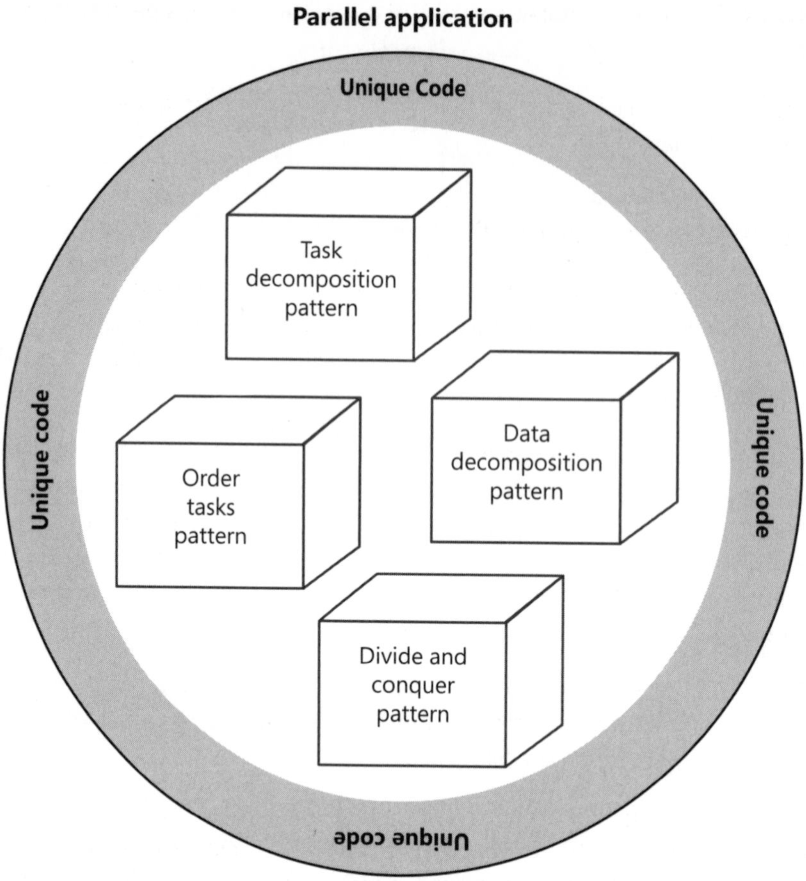

Parallel application

Design patterns should be an integral part of the software development life cycle of every application. These patterns require thorough knowledge of your problem domain. All object-oriented programs model a problem domain, and parallel applications are no exception. As applications become more complex, knowing the problem domain increases in importance.

Patterns for Parallel Programming defines four phases of parallel development:

- Finding Concurrency
- Algorithm Structures
- Support Structures
- Implementation Mechanisms

The first two phases are design and analysis, which include tasks such as finding exploitable concurrency. These phases are the precursors to actually writing code. Later, you map the analysis onto code by using the Support Structures and Implementation Mechanisms phases. The Implementation Mechanisms design phase is not reviewed in this chapter. You can consider the TPL as a generic implementation of this pattern; it maps parallel programming onto the .NET Framework.

I urge you to explore parallel design patterns so you can benefit from the hard work of other parallel applications developers.

The Finding Concurrency Pattern

The first phase is the most important. In this phase, you identify exploitable concurrency. The challenge involves more than identifying opportunities for concurrency, because not every potential concurrency is worth pursuing. The goal is to isolate opportunities of concurrency that are worth exploiting.

The Finding Concurrency pattern begins with a review of the problem domain. Your goal is to isolate tasks that are good candidates for parallel programming—or conversely, exclude those that are not good candidates. You must weigh the benefit of exposing specific operations as parallel tasks versus the cost. For example, the performance gain for parallelizing a *for* loop with a short operation might not offset the scheduling overhead and the cost of running the task.

When searching for potential parallel tasks, review extended blocks of compute-bound code first. This is where you will typically find the most intense processing, and therefore also the greatest potential benefit from parallel execution.

Next, you decompose exploitable concurrency into parallel tasks. You can decompose operations on either the code or data axis (*Task Decomposition* and *Data Decomposition*, respectively). The typical approach is to decompose operations into several units. It's easier to load balance a large number of discrete tasks than a handful of longer tasks. In addition, tasks of relatively equal length are easier to load balance than tasks of widely disparate length.

The Task Decomposition Pattern

In the Task Decomposition pattern, you decompose code into separate parallel tasks that run independently, with minimal or no dependencies. For example, functions are often excellent candidates for refactoring as parallel tasks. In object-oriented programming, functions should do one thing. However, this is not always the case. For longer functions, evaluate whether the function performs more than one task. If so, you might be able to decompose the function into multiple discrete tasks, improving the opportunities for parallelism.

The Data Decomposition Pattern

In the Data Decomposition pattern, you decompose data collections, such as lists, stacks, and queues, into partitions for parallel processing. Loops that iterate over data collections are the best locations for decomposing tasks by using the Data Decomposition pattern. Each task is identical but is assigned to a different portion of the data collection. If the tasks have short durations, you should consider grouping multiple tasks together so that they execute as a chunk on a thread, to improve overall efficiency.

The Group Tasks Pattern

After completing the Task and Data Decomposition patterns, you will have a basket of tasks. The next two patterns identify relationships between these tasks. The Group Task pattern groups related tasks, whereas the Order Tasks pattern imposes an order to the execution of tasks.

You should consider grouping tasks in the following circumstances:

- Group tasks together that must start at the same time. The Order Task pattern can then refer to this group to set that constraint.
- Group tasks that contribute to the same calculation (reduction).
- Group tasks that share the same operation, such as loop operation.
- Group tasks that share a common resource, where simultaneous access is not thread safe.

The most important reason to create task groups is to place constraints on the entire group rather than on individual tasks.

The Order Tasks Pattern

The Order Tasks pattern is the second pattern that sets dependencies based on task relationships. This pattern identifies dependencies that place constraints on the order (the sequence) of task execution. In this pattern, you often reference groups of tasks defined in the Group Task pattern. For example, you might reference a group of tasks that must start together.

Do not overuse this pattern. Ordering implies synchronization at best, and sequential execution at worst.

Some example of order dependencies are:

- **Start dependency**   This is when tasks must start at the same time. Here the constraint is the start time.
- **Predecessor dependency**   This occurs when one task must start prior to another task.
- **Successor dependency**   This happens when a task is a continuation of another task.
- **Data dependency**   This is when a task cannot start until certain information is available.

The Data Sharing Pattern

Parallel tasks may access shared data, which can be a dependency between tasks. Proper management is essential for correctness and to avoid problems such as race conditions and data corruptions. The Data Sharing pattern describes various methods for managing shared data. The goals are to ensure that tasks adhering to this pattern are thread safe and that the application remains scalable.

When possible, tasks should consume thread-local data. Thread-local data is private to the task and not accessible from other tasks. Because of this isolation, thread-local data is exempt from most data-sharing constraints. However, tasks that use thread-local data might require shared data for consolidation, accumulation, or other types of reduction. Reduction is the consolidation of partial results from separate parallel operations into a single value. When the reduction is performed, access to the shared data must be coordinated through some mechanism, such as thread synchronization. This is explained in more detail later in this book.

Sharing data is expensive. Proposed solutions to safely access shared data typically involve some sort of synchronization. *The best solution for sharing data is not to share data*. This includes copying the shared data to a thread-local variable. You can then access the data privately during a parallel operation. After the operation is complete, you can perform a replacement or some type of merge with the original shared data to minimize synchronization.

The type of data access can affect the level of synchronization. Common data access types are summarized here:

- **Read-only**   This is preferred and frequently requires no synchronization.

- **Write-only**   You must have a policy to handle contention on the write. Alternatively, you can protect the data with exclusive locks. However, this can be expensive. An example of write-only is initializing a data collection from independent values.

- **Read-write**   The key word here is the *write*. Copy the data to a thread-local variable. Perform the update operation. Write results to the shared data, which might require some level of synchronization. If more reads are expected than writes, you might want to implement a more optimistic data sharing model—for example, spinning instead of locking.

- **Reduction**   The shared data is an accumulator. Copy the shared data to a thread-local variable. You can then perform an operation to generate a partial result. A reduction task is responsible for applying partial results to some sort of accumulator. Synchronization is limited to the reduction method, which is more efficient. This approach can be used to calculate summations, averages, counts, maximum value, minimal value, and more.

The Algorithm Structure Pattern

The result of the Finding Concurrency phase is a list of tasks, dependencies, and constraints for a parallel application. The phase also involves grouping related tasks and setting criteria for ordering tasks. In the Algorithm Structure phase, you select the algorithms you will use to execute the tasks. These are the algorithms that you will eventually implement for the program domain.

The algorithms included in the Algorithm Structure pattern adhere to four principles. These algorithms must:

- Make effective use of processors.
- Be transparent and maintainable by others.
- Be agnostic to hardware, operating system, and environment.
- Be efficient and scalable.

As mentioned, algorithms are implementation-agnostic. You might have constructs and features in your environment that help with parallel development and performance. The Implementation Mechanisms phase describes how to implement parallel patterns in your specific environment.

The Algorithm Structure pattern introduces several patterns based on algorithms:

- **Task Parallelism Pattern**   Arrange tasks to run efficiently as independent parallel operations. Actually, having slightly more tasks than processor cores is preferable—especially for input/output bound tasks. Input/output bound tasks might become blocked during input/output operations. When this occurs, extra tasks might be needed to keep additional processor cores busy.

- **Divide and Conquer Pattern**   Decompose a serial operation into parallel subtasks, each of which returns a partial solution. These partial solutions are then reintegrated to calculate a complete solution. Synchronization is required during the reintegration but not during the entire operation.

- **Geometric Decomposition Pattern**   Reduce a data collection into chunks that are assigned the same parallel operation. Larger chunks can be harder to load balance, whereas smaller chunks are better for load balancing but are less efficient relative to parallelization overhead.

- **Recursive Data Pattern**   Perform parallel operations on recursive data structures, such as trees and link lists.

- **Pipeline Pattern**   Apply a sequence of parallel operations to a shared collection or independent data. The operations are ordered to form a pipeline of tasks that are applied to a data source. Each task in the pipeline represents a phase. You should have enough phases to keep each processor busy. At the start and end of pipeline operations, the pipeline might not be full. Otherwise, the pipeline is full with tasks and maximizes processor utilization.

The Supporting Structures Pattern

The Supporting Structures pattern describes several ways to organize the implementation of parallel code. Fortunately, several of these patterns are already implemented in the TPL as part of the .NET Framework. For example, the .NET Framework 4 thread pool is one implementation of the Master/Worker pattern.

There are four Supporting Structures patterns:

- **SPMD (Single Program/Multiple Data)**   A single parallel operation is applied to multiple data sequences. In a parallel program, the processor cores often execute the same task on a collection of data.

- **Master/Worker**   The process (*master*) sets up a pool of executable units (*workers*), such as threads, that execute concurrently. There is also a collection of tasks whose execution is pending. Tasks are scheduled to run in parallel on available workers. In this manner, the workload can be balanced across multiple processors. The .NET Framework 4 thread pool provides an implementation of this pattern.

- **Loop Parallelism**   Iterations of a sequential loop are converted into separate parallel operations. Resolving dependencies between loop iterations is one of the challenges. Such dependencies were perhaps inconsequential in sequential applications but are problematic in a parallel version. The .Net Framework 4 provides various solutions for loop parallelism, including *Parallel.For*, *Parallel.ForEach*, and PLINQ (Parallel Language Integration Query).

- **Fork/Join**   Work is decomposed into separate tasks that complete some portion of the work. A unit of execution, such as a thread, spawns the separate tasks and then waits for them to complete. This is the pattern for the *Parallel.Invoke* method in the TPL.

The Supporting Structure phase also involves patterns for sharing data between multiple parallel tasks: the Shared Data, Shared Queue, and Distributed Array patterns. These are also already implemented in the .NET Framework, available as collections in the *System.Collections.Concurrent* namespace.

Summary

Parallel programming techniques allow software applications to benefit from the rapid shift from single-core to multicore computers. Multicore computers will continue the growth in computing power as promised in Moore's Law; however, the price for that continued growth is that developers have to be prepared to benefit from the shift in hardware architecture by learning parallel programming patterns and techniques.

In the .NET Framework 4, Microsoft has elevated parallel programming to a core technology with the introduction of the Task Parallel Library (TPL). Previously, parallel programming was an extension of the .NET Framework. Parallel programming has also been added to LINQ as Parallel LINQ (PLINQ).

The goal of parallel programming is to load balance the workload across all the available processor cores for maximum CPU utilization. Applications should scale as the number of processors increases in a multicore environment. Scaling will be less than linear relative to the number of cores, however, because other factors can affect performance.

Multiple threads can run concurrently on the same processor core. When this occurs, the threads alternately use the processor by *interleaving*. There are benefits to concurrent execution, such as more responsive user interfaces, but interleaving is not parallel execution. On a multicore machine, the threads can truly execute in parallel—with each thread running on a separate processor. This is both concurrent and parallel execution. When oversubscription occurs, interleaving can occur even in a multicore environment.

You can coordinate the actions of multiple threads with thread synchronization—for example, to access shared data safely. Some synchronization objects are lighter than others, so when possible, use critical sections for lightweight synchronization instead of semaphores or mutexes. Critical sections are especially helpful when the duration of contention is expected to be short. Another alternative is spinning, in the hope of avoiding a synchronization lock.

Speedup predicts the performance increase from running an application in a multicore environment. Amdahl's Law calculates speedup based on the number of processors and percentage of the application that runs parallel. Gustafson's Law calculates real-world speedup. This includes using the performance dividend for more work and parallel overhead.

Parallel computing is a mature concept with best practices and design patterns. The most important phase is Finding Concurrency. In this phase, you identify exploitable concurrency—the code most likely to benefit from parallelization. You can decompose your application into parallel tasks by using Task Decomposition and Data Decomposition patterns. Associations and dependencies between tasks are isolated in the Group Tasks and Order Tasks patterns. You can map tasks onto generic algorithms for concurrent execution in the Algorithm Structure pattern. The last phase, Implementation Mechanisms, is implemented in the TPL. In the next chapter, you will begin your exploration of the TPL with task parallelism.

Quick Reference

To	Do this
Implement parallel programming in .NET Framework 4	Leverage the TPL found in the *System.Threading.Tasks* namespace.
Use LINQ with parallel programing	Use PLINQ.
Calculate basic speedup	Apply Amdahl's Law.
Find potential concurrency in a problem domain	Apply the Finding Concurrency pattern.
Resolve dependencies between parallel tasks	Use the Data Sharing pattern.
Unroll sequential loops into parallel tasks	Use the Loop Parallelism pattern.

Chapter 2
Task Parallelism

After completing this chapter, you will be able to

- Create parallel tasks.

- Handle unhandled exceptions from a task.

- Cooperatively cancel a task.

- Define relationships between tasks.

- Describe a work-stealing queue.

Chapter 1, "Introduction to Parallel Programming," introduced the concept of parallelism. This chapter is about task parallelism, and the next chapter pertains to data parallelism. Tasks are the fundamental elements of parallel programming. Task parallelism is the parallel execution of tasks across several processors. The goal of parallelism is to maximize processor utilization, and of course, improve performance. As available processors increase, your application will scale, as additional tasks run across more processors. The degree of improvement as the number of processors increases is calculated by using Amdahl's Law or, alternatively, Gustafson's Law—both of which were defined in the previous chapter.

Parallel tasks usually have inputs. In task parallelism, parallel tasks typically work on a collection of related data.

Introduction to Parallel Tasks

There are several ways to invoke parallel tasks. This section reviews the various available techniques, starting with the *Parallel.Invoke* method.

Let us assume that you have three methods (*MethodA*, *MethodB*, and *MethodC*) that have separate data input. If the methods execute sequentially, the execution time would be the sum of the duration of each method, as shown in the following image. In this example, the total time to execute the methods sequentially is 20 milliseconds (ms).

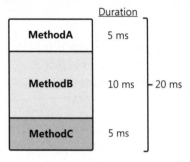

MethodA, *MethodB*, and *MethodC* have no dependencies. When the methods are converted to tasks, the tasks are completely independent, and they are said to be *embarrassingly parallel*. This is important because it means that the tasks can run in parallel without any synchronization, such as a semaphore or monitor. Performance is therefore better, and this portion of the application is more scalable. Furthermore, synchronization can add complexity, which is harder to maintain and debug. When a group of tasks execute in parallel, their duration is the elapsed time of the longest task. In the following image, TaskB takes the longest time (10 ms) to complete. Therefore, the duration of the group of tasks is 10 ms, which is half the duration of the related methods when they are executed sequentially (see the previous illustration). This assumes that there are enough processors (three, in this example) to execute the tasks in parallel and not sequentially.

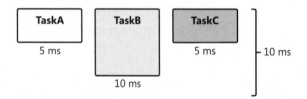

Tasks are scheduled and then assigned to a thread. The thread is then executed by a processor. In the past, threads—not tasks—were the basic unit of scheduling. A thread is an asynchronous path of execution through your process. A process is itself not active; activity is found in the threads. In fact, the Windows operating system automatically closes a process with no threads, because there is no reason to maintain a process that has no potential activity. Despite this, a process is nonetheless important. It provides the resources needed for a running program, such as the virtual memory, the working set, and the handle table. Threads require these resources to execute. Threads privately own resources as well, most notably the stack and thread local storage.

Threads

Tasks run on threads. Threads are the engine of your application and represent running code. Understanding threads helps you understand tasks. This is important because some of the overhead associated with a task pertains to threads. Therefore, threads are especially relevant when discussing parallel programming.

The Windows operating system schedules threads preemptively. Threads are assigned an adjustable priority, and in general, they are scheduled in a round-robin fashion based on thread priority. Here are some of the reasons that a thread might be preempted:

- The thread has exceeded its time slice or quantum.

- A higher-priority thread starts.

- The thread places itself into a wait condition.

- An input-output operation occurs.

Nothing is free—including threads. Threads have overhead. Most of the overhead associated with a thread involves the stack, thread local storage, and context switches. The default stack size for each thread is one megabyte (MB). For example, 200 threads would reserve 200 MB of memory for stack space, which is not trivial. Thread local storage is private memory set aside for each thread and can also be significant. In addition to the storage overhead, threads have a performance cost: context switches. Much of this cost is associated with switching between user and kernel mode when swapping the running thread for another user mode thread. The cost of context switches can reduce the benefit of additional threads.

In addition to context switches, there are other costs, such as ramping up and destroying threads. The Microsoft .NET Framework thread pool helps to manage these costs and to abstract much of the complexity of creating, starting, and destroying threads. There is one .NET Framework thread pool per managed application. Thread pools commonly reuse threads to avoid the costs of thread startup and destruction. When the thread is no longer required, the operating system reassigns additional work to the thread or suspends the thread. There is an algorithm for adjusting thread pool size dynamically based on thread utilization and other factors. The .NET Framework 4 thread pool is the default scheduler for parallel tasks in the .NET Framework. When you start a task, it is scheduled to run and placed in a queue as part of the thread pool. Later, the task is dequeued and assigned to run on an available thread. Fortunately, most of this activity is transparent to you.

To recap: A task is a group of related statements. When started, tasks are added to a queue in the thread pool. Eventually (maybe immediately), a task is executed on a thread, which is a unit of execution. This is, of course, a thread from the thread pool. Each thread is assigned to and executed initially on a particular processor, which is considered the processor unit. The following diagram shows the relationship between a task, a thread, and a processor.

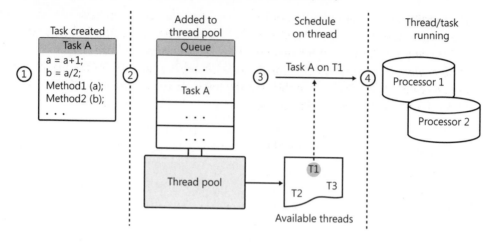

The *Task* Class

In the .NET Framework, the *Task* class is a logical abstraction of a task. You can use this class to schedule and ultimately execute a parallel task. Remember, tasks are unlike threads in that you do not start a task directly. By default, the thread pool schedules a task, places it on a queue in the thread pool, and eventually executes the task on an available thread. In this book, *starting* a task implies queuing the task first and later executing the task on an available thread from the thread pool.

Using the *Parallel.Invoke* Method

You can schedule a task in several ways, the simplest of which is by using the *Parallel.Invoke* method. The following example executes two parallel tasks—one for *MethodA* and another for *MethodB*. This version of *Parallel.Invoke* accepts an array of *Action* delegates as the sole parameter. *Action* delegates have no arguments and return *void*.

```
Parallel.Invoke(new Action[] { MethodA, MethodB });
```

The *Parallel.Invoke* method is convenient for executing multiple tasks in parallel. However, this method has limitations:

- *Parallel.Invoke* creates but does not return task objects.

- The *Action* delegate is limited—it has no parameters and no return value.

- *Parallel.Invoke* is not as flexible as other solutions and always uses an implied *Task.WaitAll* method, described in more detail later in this section.

Parallel.Invoke does not guarantee the ordering of task execution. In the previous example, the task for *MethodB* might execute first. When ordering is required, dependency is implied. You should avoid task dependencies whenever possible.

The *Parallel.Invoke* method does not return until the provided tasks have completed. For example, consider the use of *Parallel.Invoke* to execute two tasks. The first task's duration is 500 ms, and the duration of the second task is 250 ms. *Parallel.Invoke* will return in 500 ms. In other words, the duration of *Parallel.Invoke* is the execution time of the longest-running task. As with other comments in this chapter, this is a general comment. The actual duration depends on several factors, such as overhead and processor utilization.

Using the *TaskFactory.StartNew* method

Another way to execute a task is to use the *TaskFactory.StartNew* method. The *TaskFactory* class is an abstraction of a task scheduler. In the *Task* class, the *Factory* property returns the default implementation of the task factory, which employs the .NET Framework 4 thread pool. *TaskFactory* has a *StartNew* method for executing tasks using the default task factory. Here is sample code that executes two tasks by using *TaskFactory.StartNew*.

```
var TaskA = Task.Factory.StartNew(MethodA);
var TaskB = Task.Factory.StartNew(MethodB);
```

Like the *Parallel.Invoke* method, *TaskFactory.StartNew* uses an *Action* delegate. Unlike the *Parallel.Invoke* method, *TaskFactory.StartNew* returns immediately. There is no implied wait. Therefore, how do you know when the task or tasks have completed? Fortunately, the *StartNew* returns a *Task* object. You can explicitly wait for a single task by using the *Task.Wait* method, which is an instance method. A thread waiting on a task is considered to be the joining thread. If the task has already completed, *Task.Wait* returns immediately. Otherwise, the joining thread will wait (block) until the task has completed. Here's sample code that executes and waits on a single task.

```
var TaskA = Task.Factory.StartNew(MethodA);
TaskA.Wait();
```

The previous example waited on a single task. You can also wait for multiple tasks. After all, an application is not very parallel with a single task. There are two options for waiting for multiple tasks: wait for all the tasks to complete, or wait for any task to complete. *Task.WaitAll* waits for all tasks to complete. *Task.WaitAny* returns when any of the referenced tasks have completed. Both methods accept an array of tasks as a parameter. Both *Task.WaitAll* and *Task.WaitAny* methods are static methods of the *Task* class.

Important What follows is the first step-by-step tutorial procedure in this book. You'll start each tutorial by creating a console project from the New Project dialog box in Microsoft Visual Studio 2010. Add a *using* statement for the *System.Threading* and *System.Threading.Tasks* namespaces at the beginning of the application. The template for a console application includes a *Main* function, which is the entry point. You will add most of your code in the *Main* function.

Create two tasks from separate methods and wait for both tasks to complete

1. Create a console application. Before the *Main* function, add a *MethodA* and *MethodB* method. Each method should display the name of the method by using *Console.WriteLine*.

```
static void MethodA() { Console.WriteLine("MethodA"); }
static void MethodB() { Console.WriteLine("MethodB"); }
```

2. In the *Main* function, create and start two tasks with the *TaskFactory.StartNew* method. Initialize the tasks with the *MethodA* and *MethodB* methods.

```
var TaskA = Task.Factory.StartNew(MethodA);
var TaskB = Task.Factory.StartNew(MethodB);
```

3. You can now wait for both methods to complete with the *Task.WaitAll* method.

```
Task.WaitAll(new Task[] { TaskA, TaskB });
```

4. Add *Console.ReadLine()* call to the end of the *Main* method to prevent the console from closing before you can see the output. Your completed code should look like the following.

```
class Program
{
    static void MethodA() { Console.WriteLine("MethodA"); }
    static void MethodB() { Console.WriteLine("MethodB"); }


    static void Main(string[] args)
    {
        var TaskA = Task.Factory.StartNew(MethodA);
        var TaskB = Task.Factory.StartNew(MethodB);
        Task.WaitAll(new Task[] { TaskA, TaskB });
        Console.ReadLine();
    }
}
```

5. Run the program. You should see the output from both tasks in the console window.

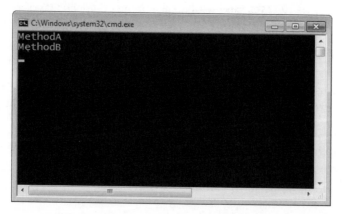

The example you just completed uses the *Task.WaitAll* method to wait for both tasks to complete. In contrast, the *Task.WaitAny* method returns as soon as any task completes. You can discover which task completed because *Task.WaitAny* returns a zero-based index into the *Task* array that was provided as a parameter. The array index identifies the task that completed.

You used the *Console.ReadLine* method to prevent the console window from closing. Of course, this makes it easier to view the results. Alternatively, you can execute the application in Release mode, which you can do by using the shortcut Ctrl+F5. This prevents the addition of an extraneous line of code. Either technique is okay.

In the previous example, you waited for all tasks to complete. In this tutorial, you just wait for the first task to complete. You will then display the task ID of that task.

Create two tasks and wait for just the first one to complete

1. Create a new console application. At the top of the source file, reference the *System.Threading* and *System.Threading.Tasks* namespaces. Before the *Main* function, add a *MethodA* and *MethodB* method. To emulate a compute bound task, you will ask each task to simply spin and burn processor cycles by using the static *Thread.SpinWait* method.

```
static void MethodA() { Thread.SpinWait(int.MaxValue); }
static void MethodB() { Thread.SpinWait(int.MaxValue/2); }
```

2. In the *Main* function, create two tasks with the *TaskFactory.StartNew* method. Initialize the tasks with the *MethodA* and *MethodB* methods.

```
var TaskA = Task.Factory.StartNew(MethodA);
var TaskB = Task.Factory.StartNew(MethodB);
```

3. Display the ID for each task.

```
Console.WriteLine("TaskA id = {0}", TaskA.Id);
Console.WriteLine("TaskB id = {0}", TaskB.Id);
```

4. Now create an array of tasks. Call *Task.WaitAny* to wait until either task has run to completion. Initialize an integer variable with the return value.

```
Task [] tasks=new Task[] {TaskA, TaskB};
int whichTask = Task.WaitAny(tasks);
```

5. *WaitAny* returns a zero-based index into the task array, which identifies the task that has finished. In this example, you can use the index to display the task ID of that task.

```
Console.WriteLine("Task {0} is the gold medal task.",
    tasks[whichTask].Id);
```

6. Keep the console open and prevent the application from exiting by using a *Console.ReadLine=* statement at the end of the application.

Here is the completed code:

```
using System;
using System.Collections.Generic;
using System.Linq;
using System.Threading;
using System.Threading.Tasks;

namespace TwoTask_WaitAny
{
    class Program
    {

        static void MethodA() { Thread.SpinWait(int.MaxValue); }
        static void MethodB() { Thread.SpinWait(int.MaxValue/2); }

        static void Main(string[] args)
        {
            var TaskA = Task.Factory.StartNew(MethodA);
            var TaskB = Task.Factory.StartNew(MethodB);

            Console.WriteLine("TaskA id = {0}", TaskA.Id);
            Console.WriteLine("TaskB id = {0}", TaskB.Id);

            var tasks=new Task[] {TaskA, TaskB};
            int whichTask = Task.WaitAny(tasks);
            Console.WriteLine("Task {0} is the gold medal task.",
                tasks[whichTask].Id);

            Console.WriteLine("Press enter to exit");
            Console.ReadLine();

        }
    }
}
```

7. Run the application. This time, when either of the methods completes, the *Console .WriteLine* code will show a message containing the ID of the task that finished first. Based on your code, TaskB will finish first.

Be careful with the *Wait* methods: *Wait*, *WaitAll*, and *WaitAny*. There is always a possibility of waiting longer than you expect; you might even deadlock. For that reason, you should always consider using the versions of these methods that have a time-out parameter. You can then set a reasonable duration for the task to complete. When the task exceeds the duration, the *Wait* method will time out and return *false*. It is important to note that the task itself is not aborted and might run until completion. However, you are no longer waiting. In this circumstance, you might decide to cancel the task. You'll see more about cooperative task cancellation later in this chapter.

Because the *Wait* method has a time-out, using the following code is safer than using the code in the previous examples. The task must complete in the allotted time, or the wait will be released. The joining thread is then allowed to continue. For simplicity, the duration is not used in general in this book unless required.

```
var TaskA = Task.Factory.StartNew(MethodA);
if (!TaskA.Wait(5000)) {
    Console.WriteLine("Task timed out");
}
```

Using the *Task.Start* Method

There is yet one more way to directly start a task. You can create an instance of the *Task* class and call the *Task.Start* method, which is an instance method. One advantage is that you can configure the task in the *Task* constructor before starting the task. Several of the options, as defined in the *TaskCreationOption* enumeration, are particularly helpful. The following table lists the options.

Option	Explanation
PreferFairness	This is a suggestion to the *TaskScheduler* that tasks should execute in an order similar to when they were scheduled.
LongRunning	In the .NET Framework 4, long-running tasks are scheduled on threads not in the thread pool.
AttachToParent	This initiates a task inside another task to create a subtask.

This example code demonstrates a couple of these options.

```
var TaskA = new Task(MethodA, TaskCreationOptions.LongRunning);
var TaskB = new Task(MethodB, TaskCreationOptions.PreferFairness);

TaskA.Start();
TaskB.Start();
```

The .NET Framework 4 thread pool is optimized for short tasks. For this reason, long-running tasks can adversely affect the performance of the .NET Framework 4 thread pool. Use the *TaskCreationOption.LongRunning* option to schedule a long-running task on a dedicated thread that is not part of the thread pool.

The .NET Framework thread pool does not promise to execute tasks in order; more often than not, tasks will run out of sequence. Therefore, you cannot predict the order of execution and should not write code predicated on this requirement. *TaskCreationOptions.PreferFairness* is a task option that indicates a preference to execute a task in its natural order. However, *TaskCreationOptions.PreferFairness* is merely a *suggestion* to execute a task in order, not an absolute directive to the Task Parallel Library (TPL).

Using Function Delegates

So far, this chapter has used *Action* delegates as tasks. *Action* delegates have no parameters and do not return a value. In some circumstances, this might be inflexible and limiting. For tasks, you can also use the *Func<TResult>* delegate, where *TResult* is the return type. When the task completes, the return or result of the task is accessible with the *Task<TResult>.Result* property. You can check for the result at any time. However, if the task has not completed, accessing the *Task<TResult>.Result* property will block the joining thread until the task is done. Execution will resume after the task has finished, when the result is returned.

In the next example, a task returns the value 42, which is the answer to life, the universe, and everything (a not-so-veiled reference to the fabulous book *The Hitchhiker's Guide to the Galaxy* by Douglas Adams). *Task<int>* indicates that the task returns an integer value.

Lambda expressions are convenient for relatively short tasks. This book alternates between using lambda expressions and formal methods/functions, to familiarize you with both approaches.

Create a task that uses a lambda expression

1. Create a new console application. In the *Main* function, create and start a new task by using the *TaskFactory.StartNew* method. The task will return an integer value. In the *TaskFactory.StartNew* method, initialize the task with a lambda expression. In the lambda expression, return the value of 42.

```
var TaskA = Task<int>.Factory.StartNew(() => {
    return 42; });
```

2. You can now wait for the task with the *TaskA.Wait* method.

```
TaskA.Wait();
```

3. Display the result of the task with the *Task.Result* property.

4. Build and run the application.

Here is the complete application.

```
class Program
{
    static void Main(string[] args)
    {
        var TaskA = Task<int>.Factory.StartNew(() =>
        {
            return 42;
        });
        TaskA.Wait();
        Console.WriteLine(TaskA.Result);
    }
}
```

Here is another example of starting a task that returns a value. Different from the previous example, this code initializes the *Task* object in its constructor with a function delegate. *Task.Start* then executes the task.

```
Task <int> TaskA=new Task<int>(() => {
    return 42;
});
TaskA.Start();
```

You now know how to execute a task that has a return value. You might also want to pass information into the task. You pass state information for a task as an additional parameter—the object type (the state information can be any type). The next example employs *TaskFactory.StartNew* to execute a task. The first parameter is the task, and the second parameter is the state.

Create a task that uses a state object, which in this example is a string

1. Create a console application. In the *Main* function, create and start a new task by using the *TaskFactory.StartNew* method. Initialize the task with a lambda expression. Pass the state object into the lambda expression as a parameter. In the lambda expression, return the length of the lambda expression.

```
var TaskA = Task<int>.Factory.StartNew(val => {
return ((string)val).Length;},
```

2. The next parameter of this version of the *TaskFactory.StartNew* method is the state object. You will provide a string value.

```
"On Thursday, the cow jumped over the moon.");
```

3. You are ready to wait for the task, which is done with the *Task.Wait* method. You can then display the result of the task by using the *Task.Result* property. Of course, the answer remains 42, since *that is truly* the answer to life, the universe, and everything.

   4. Build and run the application.

Here is the complete application.

```
class Program
{
    static void Main(string[] args)
    {
        var TaskA = Task<int>.Factory.StartNew(val => {
            return ((string)val).Length;},
            "On Thursday, the cow jumped over the moon.");
        TaskA.Wait();
        Console.WriteLine(TaskA.Result);
    }
}
```

Here's an altered version of the previous example. Instead of using *TaskFactory.StartNew*, the task constructor initializes the state object.

```
var TaskA=new Task<int>(val =>{
    return ((string)val).Length;
}, "On Thursday, the cow jumped over the moon.");

TaskA.Start();
```

Unhandled Exceptions in Tasks

Tasks are not immune to exceptions. An unhandled exception raised in a task is handled differently by the common language runtime (CLR) than a typical exception. Unhandled exceptions in tasks are not handled in the context of the task, but in the context of the joining thread. Essentially, unhandled exceptions in a task are deferred and propagated to the joining thread. The joining thread can then observe the exception as the observer.

The unhandled exception propagated to the observer is wrapped in an *AggregateException* object. If you're waiting on multiple tasks, the *AggregateException* might aggregate more than one unhandled exception from different parallel tasks. If a single exception is raised, the *InnerException* property of the *AggregateException* contains the original exception. For multiple exceptions, the *InnerExceptions* property returns a collection of Exception objects—one for each unhandled exception.

There are many ways to observe an unhandled exception raised in a task. Waiting for the task will observe the exception: *Wait*, *WaitAll*, or *WaitAny* methods. The joining thread then becomes the observer and is responsible for handling the exception. If the *Wait* method is within the scope of a *try* block (protected code), the otherwise unhandled exception of a task can be caught. You can then unbundle the *AggregateException* object and examine the original exception(s) in the *InnerException* or *InnerExceptions* property.

Remember that *Parallel.Invoke* ends with an implicit *Task.WaitAll*. This blocks the joining thread until all the tasks have completed. When *Parallel.Invoke* returns, any unhandled exceptions are observed, and if the code is running within a *try* block, you can handle the exception(s) in a *catch* block.

After scheduling a task, the TPL tracks the status of that task. The status is exposed as the *Task.Status* property, which is a *TaskStatus* type. *TaskStatus* is an enumeration. Some of the possible values are *TaskStatus.WaitingToRun*, *TaskStatus.Running*, *TaskStatus.RanToCompletion*, and *TaskStatus.Canceled*, which are self-explanatory. When a task raises an unhandled exception, the task status is *TaskStatus.Faulted*.

The following image shows a sequence diagram of a task that throws an exception. The exception is observed in a *try* block and caught in the subsequent *catch* block. Thicker vertical lines represent tasks executing on a thread.

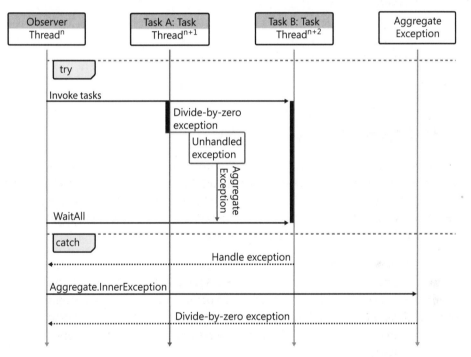

Here are the steps in the sequence diagram.

- Within a *try* block, invoke TaskA and TaskB. TaskB has the longer duration.
- TaskA throws a divide-by-zero exception, which is wrapped in an *AggregateException*.
- When TaskB completes, the *WaitAll* observes the unhandled exception raised by TaskA.
- The *catch* block retrieves the original exception as the *InnerException*.

Note that unhandled exceptions must be observed before the related task is garbage-collected; otherwise, the unhandled exception might crash the application. Here's an example of successfully handling an unhandled exception in a parallel task.

Create a task that throws an unhandled exception that is observed with a *Task.Wait* method

1. Create a console application. In the *Main* function, create a task reference, which is set to null.

    ```
    Task TaskA = null;
    ```

2. Start a *try/catch* block. You will enter code guarded for an exception in the *try* block.

    ```
    try {
    ```

3. In the *try* block, you will create and start a new task. Initialize the task with a lambda expression. In the lambda expression, define two integer variables. Set one of the integers to zero. Divide by the integer variable that has the zero value to raise the divide-by-zero exception.

    ```
    TaskA = Task.Factory.StartNew(() => {
    int a = 5, b = 0;
    a /= b;});
    ```

4. Wait for the task to complete.

    ```
    TaskA.Wait(); }
    ```

5. In the *catch* statement, catch the *AggregateException* exception. This will catch and observe the unhandled exception from the task.

    ```
    catch(AggregateException ae) {
    ```

6. In the *catch* block, display the task status and inner exception, which contains the original exception.

7. Build and run the application.

Here is the complete application.

```
class Program
{
    static void Main(string[] args)
    {
        Task TaskA = null;
        try {
            TaskA = Task.Factory.StartNew(() => {
                    int a = 5, b = 0;
                      a /= b;
                });
            TaskA.Wait();
        }
```

```
        catch(AggregateException ae) {
            Console.WriteLine("Task has "+TaskA.Status.ToString());
            Console.WriteLine(ae.InnerException);
        }
    }
}
```

Observe and iterate unhandled exceptions from three separate tasks

Different from the previous example, this walkthrough lists the separate exceptions thrown from different tasks.

1. Create a console application. Before the *Main* function, define *MethodA*, *MethodB*, and *MethodC* methods. Each method throws an explicit exception. In the exception constructor, provide the name of the task.

```
static void MethodA() { throw new Exception("TaskA Exception"); }
static void MethodB() { throw new Exception("TaskB Exception"); }
static void MethodC() { throw new Exception("TaskC Exception"); }
```

2. Start a *try/catch* block. You will enter code guarded for an exception in the *try* block.

```
try {
```

3. In the *try* block, create and start three tasks. Each task is initialized with a different method.

```
var TaskA=Task.Factory.StartNew(MethodA);
var TaskB=Task.Factory.StartNew(MethodB);
var TaskC=Task.Factory.StartNew(MethodC);
```

4. Use the *Task.WaitAll* method so that you can wait for the tasks and observe any exception.

```
Task.WaitAll(new Task[] {TaskA, TaskB, TaskC}); }
```

5. In the *catch* statement, catch the *AggregateException* exception. This will catch all unhandled exceptions of the tasks.

```
catch (AggregateException ae) {
```

6. In the *catch* block, iterate the *AggregateException.InnerExceptions* property and display each individual exception.

7. Build and run the application.

Here is the complete application.

```
class Program
{
    static void MethodA() { throw new Exception("TaskA Exception"); }
    static void MethodB() { throw new Exception("TaskB Exception"); }
    static void MethodC() { throw new Exception("TaskC Exception"); }
    static void Main(string[] args)
```

```
    {
        try {
            var TaskA=Task.Factory.StartNew(MethodA);
            var TaskB=Task.Factory.StartNew(MethodB);
            var TaskC=Task.Factory.StartNew(MethodC);
            Task.WaitAll(new Task[] {TaskA, TaskB, TaskC});
        }
        catch (AggregateException ae) {
            foreach (var ex in ae.InnerExceptions) {
                Console.WriteLine(ex.Message);
            }
        }
    }
}
```

The following code is similar to the previous example, except that it calls *Parallel.Invoke* instead of *TaskFactory.StartNew*.

```
try {
    Parallel.Invoke(new Action[] { MethodA, MethodB, MethodC });
}
catch (AggregateException ae){
    foreach (var ex in ae.InnerExceptions) {
        Console.WriteLine(ex.Message);
    }
}
```

The previous examples use a *foreach* loop to inspect and handle unhandled exceptions from different tasks. Alternatively, you can call the *AggregateException.Handle* method, which takes a callback function (delegate) as its only parameter. The delegate accepts the original exception as the single parameter and returns a *Boolean: Task<TResult>*. The return value indicates whether the unhandled exception was handled. Return *true* when you successfully handle the exception, otherwise return *false*. If you return *false*, the exception will continue to propagate up the call stack as a new aggregate exception. This new *AggregateException* will contain all the exceptions where the handler delegate returned *false*.

AggregateException calls the provided callback method for the exception from a task. For example, if there are four unhandled exceptions, it calls the callback four times. You'll practice handling exceptions with a callback in the next exercise.

Handle task exceptions with a callback function

1. Create a console application. Before the *Main* function, define *MethodA*, *MethodB*, and *MethodC* methods. Each method throws an explicit exception. In the exception constructor, provide the name of the task.

```
static void MethodA() { throw new Exception("TaskA Exception"); }
static void MethodB() { throw new Exception("TaskB Exception"); }
static void MethodC() { throw new Exception("TaskC Exception"); }
```

2. Start a *try/catch* block for handling exceptions.

```
try {
```

3. In the *try* block, execute the three methods as tasks by using the *Parallel.Invoke* method.

```
Parallel.Invoke(new Action[] { MethodA, MethodB, MethodC }); }
```

4. In the *catch* statement, catch the *AggregateException* exception. This will catch all unhandled exceptions of the tasks.

```
catch (AggregateException ae) {
```

5. Call the *Handle* method on the *AggregateException* object. Enter the callback as a lambda expression.

```
ae.Handle(ex => {
```

6. In the lambda expression, display the current exception message. Return *true* to indicate that the exception was handled.

7. Build and run the application.

Here is the complete application.

```
class Program
{
    static void MethodA() { throw new Exception("TaskA Exception"); }
    static void MethodB() { throw new Exception("TaskB Exception"); }
    static void MethodC() { throw new Exception("TaskC Exception"); }
    static void Main(string[] args)
    {
        try
        {
            Parallel.Invoke(new Action[] { MethodA, MethodB, MethodC });
        }
        catch (AggregateException ae)
        {
            ae.Handle(ex =>
            {
                Console.WriteLine(ex.Message);
                return true;
            });
        }
    }
}
```

As mentioned previously, a task can return a value, which you can inspect by using the *Task<TResult>.Result* property. If the *Task* has not completed, the current thread is suspended until the task finishes and returns a value. In addition, the *Task<TResult>.Result* property will observe an unhandled exception of the task, if any. Here is an example.

```
try{
var TaskA=Task<int>.Factory.StartNew(() =>{
            throw new DivideByZeroException();
            return 42;
});

        // Unhandled exception observed.
        Console.WriteLine(TaskA.Result);
  }
catch (AggregateException ae) {
    // handle exception
    Console.WriteLine(ae.InnerException.Message);
 }
```

Sort Examples

Sorting a collection is the one way to demonstrate task parallelism. The examples in this chapter sort an integer collection. As you are probably aware, there are various sorting algorithms; this section uses three different ones, to compare them and identify the quickest of the three—a race of sort algorithms!

The sort algorithms to compare are bubble sort, insertion sort, and pivot sort. In this example, the potential dependency is the integer collection, which is sorted simultaneously by different sort algorithms. This is a problem because the integer collection is being sorted in place. There are various techniques for resolving a dependency. One solution is to make copies of the shared data and provide each task with a private copy, which is the approach chosen here; each task (sort algorithm) gets a copy of the original integer collection as a parameter.

 Note The example code in this chapter and the remainder of the book does not have comments. Instead, it's self-documenting code that uses longer symbolic names, which makes the code more readable.

Bubble Sort

Bubble sort is a commonly used sort algorithm. However, this does not mean it is the quickest sort algorithm; in fact, it's probably one of the slowest sort algorithms. You'll see just how slow a bubble sort is when compared to other sort algorithms. Popularity does not always equate to quality.

A bubble sort performs binary comparisons. It typically begins at the start of the collection and compares the value of the first two elements. If the second element is less than the first, it swaps the element's position in the collection (assuming an ascending sort). It then performs the same comparison and swap operation on the second and third elements, and so on until the end of the collection. The sort is then repeated from the beginning until the collection is fully sorted. Here is the sample code.

```
public static void BubbleSort(List<int> sortedList) {
    int count = sortedList.Count;
    int temporary;

    for (int iteration = 0; iteration < count; ++iteration) {
        for (int index = 0; index + 1 < count; ++index) {
            if (sortedList[index] > sortedList[index + 1]) {
                temporary = sortedList[index];
                sortedList[index] = sortedList[index + 1];
                sortedList[index + 1] = temporary;
            }
        }
    }
}
```

Insertion Sort

An insertion sort iterates over the collection several times. Each iteration places a selected item in the correct location in the sort sequence. For example, the initial iteration would scan the collection and place the first element in the correct position for the sorted sequence. The second iteration would scan the list again and place the second element in the correct position. This continues until each element of the list is positioned correctly. Insertion sorts can use two lists: an unsorted list (input) and a sorted list (output); however, this example uses only one list, performing the sort in place. The sort repositions each element by using an insert, reposition, and delete operation. Here's the code.

```
public static void InsertionSort(List<int> sortedList, CancellationToken token) {
    int count = sortedList.Count;
    int currentLocation, currentValue, insertionLocation;
    sortedList.Insert(0, 0);

    for (int location = 1; location < count + 1; ++location) {
        currentLocation = location;
        insertionLocation = location - 1;
        currentValue = sortedList[currentLocation];
        while (sortedList[insertionLocation] > currentValue) {
            sortedList[currentLocation] = sortedList[insertionLocation];
            --currentLocation;
            --insertionLocation;
        }
        sortedList[currentLocation] = currentValue;
    }
    sortedList.Remove(0);
}
```

Pivot Sort

Pivot sorts are fun! A pivot sort is commonly known as a *quick sort*. The algorithm first chooses a pivot value, dividing the collection into two collections. The first collection contains the elements that are less than the pivot value, while the second collection contains values greater than the pivot. You then perform a pivot sort on the two sub-collections by using new pivot values. You continue to divide and sort collections recursively until the sub-collections each contain one element. Finally, you assemble the sorted sub-collections to create the sorted list. Because this example sorts in ascending order, it always places lesser values in the left sub-collection and greater values in the right sub-collection. Here's the sample code.

```
public static void PivotSort(List<int> integerList, int start, int end, int pivot)
{
    if (start < end)
    {
        pivot = integerList[end];
        int location = start;
        int bound = end;

        while (location < bound)
        {
            if (integerList[location] < pivot)
            {
                ++location;
            }
            else
            {
                integerList[bound] = integerList[location];
                integerList[location] = integerList[bound - 1];
                --bound;
            }
        }

        integerList[bound] = pivot;
        PivotSort(integerList, start, bound - 1, pivot);
        PivotSort(integerList, bound + 1, end, pivot);
    }
}
```

Using the *Barrier* Class

For a horse race to be fair, the horses need to start at the same time. Horse racing uses a starter gate; the .NET Framework offers the *Barrier* class. The *Barrier* class is in the *System.Threading* namespace. It is introduced in the .NET Framework 4. You use the *Barrier* classes to create logical gates or phases in your application. When you initialize a *Barrier*, you can set a maximum number of elements. Until the maximum number is reached, adding an element to the *Barrier* will block the current task. When the *Barrier* reaches capacity, it "spills." At that point, the waiting tasks execute. So when the *Barrier* is full (all the horses are at the gate), it releases all tasks and the race begins.

This diagram demonstrates a barrier with a capacity of three.

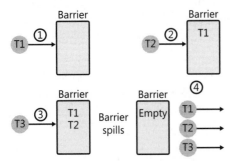

You could also think of a *Barrier* as a bucket. When the bucket is full, it will tip over. Of course, at that point, everything in the bucket is released.

Here are the helpful instance methods of the *Barrier* class:

- *Barrier constructor(int participantCount)*   This creates an instance and sets *Barrier* capacity.

- *void SignalAndWait()*   This signals that a task has reached a *Barrier.*

- *long AddParticipants(int participantCount)*   This increases the capacity of the Barrier.

- *void RemoveParticipants(int participantCount)*   This reduces the capacity of the *Barrier.*

The sorting example uses a *Barrier* to mark the start of the sorting phase. The maximum for the *Barrier* is set to three (bubble, insertion, and pivot sort). Using the *Barrier* guarantees that the three sort routines start at the same time, which makes for a fair race.

Each sort algorithm is started in a separate code region. Each region follows the same general pattern:

1. Duplicate list

2. Create task for sort algorithm

3. Task: signal barrier

4. Task: perform sort

5. Start task

Here is the Insertion Sort Region, which is one of the three sort regions.

```
// Insertion SortRegion

List<int> insertionList = integerList.ToList();
Task taskInsertionSort = new Task(() => {
    sortBarrier.SignalAndWait();
    using (new SortResults("Insertion Sort")){
        SortAlgorithms.InsertionSort(insertionList);
    }
});
taskInsertionSort.Start();
```

You also need some code to display the duration of each sort algorithm to find out which sort algorithm is the quickest. This code waits for the sorting tasks to complete, then iterates and displays the results.

```
Task.WaitAll(new Task[] { taskBubbleSort, taskInsertionSort, taskPivotSort });
foreach (string result in SortResults.results){
    Console.WriteLine(result);
}
```

When you run this, you'll get results similar to the ones below, which show the result of sorting 10,000 integers with durations in milliseconds. *And the winner is...pivot sort!* The race was not even close.

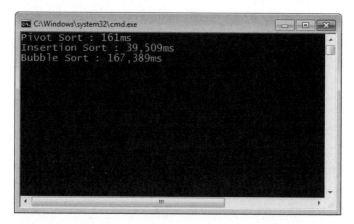

Where does the code calculate the duration? First, a *Stopwatch* class, which is defined in the *System.Diagnostics* namespace, is used to track the duration of each algorithm. In this program, the *SortResults* class is a wrapper for the *Stopwatch* class and calculates the duration of a sort algorithm.

Here is a general description of the *SortResults* class.

1. In the *SortResults* class, I create an instance of the *Stopwatch* class as a member field.

2. The constructor calls the *Start* method of the *Stopwatch* instance and sets the name of the sort algorithm.

3. The *Dispose* method calls the *Stop* method of the *Stopwatch*. The result is then format-ted and added to a results collection. The results collection is later iterated to display the results.

Here is the code for the class.

```
class SortResults : IDisposable{
    // Instance Members
    public  SortResults(string name){
        sortName = name;
        _stopwatch.Start();
    }

    private Stopwatch _stopwatch = new Stopwatch();
    private string sortName;

    public void Dispose(){
        _stopwatch.Stop();
        results.Add(string.Format("{0} : {1:N0}ms", sortName,
            _stopwatch.ElapsedMilliseconds));
    }
    // Classwise members (static)      // The rest of the class…

}
```

Each sort region uses the *SortClass* via a *using* statement (see the sort regions discussion, ear-lier in this section). Here is a snippet of code from the bubble sort region.

```
using (new SortResults("Bubble Sort")){
  // Perform sort
}
```

What is being done in the *using* statement and subsequent block? *SortResults* objects are disposable and can be instantiated in a *using* statement. In our example, an anonymous *SortResult* object is created. As shown previously, the *SortResults* object creates a *Stopwatch* and starts it in the constructor. The closing brace of the *using* statement is important. When execution reaches the closing brace, it calls the *SortResults.Dispose* method, which stops the *Stopwatch* and records the results.

Refactoring the Pivot Sort

The pivot sort algorithm performed better than the bubble and insertion sort algorithms. It is the champion. Magnifique! However, even the pivot sort could be improved. As mentioned in Chapter 1, one challenge of parallel programming is identifying potential opportunities for parallelism. Of course, not every opportunity for parallelism should be exploited. Sometimes the cost of parallelism offsets the benefits.

The pivot sort works by pivoting around a value. It creates *less than* and *greater than* collections in which the pivot value is the delineating factor between the two. It then sorts each sub-collection along a new pivot value, and so on. In the pivot sort example used previously, the sort is performed sequentially. Sorting the sub-collections in parallel could improve performance, but possibly not in every circumstance. For example, if one of the sub-collections were significantly larger than the other, sorting the collections in parallel would provide only a limited advantage. Sorting the sub-collections in parallel only makes sense when the left and right collections are relatively close to the same size.

In the following example, the code for the pivot sort has been refactored to sort sub-collections in parallel. In this example, the sub-collections must be of similar size and must contain more than 50 items to sort in parallel; otherwise, the algorithm chooses a sequential sort. These changes improve the pivot sort by about 20 percent for a collection of 10,000 integers.

These are the steps to pivot sort the sub-collections.

1. If a collection contains fewer than 50 items, don't perform a parallel sort.
2. Check whether the collections have similar sizes.
3. If the sizes are similar, sort the sub-collections in parallel.
4. When the sizes differ significantly, sort the sub-collections sequentially.

Here is the refactored sample code.

```
if (sortedList.Count >50) {
double delta = ((double)left.Count) / right.Count;
if ((delta > .75) && (delta < 1.333)) {
var taskLeft = Task.Factory.StartNew(() => PivotSort(left));
            var taskRight = Task.Factory.StartNew(() => PivotSort(right));
            rleft = taskLeft.Result;
            rright = taskRight.Result;
}
else
{
        rleft = PivotSort(left);
        rright = PivotSort(right);
}
}
```

Cancellation

The sort algorithm sample code in the preceding section allows the three sort algorithms to run to completion. But logically, because all the sort algorithms wind up with the same results, you need to sort the integer collection only once—the fastest way possible. When the fastest sort completes, you can cancel the other sorts. The .NET Framework 4 introduced the concept of *cooperative cancellation*, which is a consistent model for cancelling tasks. As the name implies, the model requires cooperation from running tasks. Tasks are responsible for regularly checking for a cancellation request. After a cancellation request has been received, a task should perform a timely and orderly shutdown. Checking for cancellation might require polling, and that can easily become a performance sink. For this reason, if it is required, be careful when implementing a polling strategy.

Here are the steps required for the cooperative cancellation model:

1. Create an instance of the *CancellationTokenSource* class, which is a wrapper for a cancellation token.

2. Pass the actual cancellation token (the *CancellationTokenSource.Token* property) as a parameter to the cooperating tasks.

3. From the original thread, call the *CancellationTokenSource.Cancel* method to make a cancellation request.

4. In the task, check the *CancellationToken.IsCancellationRequested* property for a cancellation request.

5. After preparing for cancellation, for example by preserving state information, the task should call the *CancellationToken.ThrowIfCancellationRequest* method. This throws the *OperationCanceledException* exception and cancels the task.

6. You can inspect whether a task was canceled. Check *Task.Status* for *TaskStatus.Canceled*.

The use of *CancellationTokenSource* and *CancellationToken* types is not restricted to tasks. Many of the types referenced in this book, including the cancellation types, can be used more generally with threads.

The next tutorial demonstrates the cooperative model for cancellation. In this example, you will create a *CancellationToken* that is passed into a task. In the task, you will periodically check for a cancellation request.

Create a task that throws a cancellation exception

In this procedure, the joining thread catches and handles the unhandled exception.

1. Create a console application. Before the *Main* function, add a *DoSomething* method. To emulate a compute-bound task, the task will simply spin and burn processor cycles. This is done with the *Thread.SpinWait* method.

```
static void DoSomething() { Thread.SpinWait(4000); }
```

2. In the *Main* function, create a *CancellationTokenSource* object. Afterward, initialize a cancellation token with the *CancellationTokenSource.Token* property.

```
CancellationTokenSource cancellationSource =
    new CancellationTokenSource();
CancellationToken token = cancellationSource.Token;
```

3. Start a *try/catch* block for handling exceptions.

```
try {
```

4. You can now create and start a new task by using the *TaskFactory.StartNew* method. Initialize the task with a lambda expression.

```
Task TaskA=Task.Factory.StartNew(() => {
```

5. In the lambda expression, you need a *while* loop. In the loop, call the compute-bound method. Check whether an exception is requested by using the *CancellationToken .IsCancellationRequested* property. If cancellation is requested, throw a cancellation exception. Notice that you also pass the cancellation token to the task as the last parameter of the *StartNew* method.

```
while (true) {
    DoSomething();
    if (token.IsCancellationRequested) {

        token.ThrowIfCancellationRequested();
    }
}}, token);
```

6. In the joining thread, cancel the task. Then wait for the task to complete and observe the cancellation exception.

```
cancellationSource.Cancel();
```

```
TaskA.Wait(); }
```

7. In the *catch* block, catch the cancellation exception and display the message.

8. Build and run the application.

Here is the complete application.

```
static void Main(string[] args)
{
    CancellationTokenSource cancellationSource =
        new CancellationTokenSource();
    CancellationToken token = cancellationSource.Token;
    try
    {
    Task TaskA=Task.Factory.StartNew(() =>
    {
        while (true)
        {
            DoSomething();
            if (token.IsCancellationRequested)
            {
                token.ThrowIfCancellationRequested();
            }
        }
    }, token);
    cancellationSource.Cancel();
    TaskA.Wait();
    }
    catch (AggregateException ex)
    {
        Console.WriteLine(ex.InnerException.Message);
    }
}
}
```

A Cancellation Example

Here is the sample code to implement cancellation in the bubble sort region of the sorting application. Similar changes can be made in the regions for the insertion and pivot sorts. The three sorting tasks are given the same cancellation token. Because they share the same token, all of the sorting algorithms can be cancelled as a group. For this reason, you create the cancellation token only once before entering the sort regions.

```
CancellationTokenSource cancellationSource =
    new CancellationTokenSource();
CancellationToken token = cancellationSource.Token;

// Bubble Sort Region

List<int> bubbleList = integerList.ToList();
Task taskBubbleSort = new Task(() => {
    sortBarrier.SignalAndWait();
    using (new SortResults("Bubble Sort")){
        SortAlgorithms.BubbleSort(bubbleList, token);
    }
}, token);
taskBubbleSort.Start();
```

Because each sort is different, cancellation polling occurs in different locations in each sort algorithm. When a cancellation request is detected, the code throws an *OperationCanceled Exception* exception and cancels the task.

Here is the sample code for actually canceling the sort algorithms. The joining thread calls *WaitAny*. Unlike *WaitAll*, *WaitAny* will return when the fastest task finishes, at which time you can cancel the other sort algorithms that are still running, by calling *CancellationTokenSource .Cancel*.

```
Task.WaitAny(new Task[] { taskBubbleSort, taskInsertionSort, taskPivotSort });
cancellationSource.Cancel();
```

Task Relationships

This chapter has already demonstrated several techniques for creating tasks. For example, you can start multiple tasks with the *Parallel.Invoke* method, create tasks with *TaskFactory .StartNew*, or use the *Task* constructor. Each approach varies slightly in functionality but ultimately creates a task that is scheduled and eventually started. So far, the example tasks have been independent, with no relationship to another task. However, tasks can have relationships. You can create *continuation* tasks, *subtasks*, and tasks that have a *parent-child relationship*. Task relationships help you create more sophisticated solutions.

A continuation task automatically starts after another task completes. For example, the first task might be responsible for calculating a result, and then the second task might display the result. An error might occur if the result is shown before the calculation is complete. For this reason, it is important to order the execution of these two tasks.

Continuation Tasks

Ordering parallel tasks is sometimes helpful. Naturally, executing tasks in parallel is preferable; however, for correctness, ordering of tasks is sometimes required. The next image depicts four tasks. Two of the tasks are compute bound and return a result. The other two tasks are responsible for displaying the results. As shown, the four tasks are running in parallel, which could cause problems.

The tasks should be ordered so that the display tasks start after their corresponding compute tasks. In this scenario, the compute task is termed the *antecedent*, and the display task is called the *successor*. An antecedent is the first task in an ordered sequence. The successor task is the second and is a continuation of the antecedent task. The terms *successor* and *continuation task* are used interchangeably in this book. As illustrated, *TaskB* should continue *TaskA*, and *TaskD* should continue *TaskC*.

Ordered tasks

TaskA	TaskC
Compute result	Compute result
TaskB	TaskD
Display result	Display result

The *Task* class has several methods that order tasks. These methods schedule one task to continue after another. The *ContinueWith* method, which is an instance method, is the simplest of them. Call *Task.ContinueWith* on the antecedent task. As a parameter, pass in the successor method as a delegate. The parameter is used to create the successor task that will continue after the antecedent task. Inside the successor task, you can reference the antecedent task, which is provided as a parameter.

Create an antecedent and successor task and then wait for both to complete

1. Create a console application. In the *Main* function, create a new task by using the *Task* constructor. Initialize the task with a lambda expression. In the lambda expression, display the name of the task.

```
var antecedent = new Task(() =>{
    Console.WriteLine("antecedent.");
});
```

2. Use the *Task.ContinueWith* method to create a continuation task. In the lambda expression for this task, display the name of the task. This task automatically runs when the antecedent task completes.

```
var successor=antecedent.ContinueWith((firstTask) =>
{ Console.WriteLine("successor."); });
```

3. You can now start the antecedent task. Afterward, wait for both the antecedent and successor tasks to complete.

```
class Program
{
    static void Main(string[] args)
    {
        var antecedent = new Task(() =>
        {
```

```
                    Console.WriteLine("antecedent.");
            });
            var successor=antecedent.ContinueWith((firstTask) =>
            { Console.WriteLine("successor."); });
            antecedent.Start();
            Task.WaitAll(antecedent, successor);
        }
    }
```

In the previous example code, the antecedent task did not return a result. When the antecedent returns a value, the successor task can find the results of the antecedent task in the *Task<TResult>.Result* property. Remember, the successor gets a reference to the antecedent as a parameter.

Create an antecedent task and a successor task in which the antecedent task result is checked later

1. Create a console application. In the *Main* function, define a new task by using the *Task* constructor. The task should return an integer value. Initialize the task with a lambda expression. In the lambda expression, display the current task and return a value. This is the antecedent task.

```
Task<int> calculate = new Task<int>(() =>{
    Console.WriteLine("Calculate result.");
    return 42;});
```

2. With the *Task.ContinueWith* method, create a continuation task that displays the result of the antecedent task. Pass a reference to the antecedent as a parameter. You can use the reference to access the result of the antecedent.

```
var answer=calculate.ContinueWith((antecedent) =>{
        Console.WriteLine("The answer is {0}.", antecedent.Result); });
```

3. You can now start the antecedent task. Then wait for both the antecedent and successor methods to complete.

```
class Program
{
    static void Main(string[] args)
    {
        Task<int> calculate = new Task<int>(() =>
        {
            Console.WriteLine("Calculate result."); return 42;
        });
        Task answer=calculate.ContinueWith((antecedent) =>{
                Console.WriteLine("The answer is {0}.", antecedent.Result); });
        calculate.Start();
        Task.WaitAll(calculate, answer);
    }
}
```

In the preceding example, the successor task started when the current task completed. What if you want to continue only after several tasks finish? That is possible with the static *TaskFactory.ContinueWhenAll* method. This method accepts an array of tasks as a parameter. The continuation task will begin after the last of these tasks has completed. In this case, the successor task receives an array of antecedent tasks as a parameter. You can use this array in the successor to access state information from each antecedent.

Create two antecedent tasks and check the result of both in the successor task

1. Before the *Main* function, add a *PerformCalculation* method that returns an integer value of 42.

```
static int PerformCalculation() { return 42; }
```

2. Next, create a new task that returns an integer value. Initialize the task with a lambda expression. In the lambda expression, display the current task and return the result of the *PerformCalculation* method.

```
Task<int> TaskA = new Task<int>(() =>{
    Console.WriteLine("TaskA started.");
    return PerformCalculation(); });
```

3. Now create a *TaskB*, similar to *TaskA*. *TaskA* and *TaskB* are the antecedent methods.

```
Task<int> TaskB = new Task<int>(() => {
        Console.WriteLine("TaskB started.");
        return PerformCalculation(); });
```

4. Create a continuation task to run after *TaskA* and *TaskB* have completed. You can accomplish this with the *TaskFactory.ContinueWhenAll* method. The first parameter is an array of tasks.

```
Task total=Task.Factory.ContinueWhenAll(new Task<int>[] { TaskA, TaskB },
```

5. As part of *TaskFactory.ContinueWhenAll*, you next define the continuation task as a lambda expression. Pass a reference to the antecedent tasks as the parameter. In the successor task, add and display the results of the antecedent tasks.

```
(tasks)=>Console.WriteLine("Total = {0}", tasks[0].Result+tasks[1].Result));
```

6. Start both antecedent tasks and then wait for both to complete. Afterward, wait for the continuation task to complete.

```
class Program
{
    static int PerformCalculation() { return 42; }
    static void Main(string[] args)
    {
        Task<int> TaskA = new Task<int>(() =>
        {
            Console.WriteLine("TaskA started.");
            return PerformCalculation();
```

```
        });
        Task<int> TaskB = new Task<int>(() =>
        {
            Console.WriteLine("TaskB started.");
            return PerformCalculation();
        });
        Task total=Task.Factory.ContinueWhenAll(new Task<int>[] { TaskA, TaskB },
            (tasks) => Console.WriteLine(
                "Total = {0}", tasks[0].Result + tasks[1].Result));
        TaskA.Start();
        TaskB.Start();
        Task.WaitAll(TaskA, TaskB);
        total.Wait();
    }
}
```

As shown, *TaskFactory.ContinueWhenAll* starts the continuation task (successor) after all the antecedent tasks have completed. Alternatively, there's a *TaskFactory.ContinueWhenAny*, which is an instance method that starts the continuation task after *any* listed antecedent task completes.

An interesting option when continuing a task is the *TaskContinuationOptions* parameter. With this option, you can set an event as an additional criterion for starting the continuation task. For example, suppose you want to continue a task only when the antecedent raises an exception. As another example, you might want to continue a task only when the antecedent was not canceled. *TaskContinuationOptions* is an enumeration that covers both of these scenarios and more. Here are the possible values.

- *None*
- *AttachedToParent*
- *ExecuteSynchronously*
- *LongRunning*
- *NotOnCanceled*
- *NotOnFaulted*
- *NotOnRanToCompletion*
- *OnlyOnCanceled*
- *OnlyOnFaulted*
- *OnlyOnRanToCompletion*
- *PreferFairness*

Some of the values, such as *OnlyOnFaulted*, are not available for continuation or successor tasks with multiple antecedents.

Here is a scenario. Assume that you want to perform a rollback if a task throws an unhandled exception. Exceptions can sometimes leave objects in an unknown state, so you might want to return objects to a known state; being in an unknown state is rarely good for a program. If an unhandled exception occurs in a task, you can perform the rollback in a continuation task, by using the *TaskContinuationOptions.OnlyOnFaulted* enumeration value.

Implement the preceding scenario in an application

1. Create a console application. You need to implement a custom task that can perform a rollback of an operation. First, define a new *CustomTask* class. Inherit the class from the *Task* class.

   ```
   class CustomTask : Task {
   }
   ```

2. Implement a public one-argument constructor for the *CustomTask* class with an *Action* delegate as the parameter. Pass the *Action* delegate to the base class (*Task*) constructor.

   ```
   public CustomTask(Action action)
       : base(action)
   { }
   ```

3. Add a *PerformRollback* method to the *CustomTask* class as a member method. In the real world, this method would perform a rollback. In our example, it simply displays a message.

   ```
   public void PerformRollback() { Console.WriteLine("Rollback..."); }
   ```

4. In the *Main* function, create a new *CustomTask*. This is the antecedent task. In the lambda expression for the task, throw an unhandled exception.

   ```
   CustomTask antecedent = new CustomTask(() => {
       throw new Exception("Unhandled"); });
   ```

5. Next, create a continuation task for the antecedent task by using the *Task.ContinueWith* method. Implement the continuation task as a lambda expression. Pass a reference of the antecedent task as a parameter of the lambda expression. In our example, you want to perform a rollback. Finally, you want to execute the continuation task only when the antecedent task has a fault. For that reason, add the *TaskContinuationOptions .OnlyOnFaulted* as the final parameter.

   ```
   antecedent.ContinueWith((predTask) =>
   {
       ((CustomTask)predTask).PerformRollback();
   }, TaskContinuationOptions.OnlyOnFaulted);
   ```

6. Now you can start the antecedent task. Wait for the task in a *try/catch* block.

   ```
   class CustomTask : Task {
           public CustomTask(Action action)
               : base(action)
   ```

```
                { }
                public void PerformRollback() { Console.WriteLine("Rollback..."); }
        }
        class Program
        {
            static void Main(string[] args)
            {
                CustomTask antecedent = new CustomTask(() =>
                {
                    throw new Exception("Unhandled");
                });
                antecedent.ContinueWith((predTask) =>
                {
                    ((CustomTask)predTask).PerformRollback();
                },
                TaskContinuationOptions.OnlyOnFaulted);
                antecedent.Start();
                try
                {
                    antecedent.Wait();
                }
                catch (AggregateException ex)
                {
                }
            }
        }
```

Parent and Child Tasks

So far, you haven't seen examples that create subtasks. A subtask is a task created in the context of another task. The outer task is not necessarily a parent task. There is no implied relationship. The default task scheduler (the .NET Framework 4 thread pool) handles subtasks differently than other tasks. *Work stealing*, as explained in the next section, can occur whenever subtasks are created.

In the following exercise, you will create a task and subtask.

Create an outer task and a subtask

1. Create a console application. In the *Main* function, create a new task by using the *Task* constructor. Initialize the task with a lambda expression. This will be the outer task in a task relationship.

   ```
   var outer = new Task(() => {
   ```

2. In the lambda expression, display the name of the current task.

   ```
   Console.WriteLine("Outer task.");
   ```

3. Still within the lambda expression, create and start a task. Because you are within an existing task, this is a subtask. In the lambda expression for the new task, display the name of the task.

```
var inner=Task.Factory.StartNew(() => Console.WriteLine("Inner task."));
```

4. Wait for the subtask and close the lambda expression for the outer task.

```
inner.Wait(); });
```

5. To complete the example, start and then wait for the outer task. As part of the outer task, the inner task will also be started.

```
class Program
{
    static void Main(string[] args)
    {
        Task outer = new Task(() =>
        {
            Console.WriteLine("Outer task.");
            var inner=Task.Factory.StartNew(() => Console.WriteLine(
                "Inner task."));
            inner.Wait();
        });
        outer.Start();
        outer.Wait();
    }
}
```

You can convert a subtask relationship into a parent/child relationship. You might want to do this for a variety of reasons, including creating a hierarchy of tasks. Instantiating a subtask does not immediately confer a parent and child relationship between the two tasks. In addition to a subtask, you must also choose the *TaskCreationOptions.AttachedToParent* option to indicate a parent/child relationship.

The *TaskCreationOptions.AttachedToParent* method binds the lifetime of the parent and child tasks. In other words, when waiting for the parent task, you are essentially waiting for both the parent and the child task to complete. The parent might complete before the child. If that occurs, the status of the parent task becomes *TaskStatus.WaitingForChildrenToComplete*. When the child task eventually finishes, the status of the parent task is updated appropriately, for example, to *TaskStatus.Completed* or *TaskStatus.Faulted*.

Create a parent task and a child task where the duration of the child task is longer than the parent. Report the status when the parent task completes execution.

1. Create a console application. Implement a computer-bound method.

```
static void DoSomething() { Thread.SpinWait(4000); }
```

2. In the *Main* function, create a new task by using the *Task* constructor. Initialize the task with a lambda expression. This will be the parent task.

```
var parent = new Task(() => {
```

3. In the lambda expression for the parent task, display the name of the current task.

```
Console.WriteLine("Parent task.");
```

4. Still in the lambda expression, create and start a child task by using the *TaskFactory* .*StartNew* method. In the lambda expression for the child task, sleep for 5,000 millisec-onds by using the *Thread.Sleep* method. Be sure to define a parent/child relationship with the *TaskCreationOptions.AttachedToParent* option.

```
Task.Factory.StartNew(() => { Thread.Sleep(5000); },
    TaskCreationOptions.AttachedToParent);});
```

5. Start the parent running with the *Task.Start* method. The child task is executed as part of the parent task.

```
parent.Start();
```

6. Wait for the parent to complete. If the wait operation times out, query whether the parent is waiting for child tasks to complete. If the parent task is waiting for the child, display the status of the parent task.

```
class Program
{
    static void Main(string[] args)
    {
        Task parent = new Task(() =>
        {
            Console.WriteLine("Parent task.");
            Task.Factory.StartNew(() => { Thread.Sleep(5000); },
                TaskCreationOptions.AttachedToParent);
        });
        parent.Start();
        if ((!(parent.Wait(2000)) &&
            (parent.Status == TaskStatus.WaitingForChildrenToComplete)))
        {
            Console.WriteLine("Parent completed but child not finished.");
            parent.Wait();
        }
    }
}
```

The Work-Stealing Queue

Historically, thread pools have a single global queue in which to place work items. The thread pool dequeues work items from the global queue to provide work to available threads. The thread pool exists in a multi-threaded environment, so the global queue must be thread safe.

The resulting synchronization can adversely affect the performance of the thread pool and indeed the overall application.

Because a single global queue is a potential bottleneck, the .NET Framework 4 thread pool offers a global queue and any number of local queues. This scheme allows work items to be distributed across several queues and removes a single point of synchronization. Parent tasks can be scheduled on the global queue, while subtasks are placed on local queues.

Work items in the global queue are accessed in a first-in, first-out (FIFO) manner, whereas local queues are last-in, first-out (LIFO). In addition, local queues are double-ended; they have a private side and a public side. The private side is virtually lock free and is accessible only from the current thread. Other threads access the queue from the public side, which is controlled using synchronization. This explanation is somewhat of a generalization, but hopefully it is sufficient to convey the essence of work stealing.

Ultimately, work stealing is a performance optimization. A subtask is placed on a local queue and then scheduled (FIFO) to run on an available thread in the thread pool. After the task completes, the now-available thread returns to the same local queue for additional work. When this queue is empty, the thread can freelance and help other local queues with pending work. If work is found in another local queue, a task is dequeued (LIFO) and run on the available thread. This process is called *work stealing*. Here is a typical scenario:

1. A primary task is started and placed on the global queue.

2. When the primary task runs, it creates a subtask. The new task is then placed on a local queue.

3. The subtask completes. The thread pool searches for additional work to give to the newly available thread, which it does as follows:

   a. Search the same local queue for another task to dequeue (LIFO) and execute.

   b. If the local queue is empty, find work for the thread on another local queue (LIFO).

   c. If a task is found on another local queue, it is dequeued (FIFO) and executed. In essence, the thread just "stole" work from another local queue. However, in this context, stealing is helpful.

Instead of stalling a thread, work stealing keeps a thread busy even when its local queue is empty. The stolen task is taken from the back of another local queue. This must be synchronized for thread safety, because there might be other work-stealing threads that need work at the same time. However, that synchronization is an infrequent penalty, because most tasks are taken from the private front end of the local queue.

Subtasks of long-running threads are not placed on a local queue. Long-running tasks are scheduled on a dedicated thread and not on a thread in the thread pool. Similarly, subtasks of long-running tasks are scheduled on a dedicated thread as well. Therefore, long-running tasks exist outside of the thread pool and do not benefit from work stealing.

Here is a diagram of the work-stealing process.

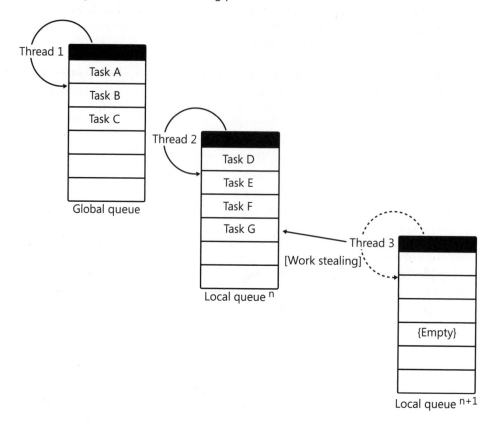

Summary

This chapter described several ways to start a parallel task:

- *Parallel.Invoke*
- *TaskFactory.StartNew*
- *Task.Start*

After a task has started, you can wait for it to complete by using one of the following methods:

- *Task.Wait*
- *Task.WaitAll*
- *Task.WaitAny*

Unhandled exceptions in a task are propagated to the joining thread. You must observe the unhandled exception in the joining thread to prevent an exception that can abort the application. For example, you can observe an exception with *Task.Wait*. Exceptions raised in a task are wrapped in an *AggregateException* exception. You can access the original exception in the *AggregateException.InnerException* property or, for multiple exceptions, the *AggregateException.InnerExceptions* property.

Tasks can be continued by using one of the *Continue* methods. The first task is the antecedent method, and the continuation task is the successor method. The successor method will start when the antecedent finishes. The *Continue* methods are as follows:

- *Task.ContinueWith*

- *TaskFactory.ContinueWhenAll*

- *TaskFactory.ContinueWhenAny*

Subtasks are tasks created within another task. Primary tasks are placed on the global queue of the thread pool, and subtasks are normally placed on a local queue. Work queue stealing occurs when a thread with no work steals work from another local queue.

Finally, *TaskCreationOptions.AttachedToParent* creates a parent/child relationship between two tasks. This binds the lifetimes of the parent and child tasks. Waiting for the parent will also wait for the child to complete.

Quick Reference

To	Do this
Invoke parallel tasks	Use the *Parallel.Invoke* method. Use the *TaskFactory.StartNew* method. Use the *Task.Start* method.
Observe an unhandled exception raised in a task	Implement exception handling in the observer, which is the joining thread. Catch *AggregateException*. Use *AggregateException.InnerException* to identify the underlying exception.
Cancel a task	Adhere to the cancellation model. Create a *CancellationTokenSource*. Pass the resulting *CancellationTokenSource.Token* to the cooperating tasks. Call the *CancellationToken.Cancel* method to cancel the parallel operation.
Continue one task with another task	Use the *Task.ContinueWith* method.
Define a parent/child relationship between two tasks	Create a subtask, and use the *TaskCreationOptions .AttachedToParent* option. This will link the lifetime of the parent and child tasks.
Add a task to a local queue	Create a subtask. Subtasks automatically use local queues versus the global queue. A local queue can also be a work-stealing queue.

Chapter 3
Data Parallelism

After completing this chapter, you will be able to

- Contrast data and task parallelism.

- Parallelize a sequential loop.

- Properly cancel a parallel loop.

- Handle unhandled exceptions arising in a parallel loop.

- Perform reductions while minimizing dependencies.

- Explain the MapReduce pattern.

The previous chapter introduced task parallelism, which involves invoking separate and distinct parallel tasks. In contrast, data parallelism applies a common operation to each element of a collection of data. An example of data parallelism could consist of applying a 10 percent price adjustment to items that have been in inventory for more than 90 days. The price increase is the common operation, and the inventory is the data collection. Naturally, data parallelism is more useful in data-centric and computing-intensive situations, such as database management, accounting, weather reporting, sales analysis, scientific applications, and even a fantasy sports league. Some portion of most applications is data centric, which provides an opportunity to implement data parallelism.

Finding concurrency in data parallelism is generally simpler than isolating opportunities for task parallelism. You look for loops. Loops are easy to locate syntactically—search for a *for*, *foreach*, *while*, or *do while* statement. A *for* or *foreach* statement typically implies a straightforward loop. In contrast, *while* loops are often used in more complex scenarios, such as circumstances that require loop dependencies. There are separate patterns for handling loop dependencies in parallel programming. Of course, there are other opportunities for data parallelism, such as calling an iterative function on a tree structure. However, searching for loops will probably find the majority of them. If iterations of the loop are independent or minimally dependent, the loop iterations can probably be "unrolled" as parallel operations. If they are entirely independent, the loop iterations can run embarrassingly parallel for optimum performance gain.

Loops often iterate collections in which an identical operation is applied to each element. Because data parallelism frequently involves parallelizing a loop, it is often called *loop-level parallelism*. Revisiting the previous example, suppose that you want to apply a 10 percent discount to certain items in inventory. The 10 percent price discount is an independent operation; discounting the price of one item should not affect another, so it can be embarrassingly parallel. For that reason, you can easily parallelize the operation, making each discount a parallel task. For the Task Parallel Library (TPL), the actual granularity is defined by the default partitioner, which defines the appropriate chunking. These tasks are then assigned to threads in the Microsoft .NET Framework 4 thread pool. You can customize partitioners and schedulers to fine-tune parallel operations. You'll see more about this topic in Chapter 6, "Customization."

Unrolling Sequential Loops into Parallel Tasks

Data parallelism typically begins by unrolling a sequential loop. For example, the code below defines a loop that runs sequentially. In this example, the code iterates over the loop body 100 times. The duration of the *for* loop is the aggregate duration of those 100 operations. Assuming an average of 100 milliseconds per operation, the *for* loop will take 10 seconds to complete (100 × 100 milliseconds).

```
for (int count = 0; count < 100; ++count)
{
    Operation();
}
```

Most importantly, the preceding code does not fully utilize the available processor cores. Look at a view of the processor cores for a computer with eight cores.

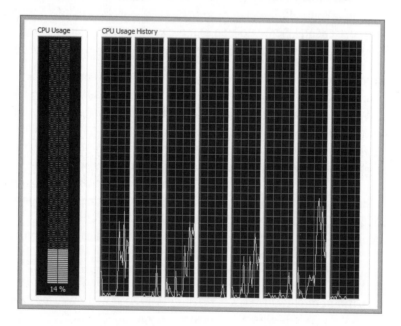

Note To display the Windows Task Manager, use the Ctrl+Shift+Esc key combination. You can then double-click anywhere in one of the CPU usage graphs to switch to the dedicated CPU usage view.

Notice that the average utilization of the cores is relatively low. Except for the first processor core, the other cores are not very busy. *A lot of processor power is being wasted!*

Here's the complete code for you to try.

```csharp
using System;+
using System.Collections.Generic;
using System.Linq;
using System.Text;
using System.Threading;
using System.Threading.Tasks;

namespace ParallelLoop
{
    class Program
    {
        static void Operation()
        {
            Thread.SpinWait(int.MaxValue);
        }

        static void Main(string[] args)
        {
            for (int count = 0; count < 100; ++count)
            {
                Operation();
            }
        }
    }
}
```

Fortunately, changing from a sequential loop to a parallel loop requires minimal changes in most circumstances. Here's the parallel version of the serial loop in the previous example.

```csharp
Parallel.For(1, 100, (count) =>
{
    Operation();
});
```

That was an easy change! Look at the processor usage graph for the parallel version. Nirvana! The graph shows 100 percent processor utilization with the parallel loop. However, there is a barely visible straight line across the top of the graph that represents 100 percent utilization.

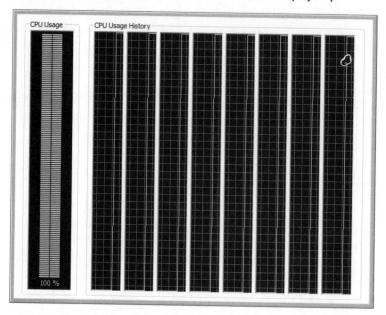

You'll delve into the syntactical nuances of *Parallel.For* shortly. The important point now is that this code successfully parallelizes the operation as a basket of tasks scheduled across the available cores. There are enough tasks to keep the processor cores busy, which is an important goal of parallel programming.

The key to high-performing data parallelism is independent iterations, which prevent dependencies when converted to parallel tasks. Only with independent iterations can you unroll the loops successfully. You can accomplish some dependencies, such as *reduction*, with minimal effect on performance. Reduction reduces a series of operations to a scalar value and is discussed later in this chapter. Not all dependencies are obvious. Here is a partial list of possible dependencies:

- Indexes
- Shared memory
- Shared files
- Order restrictions

Can you identify the dependency in the next loop? The following code is a parallel loop that squares the current index, which is then written into a file. The program generates unexpected results. This is because of a not-so-subtle dependency.

```
StreamWriter sw = new StreamWriter(filename);
Parallel.For (0, 100, (i)=>sw.WriteLine(i * i));
sw.Close();
```

The problem is the shared file reference. The code could attempt to write to the same file simultaneously from two or more parallel tasks—and files are not implicitly thread safe. In addition, the order of the writes is not assured, because the *Parallel.For* method does not guarantee the order in which tasks are executed. The largest reported value should be 10,000 (100×100). This is a partial listing from the file.

```
6084
4900
705662415041
7225
6400
9216
73966561
```

None of the preceding values is less than 1,000! The problem occurs because of data corruption from simultaneous writes to the file, which demonstrates the potential problem that dependencies pose for data parallelism. The shared file was an obvious dependency, but unfortunately, most dependencies are more subtle and often go undetected. This underscores the importance of performing rigorous unit testing, stress testing, and concurrency testing when converting routines from sequential to parallel. Converting syntax is simple, but maintaining correctness is a greater challenge.

There are techniques and tricks to identifying dependencies. One technique is to reverse the iteration of a sequential loop. In other words, you change the iteration from ascending to descending. If the reversal causes the application to generate different results or crash, that change in results indicates the likelihood of a dependency.

Evaluating Performance Considerations

Not every sequential loop should be unrolled into parallel tasks. One consideration is performance.

If the proposed tasks are relatively small, the overhead for parallel execution—thread pool scheduling, context switching, and other overhead—might exceed the gain that parallelization would provide. You should always conduct performance benchmarks to confirm potential performance improvements. When there is minimal or no performance gain, one solution is to change the chunk size. The default chunk size is set by the default partitioner of the TPL. When a larger chunk size is requested, the larger chunk size increases the amount of work assigned to an individual task. This will lower the relative percentage of parallelization overhead and hopefully improve overall performance.

Data parallelization typically iterates the same operation. However, identical operations are not guaranteed to run for the same duration. Look at the following code, which prints out a series of prime numbers. Each loop performs exactly the same operation; however, the duration of each task could vary widely. Depending on the implementation, calculating whether

1,000 is a prime number takes considerably longer than performing the same test on the number 81. This inequity of workload can cause inefficient parallelization. In this circumstance, you might create a custom partitioner that uses a weighted algorithm to dynamically determine the chunk size to keep the workload balanced across processors. This would improve task scheduling and processor core utilization.

Here is the abstracted code for rendering prime numbers.

```
Parallel.For(1, 1000, (index) =>
{
    if(IsPrime(index))
    {
        Console.WriteLine(index);
    }
});
```

Remember, the *Parallel.For* method might not perform the prime number calculation in sequential order. In addition, *Console.WriteLine* is synchronized internally, which assures that the output is thread safe.

The Parallel *For* Loop

In most programming languages, the *for* loop is the most commonly used statement for iterations. The following example is a serial *for* loop, which performs each iteration in sequence. The loop iterates from 0 to 1000 while performing some operation. When the count is equal to or greater than 1000, the loop stops.

```
for (int count = 0; count < 1000; ++count)
{
    DoSomething();
}
```

In the Task Parallel Library (TPL), the equivalent statement uses a *Parallel.For* method. Instead of performing the iterations sequentially, the code runs them in parallel. You can find the *Parallel* class in the *System.Threading.Tasks* namespace. For the basic overload, the first two parameters are the starting and maximum value exclusively. The increment is 1. The last parameter is an *Action* delegate. For this parameter, you can provide a delegate, a lambda expression, or even an anonymous method that takes the current index as its only parameter. *Parallel.For* returns a *ParallelLoopResult* structure that contains the status of the *Parallel.For* loop. Here is the prototype for the *Parallel.For* method.

```
public static ParallelLoopResult For(
    int fromInclusive,
    int toExclusive,
    Action<int> body
)
```

Next is an example of an equivalent *Parallel.For* loop that executes an operation 100 times. Unlike the *for* loop's iterations, the parallel iterations might not execute in linear sequence, so the seven-hundredth iteration might precede the tenth. However, unless the loop is canceled or interrupted with a *ParallelLoopState.Break* or *ParallelLoopState.Stop* statement, all iterations will run—just not necessarily in order.

```
Parallel.For(0, 100, (count) =>
{
   DoSomething();
});
```

The *Parallel.ForEach* method in the TPL is the parallel equivalent to the standard Microsoft Visual C# *foreach* statement. Use the *Parallel.ForEach* method to enumerate a collection in parallel using the same operation. For the basic overload of the method, the first parameter is the source collection. The next parameter is an *Action* delegate and is the operation to be performed on each element of the collection. The *Action* delegate takes a single parameter, the current element.

```
public static ParallelLoopResult ForEach<TSource>(

   IEnumerable<TSource> source,

   Action<TSource> body
)
```

Here is a standard *foreach* loop. Of course, this loop is performed sequentially.

```
foreach (int item in aList)
{
  Operation(item);
}
```

And here's the same loop rewritten using the *Parallel.ForEach* method. Each iteration is a parallel task, executed not sequentially but in parallel.

```
Parallel.ForEach(aList, (item)=> {
   Operation(item);
} );
```

To put this into practice, in this next exercise, assume that you have a retail store with inventory. Once a month, you adjust pricing for items that have been in stock for more than 90 days, discounting inventory items priced under $500.00 by 10 percent and higher-priced items by 20 percent. Higher-priced items have an additional profit margin.

Create a *Parallel.For* loop to adjust inventory pricing

1. Create a console application for C# in Microsoft Visual Studio 2010. With the *using* statement, add the namespace *System.Threading.Tasks* to the list of namespaces. At class scope (before the *Main* method), define a static integer array that contains pricing of items in stock more than 90 days.

```
static int[] inventoryList = new int []
    {100, 750, 400, 75, 900, 975, 275, 750, 600, 125, 300};
```

2. In the *Main* method, define a *Parallel.For* loop to enumerate the inventory.

```
Parallel.For( 0, inventoryList.Length, (index) => {
```

3. You can now write the parallel operation. Define a temporary variable to hold the price of the current inventory item. If the price is greater than $500.00, apply a 20 percent discount. Otherwise, use a 10 percent discount.

```
var price= inventoryList[index];
if (price> 500)
{
    inventoryList[index] = (int)(price* .8);
}
else
{
    inventoryList[index] = (int)(price* .9);
}
```

4. Use *Console.WriteLine* to display the adjusted price.

5. At the end of the program, add a *Console.ReadLine* method to prevent the program from ending before you can view the results. You might also want to display an informative message to the user.

```
Console.WriteLine("Press enter to exit");
Console.ReadLine();
```

 Note I'll omit the previous step in future examples, but feel free to add it at your discretion.

6. Build and run the application.

Your completed code should look like the following.

```
namespace PriceIncrease
{
    class Program
    {
        static int[] inventoryList = new int [] {100, 750, 400, 75, 900, 975, 275,
            750, 600, 125, 300};
```

```
static void Main(string[] args)
{
    Parallel.For( 0, inventoryList.Length, (index) =>
    {
        var price = inventoryList[index];
        if (price> 500)
        {
            inventoryList[index] = (int)(price* .8);
        }
        else
        {
            inventoryList[index] = (int)(price* .9);
        }

        Console.WriteLine("Item {0,4} Price: {1, 7:f}",
            index, inventoryList[index]);
    });

    Console.WriteLine("Press enter to exit");
    Console.ReadLine();
}
}
}
```

Here's the output for the application. Notice that the inventory items were not handled in sequential order. Your results might vary from these results. In addition, the results of a parallel application might change between instances. For example, the order of execution of a *Parallel.For* loop is not guaranteed and could change between instances.

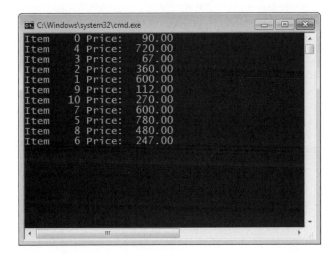

Interrupting a Loop

In a normal C# *for* or *foreach* loop, you can break or continue loop iteration by using the *break* and *continue* statements, respectively. The *break* statement interrupts the current iteration and cancels any remaining loop iterations. The *continue* statement skips the balance of the current iteration but continues with the remaining iterations. Because *Parallel.For* and *Parallel.ForEach* don't execute sequentially, cancellation is a more complex operation. Specifically, you cannot use the *break* or *continue* statement in a parallel *for* loop. This is because *Parallel.For* and *Parallel.ForEach* are methods and not language-intrinsic loops. Instead, there are special constructs for canceling a parallel loop.

To interrupt a loop, you need to pass a *ParallelLoopState* object as the second parameter of the *Action* delegate used for the parallel operation. You can then interrupt a parallel loop with the *ParallelLoopState.Break* method. At that time, other tasks might have completed, be running, or not have started. For a long-running task, you should period-ically check for a pending interruption. To confirm a pending interruption, check the *ParallelLoopState.ShouldExitCurrentIteration* property. If it's true, there is a pending cancelation. You can find the index of the cancellation task in the *ParallelLoopState.LowestBreakIteration* property. Tasks with a higher index value should voluntarily cancel at a convenient time. Tasks with lower indexes can run to completion. Tasks not started but with a lower indexed value should be allowed to start and run to completion, but tasks with higher indexes that have not started should never run.

The following image illustrates the *ParallelLoopState.Break* method. This example is a sample scenario. The results might vary based on several factors. In Phase 1, the *Parallel.For* method queues six tasks to the .NET Framework 4 thread pool, and Tasks 1, 2, 4, and 5 start running. Available processor cores are not available for Tasks 3 and 6. At the end of Phase 2, Task 4 calls the *ParallelLoopState.Break* method to cancel the loop. In Phase 3, Tasks 1, 2, and 3 are allowed to complete despite the cancellation, because those tasks have a lower index value than the canceling task. For that reason, Task 3 is allowed to start and stop. Task 5 detects the cancellation and voluntarily stops. Because Task 6 has an index value greater than the can-cellation index, it is not even allowed to start.

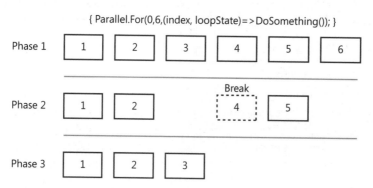

The *ParallelLoopState.Stop* method is an alternative cancellation model. Using this method, *all* running tasks are expected to cancel as soon as conveniently possible. Running tasks can confirm cancellation with the *ParallelLoopState.IsStopped* method. When the *ParallelLoopState.Stop* property is *true*, tasks are expected to voluntarily stop as soon as possible. Unlike the *ParallelLoopState.Break* method, unstarted tasks are not allowed to run, regardless of their index value. For these reasons, with the *ParallelLoopState.Stop* model, fewer tasks are allowed to start or continue when compared to *ParallelLoopState.Break*. This is a cleaner cancellation model.

The next image illustrates the *ParallelLoopState.Stop* method. In Phase 1, six tasks are scheduled but not started. Tasks 1, 2, 4, and 5 are running in Phase 2. At that point, Task 4 calls the *ParallelLoopState.Stop* method. Tasks 1, 2, and 5 eventually notice the cancellation and stop. There are no tasks running at the end of Phase 3.

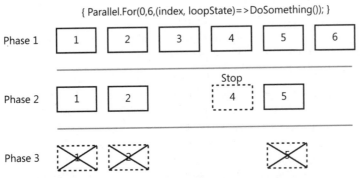

In this example, you will start and cancel a *Parallel.For* loop, reading the cancellation index from the command line.

Create and cancel a *Parallel.For* loop

1. Create a console application for C# in Visual Studio 2010. With *using* statements, add the *System.Threading.Tasks* and *System.Threading.Tasks* namespaces to the source file.

2. Before the *Main* method, create a static function named *HalfOperation*. This function will represent half of the operation for each iteration. The function has no parameters and returns *void*. In the function, call *Thread.SpinWait* for half of the maximum *int* value.

```
static void HalfOperation()
{
    Thread.SpinWait(int.MaxValue / 2);
}
```

3. In the *Main* method, you need to convert the first command-line parameter to an index value for cancellation. The *int.TryParse* method is convenient and avoids raising an exception for invalid values or miscasts. If the parameter contains an invalid value, just return.

```
int cancelValue;
if(!int.TryParse(args[0], out cancelValue))
{
    return;
}
```

4. Start a parallel loop with a minimum value of 0 and maximum of 12. Create a lambda expression for the loop operation. Pass the loop index and *ParallelLoopState* parameter into the lambda expression.

```
Parallel.For(0, 12, (index, loopState) =>
```

5. In the lambda expression, display the index of the current task and call the *HalfOperation* method. Next, check whether this is the cancellation task. If so, call the *ParallelLoopState.Break* method. Afterward, display a message about the cancellation and stop the current task.

```
Console.WriteLine("Task {0} started...", index);
HalfOperation();
if (cancelValue == index)
{
    loopState.Break();
    Console.WriteLine("Loop Operation cancelling. Task {0} cancelled...", index);
    return;
}
```

6. Tasks should periodically check for a cancellation. First check whether a cancellation is pending in the *ParallelLoopState.LowestBreakIteration.HasValue* property. If a cancellation is pending, check the cancellation index. If it's greater than the index of the current task, end the task. Of course, display appropriate messages.

```
if (loopState.LowestBreakIteration.HasValue)
{
    if (index > loopState.LowestBreakIteration)
    {
        Console.WriteLine("Task {0} cancelled", index);
        return;
    }
}
HalfOperation();
Console.WriteLine("Task {0} ended.", index);
```

Here is the complete code.

```
using System;
using System.Collections.Generic;
using System.Linq;
using System.Text;
using System.Threading;
using System.Threading.Tasks;

namespace ParallelLoopBreak
{
    class Program
```

```
{
    static void HalfOperation()
    {
        Thread.SpinWait(int.MaxValue / 2);
    }
    static void Main(string[] args)
    {
        int cancelValue;

        if(!int.TryParse(args[0], out cancelValue))
        {
            return;
        }

        Parallel.For(0, 20, (index, loopState) =>
            {
                    Console.WriteLine("Task {0} started...", index);
                    HalfOperation();
                    if (cancelValue == index)
                    {
                        loopState.Break();
                        Console.WriteLine(
                            "Loop Operation cancelling. " +
                            "Task {0} cancelled...", index);
                        return;
                    }
                    if (loopState.LowestBreakIteration.HasValue)
                    {
                        if (index > loopState.LowestBreakIteration)
                        {
                            Console.WriteLine("Task {0} cancelled", index);
                            return;
                        }
                    }
                    HalfOperation();
                    Console.WriteLine("Task {0} ended.", index);
            });
        Console.WriteLine("Press enter to end");
        Console.ReadLine();his
    }

}
}
```

The following image shows some partial output from the application. Your output should look similar. In this example, cancellation occurred at Task 12. At that time, several other tasks had already started.

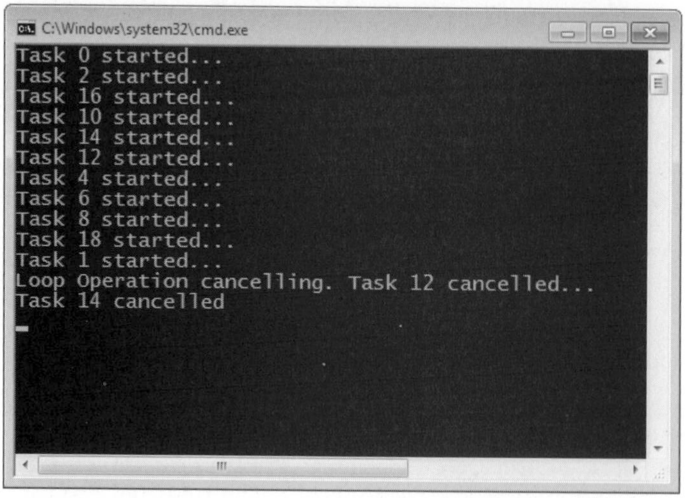

And the next image shows some output from the end of that same application. Notice that tasks with an index value less than 12 were allowed to start or run to completion.

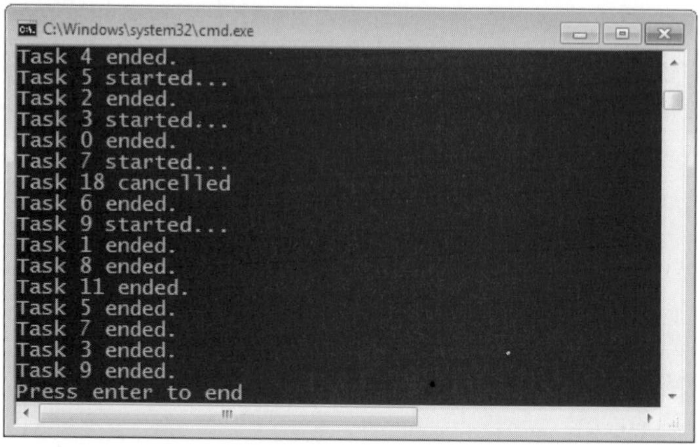

Handling Exceptions

You can raise an exception in a parallel loop, but you should consider several factors when the need to do this occurs:

- Parallel tasks already running are allowed to run until completion. This means that tasks might continue to run after the unhandled exception occurs.

- In most circumstances, iterations not started are not allowed to run after the exception.

- Long-running tasks should check the *ParallelLoopState.IsExceptional* property for pending exceptions. The property returns *true* when an exception is pending. If a pending exception is discovered, the task should end at the earliest convenient moment.

- Because tasks are running in parallel, the possibility exists that more than one exception might be raised. For that reason, the method throws an *AggregateException*. You can use the *AggregateException.InnerExceptions* property to enumerate the underlying exceptions.

- Unhandled exceptions within a parallel loop are caught on the joining thread. If the parallel call was not made within the scope of a *try/catch* block, the exception might cause the application to fail.

- An unhandled exception takes precedence over a *ParallelLoopState.Break* or *ParallelLoopState.Stop*.

The following code demonstrates the proper technique to handle an unhanded exception that occurs within a parallel loop. The code purposely raises an unhandled exception in the fourth task. Remember, the *Parallel.For* statement must be within the scope of a *try* block so that if an unhandled exception is raised, execution gets transferred to the joining thread— and ultimately to the *catch* filter, where you actually catch an *AggregateException* exception. Internally, the *catch* block enumerates the *AggregateException.InnerExceptions* collection and displays the unhandled exceptions.

```
try
{
    Parallel.For(0, 6, (index) =>
    {
        Console.WriteLine("Task {0} started.", index);
        if (index == 4)
        {
            throw new Exception();
        }
        DoSomething();
        Console.WriteLine("Task {0} ended.", index);
    });
}
catch (AggregateException ax)
{
    Console.WriteLine("\nError List: \n");
    foreach(var error in ax.InnerExceptions)
    {
        Console.WriteLine(error.Message);
    }
}
```

Here's the output from the preceding code.

```
C:\Windows\system32\cmd.exe
Task 0 started.
Task 3 started.
Task 2 started.
Task 4 started.
Task 1 started.
Task 5 started.
Exception raised in Task 4.
Task 0 ended.
Task 1 ended.
Task 5 ended.
Task 3 ended.
Task 2 ended.

Error List:

Exception of type 'System.Exception' was thrown.
Press any key to continue . . . _
```

Dealing with Dependencies

You should strive for independent loop iterations, because that provides the maximum parallel performance, allowing you to use embarrassingly parallel loops. However, not every loop
has perfectly independent iterations. This is particularly true when you are porting sequential code to parallel code, where the original developer was working under entirely different
assumptions and constraints. Dependencies, if handled incorrectly, can cause unreliable
results and, in some circumstances, application crashes. Dependencies are typically resolved
through some degree or synchronization, which can adversely affect performance. However,
correctness is sometimes more important than performance. There are various techniques
for handling dependencies in the parallel code, many of which are beyond the scope of this
book, but the most common dependency is reduction, which is covered in the next section.

Reduction

Reduction reduces a collection to a value. For example, you could calculate the sum of a collection of values. Look at the following loop. The dependency is the scalar variable, which is
shared between tasks. In particular, the scalar variable is shared across threads, where each
thread hosts one or more parallel tasks. The problem is not necessarily between tasks but
between threads.

```
int [] values=new int [] {1,2,3,4,5,6,7,8,9,10,

    11,12,13,14,15,16,17,18,19,20};
int total = 0;
Parallel.ForEach(values, (item) =>
{
  total += item;
});
```

The challenge is to make the preceding code thread-safe without sacrificing significant performance.

In the TPL, you perform reduction by using a private thread-local variable that is shared by parallel tasks on the same thread. The thread-local variable can be accessed serially by tasks running on the same thread; therefore, it's thread safe in that context. For this reason, no overt synchronization is required within tasks on the same thread. When the parallel loop completes, there are partial results on each thread. A special function is then called to combine the partial results into a final result. This is the only operation that would access the global variable and require synchronization. For this to work, the parallel operation must be both commutative and associative. The following image shows how reduction is performed for a parallel loop.

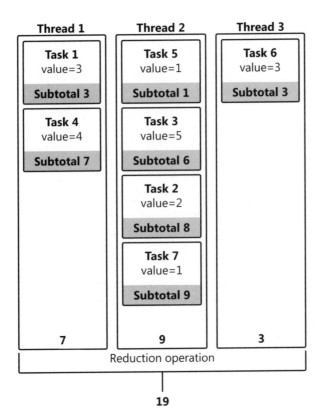

As mentioned, you should not parallelize operations that are neither commutative nor associative. The *commutative* property means that the order of operations is not important: you might remember the commutative property from Algebra 1, from the common example *a+b=b+a.* The commutative property is most commonly associated with addition and multi-plication—but not subtraction. The *associative* property means that two or more operations will return the same result—regardless of the sequence in which those operations are per-formed. Basically, the textual order of operations is important but not the sequencing. For example, *(a+b)+c=a+(b+c).*

Both *Parallel.For* and *Parallel.ForEach* have overloads with a couple of additional parameters for reduction: the *localInit* and *localFinally* parameters. You initialize the private thread-local variable by using the *localInit* function and perform the reduction in the *localFinally* function, which is an *Action* delegate. This *localFinally* function gets called after the parallel operation is complete. The parameters for *localFinally* are the current array element, the loop state, and the thread-local variable. In this function alone, you need to synchronize access to the shared variable, which you can do by using a variety of techniques, such as a *Monitor* class, an *Interlocked* class, or the *lock* statement.

Here's the basic *Parallel.For* syntax for reduction.

```
public static ParallelLoopResult For<TLocal>(
    int fromInclusive,
    int toExclusive,
    Func<TLocal> localInit,
    Func<int, ParallelLoopState, TLocal, TLocal> body,
    Action<TLocal> localFinally
)
```

This is the *Parallel.ForEach* syntax.

```
public static ParallelLoopResult ForEach<TSource, TLocal>(
    IEnumerable<TSource> source,
    Func<TLocal> localInit,
    Func<TSource, ParallelLoopState, TLocal, TLocal> body,
    Action<TLocal> localFinally
)
```

In this tutorial, you will count the number of values in an array that are greater than 5. The reduction reduces the collection to a single count.

Reduce a collection to a count

1. Create a new C# console project in Visual Studio 2010. Add a *using* statement for the *System.Threading.Tasks* namespace to the source code. At class scope, define a static integer array containing these values: 1, 10, 4, 3, 10, 20, 30, 5, and an integer count variable.

   ```
   static int[] intArray = new int [] { 1, 10, 4, 3, 10, 20, 30, 5 };
   static int count=0;
   ```

2. In the *Main* method, iterate over the integer array by using a *Parallel.For* method. In the *localInit* method, initialize the thread local variable to 0. You also need to define the parameters for the *localFinally* delegate, the last parameter of the *Parallel.For* method.

```
Parallel.For(0, intArray.Length, ()=>0, (value, loopState, subtotal)
```

3. In the lambda expression for the loop operation, check the current integer value. If it's greater than 5, increment the counter. At the end, display the thread identifier, index, current value, and partial result. Return this partial result to be used by the next iteration on the same thread.

```
if (intArray[value] > 5)
{
    ++subtotal;
    Console.WriteLine("Thread {0}: Task {1}: Value {2}, Partial {3}",
    Thread.CurrentThread.ManagedThreadId, index,
    intArray[index], subtotal);
}
return subtotal;
```

4. After the parallel loop completes, the *localFinally* method is called. You can use the *Interlocked.Add* method to combine the partial results and calculate the total in a thread-safe manner.

```
Interlocked.Add(ref count, subtotal);
```

5. After the *Parallel.For* method, display the results.

```
Console.WriteLine("Count is {0}", count);
```

Your completed code should look similar to the following.

```
using System;
using System.Collections.Generic;
using System.Linq;
using System.Text;
using System.Threading.Tasks;
using System.Threading;

namespace Count
{
    class Program
    {
        static int[] intArray = new int [] { 1, 10, 4, 3, 10, 20, 30, 5 };
        static int count=0;

        static void Main(string[] args)
        {
            Parallel.For(0, intArray.Length, ()=>0, (index, loopState, subtotal) =>
                {
                    if (intArray[index] > 5)
```

```
                        {
                            ++subtotal;
                            Console.WriteLine("Thread {0}: Task {1}: Value {2}, Partial {3}",
                                Thread.CurrentThread.ManagedThreadId, index,
                                intArray[index], subtotal);                    }
                            return subtotal;
                        },
                        (subtotal)=>
                        {
                            Interlocked.Add(ref count, subtotal);
                        });

                Console.WriteLine("Count is {0}\n", count);

                Console.WriteLine("Press Enter to Continue");
                Console.ReadLine();
            }
        }
    }
```

The following figure shows my results in the console window.

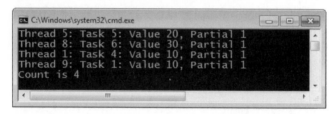

The preceding example calculated each partial result on a different thread. Therefore, you have four partial results reduced to a final total. As with most examples in this book, the actual result varies with the number of cores in your machine.

In the next tutorial, you will use the *Parallel.ForEach* method to calculate factorials. A factorial is the summation of contiguous values. For example, 5 factorial (*5!*) is *5×4×3×2×1*, or *120*. As in the previous example, the shared variable is the final result.

Reduce a collection of integers to a series of factorials

1. Create a console project in Visual Studio 2010 for C#. Add a *using* statement for the *System.Threading.Tasks* namespace to the source code. Prior to the *Main* method, declare a static integer named *total*, initialized to 1. Also define a constant called *EXCLUSIVE* and assign the value 1. You use this variable to adjust the loop boundary to include the maximum value. Finally, define a generic object that you will use as a lock later in the program.

```
static int total=1;
const int EXCLUSIVE = 1;
static object mylock = new object();
```

2. You will calculate 5 factorial (*5!*). Define a *Parallel.ForEach* statement that starts at *1* and finishes at (*5+EXCLUSIVE*). This is the range of the factorial. Initialize the subtotal to 1.

```
Parallel.For(1, 5+EXCLUSIVE, () => 1, (value, loopState, accumulator) =>
```

3. In the parallel operation, multiply the accumulator (partial result) with the input value, and return the result.

```
accumulator*=value;
return accumulator;
```

4. Define a lambda expression for the *lastFinally* delegate with the accumulator as the only parameter. In the lambda expression, define a lock that protects access to the shared variable. In the block, calculate the product of the partial result and the current total.

```
lock (mylock)
{
    total *= accumulator;
}
```

5. Display the results.

```
Console.WriteLine("The result is {0}", total);
```

Here is the entire program.

```
using System;
using System.Collections.Generic;
using System.Linq;
using System.Text;
using System.Threading.Tasks;

namespace Factorial
{
    class Program
    {
        static int total=1;
        const int EXCLUSIVE = 1;
        static object mylock = new object();
        static void Main(string[] args)
        {
            Parallel.For(1, 5+EXCLUSIVE, () => 1, (value, loopState, accumulator) =>
            {
                accumulator*=value;
                return accumulator;
            },
            (accumulator) =>
            {

                lock (mylock)
                {
                    total *= accumulator;
                }
            });
```

```
                Console.WriteLine("The result is {0}", total);

                Console.WriteLine("Press enter to <end>");
                Console.ReadLine();
            }
        }
    }
```

All examples, including the previous examples, are just that—examples. They are provided to illustrate some portion or topic in this book. For this reason, the context of this book sometimes makes it impossible to provide real-world or detailed examples.

Using the MapReduce Pattern

MapReduce is a well-known pattern introduced in 2004 in a paper titled "MapReduce: Simplified Data Processing on Large Clusters" by Jeffrey Dean and Sanjay Ghemawat. The link for the document is *http://labs.google.com/papers/mapreduce-osdi04.pdf*. The MapReduce pattern is designed to handle the reduction of vast amounts of data separated across multiple computers. However, the pattern is applicable even on a much smaller scale, such as a modern multicore computer. The MapReduce pattern is a complex application of data parallelism, dependencies, and reduction.

There are three collections in the MapReduce pattern. The first collection is the input for the MapReduce pattern. It is a collection of key and value pairs. You perform some transformation on the input collection to create a second, intermediate collection, which is a non-unique collection of key and value pairs. The third collection is a reduction of the non-unique keys from the intermediate collection.

An example might provide some clarification. There is an excellent application of the MapReduce pattern in "Patterns for Parallel Programming: Understanding and Applying Parallel Patterns with the .NET Framework 4," written by Colin Campbell, Ralph Johnson, Ade Miller, and Stephen Toub; it's available at *http://msdn.microsoft.com/en-us/library/ff963553.aspx*. This book uses the MapReduce pattern to perform a word count across multiple documents. The files act as the input collection, where the filenames are the keys and their locations are the values. In this example, you derive the intermediate collection—a list of words and word counts—from the input collection. For example, if the word *apple* appeared in three of the files, there would be identical entries for *apple* in the intermediate list. The word "apple" would be the key, and the value for each key would be the number of times that word (the key) appears in each file. For the reduction, you want to reduce non-unique keys to totals. The following diagram illustrates this example.

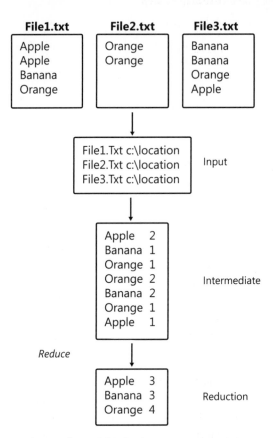

Implementing a MapReduce pattern requires multiple iterations and levels of data parallelism. Parallel Language Integrated Query (PLINQ) provides an implementation of the MapReduce pattern that you'll review in the next chapter, but otherwise, TPL offers no implementation of the MapReduce pattern. However, this chapter includes an implementation of this pattern in a MapReduce class.

> **Note** The *MapReduce* library is available in the companion content for this book. See the Introduction for download instructions.

The *MapReduce* class resides in the *ParallelBook* namespace. When you create a *MapReduce* object, you initialize it with a source collection. The *MapReduce* class has only two methods. The first, *MapReduce.Map*, is responsible for transforming the source collection to an intermediate collection. The first parameter is the mapping function, which performs the transformation. The last parameter is an *out* parameter, which is the intermediate collection. The second method is the *MapReduce.Reduce* method, which accepts and reduces the intermediate collection—its first parameter. The next parameter is the reduction operation. The *Map* and *Reduce* methods are exposed separately in the interface to allow multiple reductions of an intermediate collection. The last parameter is the *group* operation, which groups the keys of the intermediate collection. This is important because the intermediate collection is reduced along group boundaries. The default is to reduce by matching keys.

Here is the *MapReduce.Map* prototype.

```
public void Map<KEY2, VALUE2>(Func<Tuple<KEY, VALUE>,
    IEnumerable<Tuple<KEY2, VALUE2>>> mapFunc,
    out IEnumerable<Tuple<KEY2, VALUE2>> TupleCollection
)
```

And here's the *MapReduce.Reduce* prototype.

```
public IEnumerable<Tuple<KEY2, VALUE2>> Reduce<KEY2, VALUE2>(
    IEnumerable<Tuple<KEY2, VALUE2>> intermediate,
    Func<KEY2, VALUE2[], VALUE2> reduceFunc,
    Func<IEnumerable<Tuple<KEY2, VALUE2>>, Dictionary<KEY2, VALUE2[]>>
    groupFunc= null
)
```

This next exercise involves using the *MapReduce* class. You will create a collection of key and value pairs. The keys are string values, and the values are integers. The intermediate collection simply squares the values of the input collection. The reduction will then reduce keys by summation.

Create a *MapReduce* class to square the values of a source collection, and then reduce the collection by summing the keys

1. Create a console project in Visual Studio 2010 for C#. Add a *using* statement for the *System.Threading.Tasks* namespace to the source code. Add a reference to the project for *MapReduce.dll*.

2. In the *Main* method, define and initialize an array of binary tuples for string and integer pairs.

```
Tuple<string, int>[] tuples = new Tuple<string, int>[] {
    new Tuple<string, int>("a", 3),
    new Tuple<string, int>("b", 2),
    new Tuple<string, int>("b", 5)
};
```

3. Create an instance of the *MapReduce* class. In the constructor, initialize the object with the tuples array.

```
MapReduce<string, int> letters = new MapReduce<string, int>(tuples);
```

4. Now you will transform the source collection. First, define a collection of tuples to hold the intermediate results. Your mapping operation simply squares the value of each tuple and places the results in an *out* variable.

```
IEnumerable<Tuple<string, int>> newmap;
letters.Map<string, int>((input) =>
{
    return new Tuple<string, int>[] { new Tuple<string, int>(input.Item1,
        input.Item2 * input.Item2) };
}, out newmap);
```

5. Reduce the collection with the *MapReduce.Reduce* method. Provide the intermediate collection as the input. In the reduction method, sum the totals of each group.

```
IEnumerable<Tuple<string, int>> reduction =
letters.Reduce<string, int>(newmap, (key, values) =>
{
    int total = 0;
    foreach (var item in values)
    {
        total += item;
    }
    return total;
});
```

6. Display the results, which are returned from the *MapReduce.Reduce* method. The answer should be a=9 and b=29.

```
foreach (var item in reduction)
{
    Console.WriteLine("{0} = {1}", item.Item1, item.Item2);
}
```

Here is the entire program.

```
using System;
using System.Collections.Generic;
using System.Linq;
using System.Text;
using System.Threading.Tasks;

namespace Letters
{
    class Program
    {
        static void Main(string[] args)
        {
            Tuple<string, int>[] tuples = new Tuple<string, int>[] {
                new Tuple<string, int>("a", 3),
                new Tuple<string, int>("b", 2),
                new Tuple<string, int>("b", 5) };

            MapReduce<string, int> letters = new MapReduce<string, int>(tuples);
            IEnumerable<Tuple<string, int>> newmap;

            letters.Map<string, int>((input) =>
            {
                return new Tuple<string, int>[] { new Tuple<string,
                    int>(input.Item1, input.Item2 * input.Item2) };
            }, out newmap);
```

```
        IEnumerable<Tuple<string, int>> reduction = letters.Reduce<string,
          int>(newmap, (key, values) =>
        {
            int total = 0;
            foreach (var item in values)
            {
                total += item;
            }
            return total;
        });

        foreach (var item in reduction)
        {
            Console.WriteLine("{0} = {1}", item.Item1, item.Item2);
        }

        Console.WriteLine("Press enter to <end>.");
        Console.ReadLine();
    }
  }
}
```

A Word Count Example

There are more things in heaven and earth, Horatio, than are dreamt of in your philosophy.

– William Shakespeare

Shakespeare is timeless. He also tends to use many of the same words in his various works. This makes Shakespeare ideal for a word count example. In addition, this section will provide a more complete demonstration of using the *MapReduce* class.

This example uses four common Shakespearean sonnets. Fortunately, you can find these sonnets in many places online. The goal is to count the instances of every word across the four sonnets. Small words, such as *a*, *be*, *we*, and so on, would clutter the results. For that reason, exclude small words from the list. Fortunately, there is a function for this purpose. An overload of the *MapReduce.Map* method has a *Filter* parameter, which is a function delegate. The *Filter* method accepts a key-value pair. If the method returns *true*, the entry is added to the intermediate collection. If it returns *false*, the item is omitted.

The source collection is comprised of the name and location of four sonnets, used to initialize an instance of a *MapReduce* class.

```
Tuple<string, string>[] sonnets = new Tuple<string, string>[] {
new Tuple<string, string>("Sonnet 1.txt",@"C:\shakespeare"),
new Tuple<string, string>("Sonnet 2.txt",@"C:\shakespeare"),
new Tuple<string, string>("Sonnet 3.txt",@"C:\shakespeare"),
new Tuple<string, string>("Sonnet 4.txt",@"C:\shakespeare") };
MapReduce<string, string> wordCount = new MapReduce<string, string>(sonnets);
```

The *MapReduce.Map* method will map the file names to a word count.

1. Read the text from the sonnets.

2. Define word delimiters.

3. Create a *Dictionary* object. For each word, check whether the word is in the dictionary. If not, add the word to the dictionary and set the count to 1. Otherwise, when the word already exists in the dictionary, increment the count of the existing word in the dictionary. When the process completes, return the values portion of the dictionary object as the intermediate collection. The intermediate collection will have the individual count per word for each file.

Here is the code for the word count example.

```
IEnumerable<Tuple<string, int>> wordCollection;
wordCount.Map<string, int>((input) =>
{
    StreamReader sw = new StreamReader(input.Item2 + @"\" + input.Item1);
    string data = sw.ReadToEnd();
    string[] words = data.Split(new[] {' ','.',',',';',':','=','+', '-', '*', ')',
        '(',
'!', '#', '$', '\n', '\r'});
    Dictionary<string, Tuple<string, int>> rawCount =
        new Dictionary<string          Tuple<string, int>>();
    foreach (var word in words)
    {
        Tuple<string, int> value;
        if (rawCount.TryGetValue(word, out value))
        {
            int increment = rawCount[word].Item2 + 1;
            rawCount[word] = new Tuple<string, int>(word, increment);
        }
        else
        {
            rawCount.Add(word, new Tuple<string, int>(word, 1));
        }
    }
    return rawCount.Values;
},
```

After the mapping function, you have the *Filter* function. For brevity, words less than three characters in length are excluded from the final intermediate collection.

```
(key, value) =>
{
    if (key.Length < 3)
    {
        return false;
    }
    else
    {
        return true;
```

```
    }
},
out wordCollection);
```

The *MapReduce.Reduce* method is simple. The reduction method reduces the key groupings to totals that represent the aggregate total count of each word in the four files.

```
IEnumerable<Tuple<string, int>> reduction = wordCount.Reduce(
    wordCollection,
(key, values) =>
    {
        return values.Sum();
    }
);
```

Lastly, you can the show the results.

```
foreach (var item in reduction)
{
    Console.WriteLine("{0} {1}", item.Item1, item.Item2);
}
```

Here is the partial output from the Word Count example.

Summary

Data parallelism applies a parallel operation to a collection of data. In TPL, you use the *Parallel.For* and *Parallel.ForEach* methods for data parallelism. As long as there are no dependencies, converting a sequential *for* loop to parallel is simple. The default partitioner will decide the chunk size of the parallel operation.

You can interrupt a parallel loop by using the *ParallelLoopState.Break* or *ParallelLoopState.Stop* methods. The *ParallelLoopState.Stop* method cancels the parallel operation faster; however, for both methods, loop iterations might continue to run after the cancellation. Long-running tasks should periodically check whether a cancellation is pending.

You catch and handle unhandled exceptions from a parallel loop in the joining thread. Because multiple unhandled exceptions can be raised in parallel tasks, any unhandled exception gets propagated to the joining thread as an *AggregateException*. Enumerate the individual unhandled exceptions in the *AggregateException.InnerExceptions* property. When an unhandled exception is raised, already-running tasks should check for a pending exception and stop as soon as possible. *ParallelLoopState.IsExceptional* returns *true* if an exception is pending.

Reduction reduces a collection to a value. Both *Parallel.For* and *Parallel.ForEach* methods have overloads that support reduction. Iterations sharing a task use a private thread-local variable to create a partial result and avoid synchronization. When the partial result operations are completed, the *lastFinally* operation is called to consolidate the partial results into a single value.

The MapReduce pattern is useful for reducing vast amounts of data distributed across multiple servers but is also applicable to a multicore single computer environment. PLINQ has an implementation of the MapReduce pattern. You can also download an implementation of a *MapReduce* class with the companion content for this book.

Quick Reference

To	Do this
Iterate a collection with parallel tasks	Use the *Parallel.For* method.
Directly iterate the elements of a collection with parallel tasks	Use the *Parallel.ForEach* method.
Cancel a *Parallel.For* loop	Use *ParallelLoopState.Break* or *ParallelLoopState.Stop* to support cooperative cancellation. The *ParallelLoopState.Stop* method is cleaner and cancels current and future tasks.
Handle an exception in a parallel task	Catch the *AggregateException* in the joining thread. The underlying exception is found in *AggregateException.InnerException*. If more than one *AggregateException* is raised, iterate *AggregateException.InnerExceptions*.
Perform a reduction, such as a summation	Use the *localInit* and *localFinally* parameters of the *Parallel.For* and *Parallel.ForEach* methods.

Chapter 4
PLINQ

After completing this chapter, you will be able to

- Explain the benefits of LINQ.

- Create basic LINQ expressions.

- Define PLINQ.

- Set a degree of parallelism.

- Catch unhandled exceptions in PLINQ.

- Understand the cancellation model for PLINQ.

- Use reduction in PLINQ.

- Implement the MapReduce pattern for PLINQ.

The previous chapter introduced data parallelism. PLINQ (Parallel Language Integrated Query), which is the topic of this chapter, is one implementation of data parallelism in the Microsoft .NET Framework 4.

LINQ (Language Integrated Query) was introduced in the .NET Framework 3.5 and is a general-purpose query language. By using LINQ, you can create data queries that are domain agnostic. In other words, LINQ is a *portable* query language, meaning that a single LINQ query can be applied to different realms of data. For example, you can create a LINQ query for Microsoft SQL Server, and later use that same query with arrays of objects, a collection, or even an XML file. Prior to LINQ, developers had to learn different query syntax for each data domain. For example, a SQL query would not work when applied to an XML file, a query for an XML file could not be applied to a collection, and so on. LINQ is convenient because you can use the same query across data domains.

LINQ is the core technology of a circle of technologies. LINQ to Objects queries in-memory objects derived from the *IEnumerable* interfaces. There is also LINQ to SQL, LINQ to XML, and other related technologies within the LINQ sphere, as shown in the following diagram.

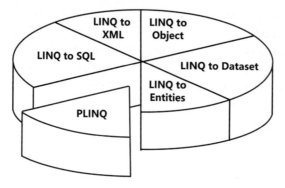

PLINQ is the most recent addition to the LINQ sphere and is included in the .NET Framework 4. It is implemented in the *System.Linq.ParallelEnumerable* class, which is part of the *System.Linq* namespace.

Introduction to LINQ

The process of understanding PLINQ starts with an understanding of LINQ. For this reason, an introduction to LINQ might be helpful. If you are already familiar with LINQ, you can skip to the next section in this chapter.

> **Note** This chapter does not review all the LINQ clauses, such as *select* and *order by*, in any detail; it covers them only very briefly. For a detailed explanation of LINQ, *Programming Microsoft LINQ in Microsoft .NET Framework 4* by Paolo Pialorsi and Marco Russo (Microsoft Press, 2010) is an excellent source.

You are probably accustomed to building query commands for conventional database sources. Here is a SQL query example in which the *SELECT* and *FROM* clauses select the *ISBN*, *FirstName*, *LastName*, *Title*, and *Publisher* fields from the *Books* table in a SQL database. The *Where* clause filters the results and returns only the records where Lucerne Publishing is the publisher. The *OrderBy* clause sorts the records by the title of the book.

```
SELECT ISBN, FirstName, LastName, Title, Publisher FROM Books
WHERE Publisher="Lucerne Publishing" ORDER BY Title
```

As mentioned, one of the advantages of LINQ is the ability to apply similar queries to a variety of domains. In the following code, the *Book* class is an encapsulation of the operations and attributes of a book. Using LINQ, you search through a collection of books as easily as searching a SQL Server database. Here is the LINQ to Objects query of a book collection.

```
from book in books where book.Publisher=="Lucerne Publishing"
    orderby book.Title select book;
```

The LINQ query starts with the *from* clause and ends with the *select* clause—the reverse of the SQL query. The *in* clause is used differently than it is in SQL. In LINQ, the *in* clause identifies the data source. The double equal sign (==), not a single equal sign (=), signifies equality. There are other differences as well; however, there is sufficient similarity that most people familiar with a modern SQL language should become somewhat comfortable with LINQ very quickly.

Here is an expanded example of a LINQ query.

```
var books = new[] {new Book{Publisher="Lucerne Publishing",
                        First="David",
                        Last="Hamilton",
                        Title="David Hamilton Book",
                        ISBN="ISBN Number" },
                new Book{Publisher="Lucerne Publishing",
                        First="Stefan",
                        Last="Hesse",
                        Title="Stefan Hesse Book",
                        ISBN="ISBN Number"},
                new Book{Publisher="Lucerne Publishing",
                        First="Mike",
                        Last="Ray",
                        Title="Mike Ray Book",
                        ISBN="ISBN Number"},
                new Book{Publisher="Lucerne Publishing",
                        First="Nuno",
                        Last="Bento",
                        Title="Nuno Bento Book",
                        ISBN="ISBN Number"}};

var titles=from book in books.AsParallel() where book.Publisher=="Lucerne Publishing"
        orderby book.Title select book;
```

The preceding example returns an array of books. You can read the LINQ query as follows: From the *books* collection, return each book where the *book.Publisher* attribute is *Lucerne Publishing*. Sort the results by the *book.Title* attribute.

LINQ queries do not execute immediately. In fact, they don't execute until you iterate the result, a process called *deferred execution*. Every time you iterate the query results, LINQ reapplies the query operation. For this reason, successive queries might generate different results, because the underlying data might have changed. There are exceptions, such as in a reduction, where a LINQ query returns a scalar value. LINQ queries that return a scalar value are executed immediately.

This tutorial demonstrates deferred execution. You will create a LINQ query and then iterate the results. In the *Where* clause, you will display a message. The message is displayed when the results are iterated and not when the LINQ query is defined. This demonstrates that the query is not executed until the results are iterated.

Execute a LINQ query and then iterate and display the results

1. Create a console application for Microsoft Visual C# in Microsoft Visual Studio 2010. By default, C# projects include a *using* statement for the LINQ namespace, which is *System.Linq*. In the *Main* method, define an *integer* array that contains 10 values.

```
var intArray =new [] {1, 2, 3, 4, 5, 6, 7, 8, 9, 10 };
```

2. Next, use a LINQ query to return the array values greater than five. Write the LINQ query by using the imperative syntax. You can then write the *Where* clause as a lambda expression to perform the appropriate selection. The lambda expression accepts a single variable, the array index. The *Where* method (as well as other LINQ methods) is implemented as an extension method of the *IEnumerable* type. Lambda expressions for the *Where* method must return *true* or *false*. Returning *true* selects the current element, and returning *false* excludes the element.

```
var numbers = intArray.Where((index) =>
```

3. In the lambda expression, if the current array element is greater than five, return *true*. Otherwise, return *false*. If it is *true*, also display the value of the current element.

```
if (intArray[index] > 5)
{
Console.WriteLine("intArray[{0}]={1}",
index, intArray[index]);
return true;
}
else
{
return false;
}
```

4. Iterate the results in a *foreach* loop. Just prior to the *foreach* method, display a message that shows the location where the program is executing. In the *foreach* loop, *do nothing*! Because of deferred execution, the LINQ query will be performed at this point, displaying the values of the selected items in the *Where* clause.

5. At the end of the program, the *Console.ReadLine* method prevents the program from ending prematurely. You might also want to display a helpful message to the user.

Note This step will be omitted in future examples in this chapter. Feel free to add these statements at your discretion.

6. Build and run the program.

Here is the complete application.

```
using System;
using System.Collections.Generic;
using System.Linq;
using System.Text;

namespace Deferred
{
    class Program
    {
        static void Main(string[] args)
        {
            var intArray =new [] {0, 1, 2, 3, 4, 5, 6, 7, 8, 9, 10 };
            var numbers = intArray.Where((index) =>
            {
                if (intArray[index] > 5)
                {
                    Console.WriteLine("intArray[{0}]={1}",
                        index, intArray[index]);
                    return true;
                }
                else
                {
                    return false;
                }
            });

            Console.WriteLine("Before foreach method.");
            foreach (var number in numbers)
            {
                // no code
            }

            Console.WriteLine("Press Enter to Continue");
            Console.ReadLine();
        }

    }
}
```

The following image shows the output for the application. Notice that nothing is displayed before the *foreach* loop. The results are displayed after the *Where* method actually executes, which occurs inside the *foreach* loop.

You now have a basic understanding of LINQ and are ready to explore PLINQ.

PLINQ

PLINQ is the parallel version of LINQ. The objective of parallel programming is to maximize processor utilization with increased throughput in a multicore architecture. For a multicore computer, your application should recognize and scale performance to the number of available processor cores. As shown earlier, the LINQ query executes when you iterate over the results, and it executes sequentially. With PLINQ, the iterations are performed in parallel, as tasks are scheduled on threads running in the .NET Framework 4 thread pool.

One of the best features of PLINQ is that it's easy to convert LINQ queries to PLINQ. You can simply add the *AsParallel* clause. Here is the LINQ query shown earlier in this chapter that returned a selection of books. The results are generated sequentially.

```
from book in books where book.Publisher=="Lucerne Publishing"
orderby book.Title select book;
```

Now, here's the same query updated for PLINQ. Note that the only addition to the code is the call to the *AsParallel* method of the *books* collection. This minor change, however, completely alters how the query is performed. When you iterate over the results, the query is performed with parallel tasks.

```
from book in books.AsParallel() where book.Publisher=="Lucerne Publishing"
orderby book.Title select book;
```

This next tutorial contrasts the productivity of standard LINQ and PLINQ. You can perform the example query either sequentially or in parallel. You'll display information to compare the performance of both approaches. The task and thread identifiers are also displayed to highlight the underlying differences between parallel and sequential execution. Because the sequential version of the query does not use the Task Parallel Library (TPL), the task IDs are blank. In addition, the sequential version will execute on a single thread.

Perform a sequential query and a parallel query on an *integer* array, and imperatively invoke the *Where* clause

1. Create a console application for C# in Visual Studio 2010. Add *using* statements for both the *System.Threading* and *System.Diagnostics* namespaces.

2. Above the *Main* method, create a static method called *Normalize* that returns a *bool*. You'll call this method in the *Where* clause. In the *Normalize* method, display the current task and thread identifiers. Use the *Thread.SpinWait* method to simulate a real-world normalization operation. Return *true* to select and add the current element to the result collection.

```
static bool Normalize()
{
Console.WriteLine("Normalizing [Task {0} : Thread {1}]",
Task.CurrentId, Thread.CurrentThread.ManagedThreadId);
Thread.SpinWait(int.MaxValue);
return true;
}
```

3. In *Main*, create an instance of the *Stopwatch* class. The *Stopwatch* is used to calculate the duration of both the sequential and the parallel versions of the PLINQ query. Also, define an *integer* array that has four elements. This is the array you will query.

```
Stopwatch sw = new Stopwatch();
var intArray = new [] { 1, 2, 3, 4 };
```

4. Perform a sequential query on the array by using LINQ to Objects. Call the *Where* method. Evaluate a lambda expression and call the *Normalize* method as a parameter. The *Where* method—and consequently *Normalize*—will be called for each element of the array. Because the lambda expression returns *true* for each element, all elements of the array are included in the results. On the next line, repeat the query but use PLINQ. Add the *AsParallel* method. For now, comment out the parallel version of the query. You will initially run only the sequential query.

```
var result = intArray.Where((index)=>Normalize());
//var result = intArray.AsParallel().Where((index) => Normalize());
```

5. Start the *Stopwatch*, and then iterate the results of the query. Display the results of the operation. Because of deferred execution, this is when the query actually executes.

```
foreach (int item in result)
{
Console.WriteLine("Item={0}", item);
}
```

6. Call the *Stop* method on the *Stopwatch* class and display the duration.

```
sw.Stop();
Console.WriteLine("Elapse time: {0}: seconds",
    sw.ElapsedMilliseconds / 1000);
```

Here is the entire program.

```
using System;
using System.Collections.Generic;
using System.Linq;
using System.Text;
using System.Threading;
using System.Diagnostics;
using System.Threading.Tasks;

namespace Performance
{
    class Program
    {
        static bool Normalize()
        {
            Console.WriteLine("Normalizing [Task {0} : Thread {1}]",
                Task.CurrentId, Thread.CurrentThread.ManagedThreadId);
            Thread.SpinWait(int.MaxValue);
            return true;
        }

        static void Main(string[] args)
        {
            Stopwatch sw = new Stopwatch();
            var intArray = new [] { 1, 2, 3, 4 };
            var result = intArray.Where((index)=>Normalize());
            //var result = intArray.AsParallel().Where((index) => Normalize());

            sw.Start();
            foreach (int item in result)
            {
                Console.WriteLine("Item={0}", item);
            }
            sw.Stop();
            Console.WriteLine("Elapsed time: {0}: seconds",
                sw.ElapsedMilliseconds / 1000);

            Console.WriteLine("Press Enter to Continue");
            Console.ReadLine();
        }
    }
}
```

Build and run the application. Because the statement containing the PLINQ query is commented, the code executes only the standard LINQ query. Each operation is therefore performed sequentially and on the same thread, which you can see from the output in the console window as shown in the following image. Because parallel tasks are not used, task IDs are not displayed. The duration is essentially the sum of running each of the operations in order.

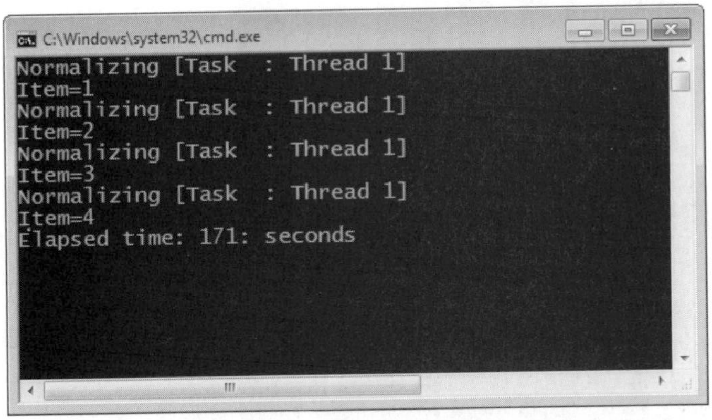

```
C:\Windows\system32\cmd.exe
Normalizing [Task   : Thread 1]
Item=1
Normalizing [Task   : Thread 1]
Item=2
Normalizing [Task   : Thread 1]
Item=3
Normalizing [Task   : Thread 1]
Item=4
Elapsed time: 171: seconds
```

Now uncomment the statement containing the PLINQ command and comment out the LINQ query instead. Rerun the application. This time, the results are entirely different. The *Where* method runs in parallel and on different threads, as shown in the output window in the following image. The PLINQ query leverages the multicore processor architecture; the results are specific to this example and the current hardware architecture. In this example, each iteration of a query operation is a different task. For this reason, the query runs faster.

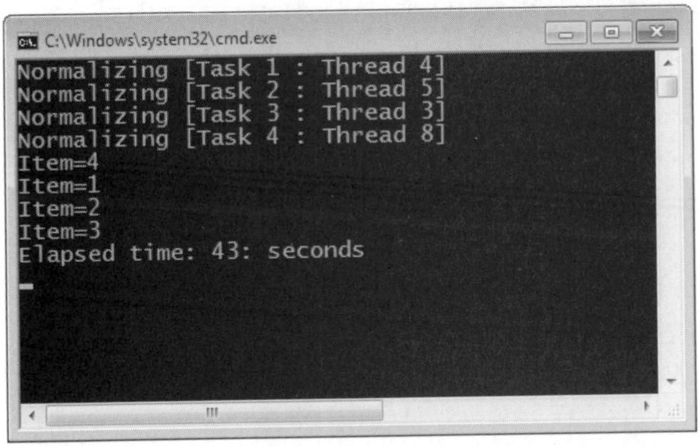

```
C:\Windows\system32\cmd.exe
Normalizing [Task 1 : Thread 4]
Normalizing [Task 2 : Thread 5]
Normalizing [Task 3 : Thread 3]
Normalizing [Task 4 : Thread 8]
Item=4
Item=1
Item=2
Item=3
Elapsed time: 43: seconds
```

The difference in performance of the two versions is depicted in Processor Utilization of the Task Manager. The next image shows a screen shot of processor utilization from the LINQ version of the application. In this example, average processor utilization is about 12 percent. Most of the processor computing capability is unused!

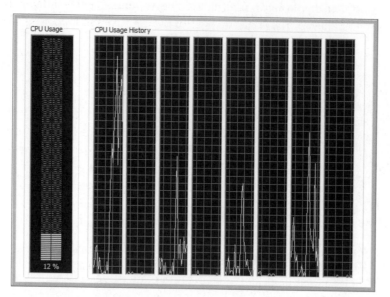

However, the PLINQ version of the application is much more efficient. In the following image, you can see a considerably higher utilization—more than 50 percent.

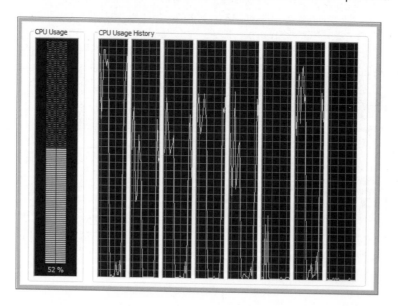

PLINQ Operators and Methods

You can modify the behavior of a PLINQ query with a variety of clauses and methods that are actually extension methods of *ParallelQuery<TSource>*. Most of these are the same clauses and methods available to LINQ. You can use these operators either independently or together to affect the behavior of a PLINQ query. However, PLINQ also introduces some new constructs, which are introduced in this section.

The *ForAll* Operator

You create a PLINQ query to parallelize your code. In most circumstances, the next step is to iterate the results by using a *foreach* or *for* method. At that time, the query is most likely performed by using deferred execution. The results are processed in iterations of the *foreach* loop. There is only one problem: the *foreach* loop is sequential. This is a classic "hurry-up-and-wait" scenario. After executing a PLINQ query, you might want to extend parallelism to handle the results in parallel as well.

In the previous chapter, you learned that the *Parallel.ForEach* method is useful for parallelizing the same operation over a collection of values. It would appear natural to adhere to the same model to process the results of a PLINQ query. PLINQ returns a *ParallelQuery<TSource>* type, which represents multiple streams of data. However, *Parallel.ForEach* expects a single stream of data, which is then parsed into multiple streams. For this reason, the *Parallel.ForEach* method must recognize and convert multistream input to a single stream. There is a performance cost for this conversion.

The solution is the *ParallelQuery<TSource>.ForAll* method. The *ForAll* method directly accepts multiple streams, so it avoids the overhead of the *Parallel.ForEach* method. Here is a prototype of the *ForAll* method. The first parameter is the target of the extension method, which is a *ParallelQuery* type. The last parameter is an *Action* delegate. For the *Action* delegate, you can use a delegate, a lambda expression, or even an anonymous method. The next element of the collection is passed as a parameter to the delegate.

```
public static void ForAll<TSource>(
        this ParallelQuery<TSource> source,
        Action<TSource> action
)
```

Here is a short tutorial that demonstrates the *ForAll* operator. In this example, you will perform a parallel query on a *string* array and then select and display strings longer than two characters in length.

Perform a parallel query of a string array

1. Create a console application for C# in Visual Studio 2010. In the *Main* method, define a *string* array.

```
string [] stringArray = { "A", "AB", "ABC", "ABCD" };
```

2. Perform a PLINQ query on the *string* array. Select strings with a length greater than two.

```
var results=from value in stringArray.AsParallel() where value.Length>2 select value;
```

3. Call the *ForAll* operator on the results. In the lambda expression, display the current item.

```
results.ForAll((item) => Console.WriteLine(item));
```

Here is the source code for the entire application.

```
using System;
using System.Collections.Generic;
using System.Linq;
using System.Text;

namespace ForAll
{
    class Program
    {
        static void Main(string[] args)
        {
            string[] stringArray = { "A", "AB", "ABC", "ABCD" };
            var results = from value in stringArray.AsParallel()
where value.Length > 2 select value;
            results.ForAll((item) => Console.WriteLine(item));

            Console.WriteLine("Press Enter to Continue");
            Console.ReadLine();
        }
    }
}
```

The application will display *ABC* and *ABCD* as the result.

ParallelExecutionMode

So far in this chapter, you have used the *AsParallel* method to convert LINQ to PLINQ. It is a simple change to a LINQ query that alters the semantics completely.

A PLINQ query is not guaranteed to actually execute in parallel. Overhead from executing the parallel query in parallel, such as thread-related costs, synchronization, and the parallel-ization code, can exceed the performance gain. Determining the relative performance benefit of the PLINQ query is an inexact science based on several factors. Here are some of the considerations that might affect the performance of a PLINQ query:

- Length of operations

- Number of processor cores

- Result type

- Merge options

One of the biggest factors is the duration of the parallel operations, such as the *Select* clause. Dependencies and the synchronization that results from them adversely affect the performance of any parallel solution. Furthermore, shorter operations might not be worth parallelizing, because the associated overhead might exceed the duration of the operation. For small operations, you could change the chunking to improve the balance of execution to overhead. Custom partitioners, including those that change the chunk size, are reviewed in Chapter 6, "Customization."

The number of processor cores might affect the performance of your parallel application, including PLINQ. However, you should typically ignore the number of processor cores, because that's mostly beyond your control. Maintaining hardware independence in your application is important for both scalability and portability.

PLINQ does not consider all of the above factors when deciding to execute a query in parallel. Based on the shape of the query and the clauses used, PLINQ decides to execute a query either in parallel or sequentially. You can override this default by using the *WithExecutionMode* clause with the *ParallelExecutionMode* enumeration as a parameter. The two options are *ParallelExecutionMode.ForceParallelism* and *ParallelExecutionMode.Default*. Use the *ParallelExecutionMode.ForceParallelism* enumeration to require parallel execution. The *ParallelExecutionMode.Default* value defers to the PLINQ for the appropriate decision on the execution mode. Here is an example that forces a parallel PLINQ query.

```
from item in data.AsParallel().WithExecutionMode(ParallelExecutionMode.ForceParallelism)
select item;
```

WithMergeOptions

How the result of your query expression is handled can also affect performance. For example, the following PLINQ query returns *a List<T>* type. Converting the PLINQ to a list requires that the results be buffered to return an entire list.

```
intArray.AsParallel().Where((value)=>value>5).ToList();
```

As mentioned, for the above code, the results are buffered. In some circumstances, PLINQ might buffer the results, but that is mostly transparent to your code.

Using the .NET Framework 4 thread pool, PLINQ uses multiple threads to execute the query in parallel. The results of these parallel operations are then merged back onto the joining thread. The merge option describes the buffering used when merging results from the various threads.

Here are the merge options as defined in the *ParallelMergeOptions* enumeration:

- **NotBuffered**   The results are not buffered. For operations such as the *ForAll* operation, *NotBuffered* is the default.

- **FullyBuffered**   The results are fully buffered, which can delay receipt of the first result.

- **AutoBuffered**   This option is similar to *NotBuffered*, except that the results are returned in chunks.

- **Default**   The default is *AutoBuffered*.

You can override the default buffer preference with the *WithMergeOptions* operator.

AsSequential

The difference between PLINQ and LINQ starts with the *AsParallel* clause. As shown in this chapter, converting from LINQ to PLINQ is often as simple as adding the *AsParallel* method to a LINQ query. Here is a basic LINQ query.

```
numbers.Select(/* selection */ ).OrderBy( /* sort */ );
```

Here is a parallel version of the same query, with the required *AsParallel* method added.

```
numbers.AsParallel().Select(/* selection */ ).OrderBy( /* sort */ );
```

So far, you've seen the *AsParallel* method prefixed to only the *Select* clause. However, *Select* is only one of the LINQ clauses that can take the *AsParallel* method as a prefix. Starting at that clause, the remainder of the query is conducted in parallel. Methods preceding the *AsParallel* clause in the query statement execute sequentially. In this example, the *Select* clause executes sequentially, but the *GroupBy* and *OrderBy* clauses execute in parallel.

```
numbers.Select(/* selection */ ).AsParallel().GroupBy( /* categorize */ )
.OrderBy( /* sort*/ );
```

AsSequential is the opposite of the *AsParallel* clause. *AsSequential* serializes portions of your LINQ query. You might choose this to resolve dependencies in a PLINQ query. You can then use *AsSequential* to isolate the dependency and make a part of a PLINQ query sequential. You might also decide that a portion of a PLINQ query is more efficiently run in parallel as opposed to sequentially.

Use *AsParallel* and *AsSequential* as gates for parallel and sequential execution, as shown in the following diagram. Although it is not common, a single PLINQ query can have multiple *AsParallel* and *AsSequential* clauses. Similar to the *AsParallel* clause, *AsSequential* can be used to prefix a LINQ method. From that position of the query forward, the remainder of the LINQ query executes sequentially—at least until it encounters an *AsParallel* clause. The following diagram illustrates a PLINQ query with both *AsParallel* and *AsSequential* clauses. The *Select* and *Groupby* clauses execute in parallel, while the *OrderBy* clause is sequential.

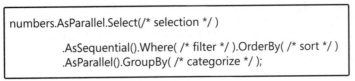

```
numbers.AsParallel.Select(/* selection */ )

        .AsSequential().Where( /* filter */ ).OrderBy( /* sort */ )
        .AsParallel().GroupBy( /* categorize */ );
```

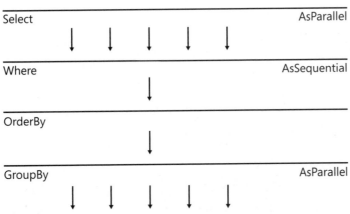

AsOrdered

For some, an orderly universe is important. Unfortunately, this is contrary to the default behavior of PLINQ. The following code squares and renders the values of an *integer* list.

```
int[] numbers = { 0, 1, 2, 3, 4, 5, 6, 7, 8, 9 };
var result = from number in numbers.AsParallel() select number * number;
```

You might be surprised by the results, which are indeed squared but do not appear in the same order as the underlying list.

```
0 4 16 25 36 49 64 81 1 9
```

PLINQ creates tasks for the query. Each task is then scheduled and placed on a queue in the .NET Framework 4 thread pool. The tasks are then scheduled on processor cores and executed. But PLINQ does not guarantee the order in which tasks will execute, so it is likely, if not probable, that the list iteration is unordered.

If you prefer ordered results, use the *AsOrdered* clause. The PLINQ query still executes in an unordered fashion to improve performance and fully utilize the available processor cores. However, the results are buffered and then reordered at the completion of the query. This localizes the performance degradation to the *AsOrdered* clause.

Here is the modified query.

```
int[] numbers = { 0, 1, 2, 3, 4, 5, 6, 7, 8, 9 };
var result = from number in numbers.AsParallel().AsOrdered()
select number * number;
```

The results are now ordered.

```
 0 1 4 9 16 25 36 49 64 81
```

WithDegreeOfParallelism

By default, PLINQ uses the available processor cores, up to a maximum of 64. The goal, of course, is to keep the available processor cores busy with active work, as shown in the following graph. The graph depicts 100% utilization, which is ideal. This graph was taken during a PLINQ query where the parallel clauses were compute bound.

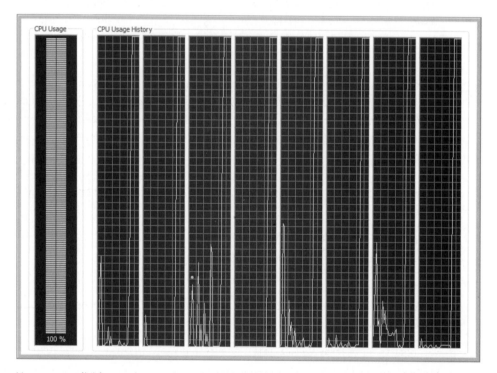

You can explicitly set the maximum number of processor cores with the *WithDegreeOf Parallelism* clause. There are two primary reasons for using this clause. First, this is useful when operations are I/O bound. I/O-bound threads are sometimes suspended, which causes processor cores to be underutilized. In this circumstance, you want to increase the degree of parallelism to exceed the number of processor cores. Conversely, you can decrease the number of tasks used in a PLINQ query with the *WithDegreeOfParallelism* clause. For example, you could create a more cooperative environment for other running applications by purposely reducing the degree of parallelism to less than the number of available cores.

Assuming eight available processor cores, the following code reduces the degree of parallelism. The amount of reduction depends on the number of available cores.

```
int[] numbers = { 0, 1, 2, 3, 4, 5, 6, 7, 8, 9 };
var result = numbers.AsParallel().WithDegreeOfParallelism(2).
Select(number=>PerformSelect(number)).ToList();
```

Handling Exceptions

Unhandled exceptions raised in a PLINQ query are propagated to the joining thread. Because there can be one or more parallel tasks, multiple unhandled exceptions could occur concurrently. For that reason, unhandled exceptions are raised as an *AggregateException*. You can enumerate the *AggregateException.InnerExceptions* property to retrieve the original exceptions raised. This is the same model for unhandled exceptions described in Chapter 2, "Task Parallelism" and Chapter 3, "Data Parallelism," and those chapters cover the subject in more detail.

You will use this exception model in the following tutorial to catch unhandled exceptions in PLINQ. In this example, you iterate an array of integers. Each element is then used as a divisor in a calculation. Unfortunately, a couple of the values in the array are zero. This throws the expected divide-by-zero exceptions. You will successfully catch and display the divide-by-zero exceptions.

Catch an exception in a PLINQ query as an *AggregateException* and display the results

1. Create a console application for C# in Visual Studio 2010. In the *Main* method, define an *integer* array. Notice that there are two zeros in the array list.

   ```
   int [] intArray = { 5, 1, 2, 7, 4, 0, 6, 2, 9, 0 };
   ```

2. Perform a PLINQ query that iterates the *integer* array. In the *Select* clause, return a 1000/nth calculation.

   ```
   var results = intArray.AsParallel().Select(item =>  (int)1000 / (int) item);
   ```

3. Define a *try* and *catch* block. In the *try* block, iterate over the results by using a *ForAll* method.

   ```
   try
   {
      results.ForAll((item) => Console.WriteLine(item));
   }
   ```

4. In the *catch* statement, catch an *AggregateException*. Then iterate over its *InnerExceptions* property and display the original underlying exceptions.

```
catch(AggregateException ex)
{
    foreach (var inner in ex.InnerExceptions)
    {
        Console.WriteLine(inner.Message);
    }
}
```

Here is the entire code.

```
using System;
using System.Collections.Generic;
using System.Linq;
using System.Text;

namespace Exception
{
    class Program
    {
        static void Main(string[] args)
        {
            int [] intArray = { 5, 1, 2, 7, 4, 0, 6, 2, 9, 0 };

            var results = intArray.AsParallel().Select(item =>  (int)1000 / (int) item);

            try
            {
                results.ForAll((item) => Console.WriteLine(item));
            }
            catch(AggregateException ex)
            {
                foreach (var inner in ex.InnerExceptions)
                {
                    Console.WriteLine(inner.Message);
                }
            }
            Console.WriteLine("Press enter to exit");
            Console.ReadLine();
        }
    }
}
```

Here's the output from the application, which shows two unhandled exceptions. Why? There is one exception for each zero in the *integer* list. Each will cause an unhandled exception in a separate task.

```
C:\Windows\system32\cmd.exe
200
1000
250
166
500
500
142
111
Attempted to divide by zero.
Attempted to divide by zero.
```

Cancellation

The cancellation model for parallel programming and the .NET Framework was introduced in the previous two chapters. This chapter applies the cancellation model to PLINQ. For a complete discussion of the cancellation model, review Chapters 2 and 3.

You cancel a PLINQ query with a *CancellationTokenSource* and *CancellationToken* object. *CancellationToken* is a property of the *CancellationTokenSource* class. Using the *WithCancellation* clause, you provide a cancellation token to a PLINQ query. You can then call *CancellationToken.Cancel* to cancel the query operation. When you cancel the operation, it throws an *OperationCanceledException* exception. Here are the basic steps of the cancellation model with PLINQ.

1. Define a *CancellationTokenSource*.

2. Execute the PLINQ query within a *try* block.

3. Add the *WithCancellation* clause to the PLINQ query. The only parameter is the *CancellationToken*.

4. Call the *CancellationTokenSource.Cancel* method to assert a cancellation. This will throw an *OperationCanceledException* in the PLINQ query.

5. In a *catch* block, catch and handle the *OperationCanceledException*.

Review the following example code. Note that it catches both the *OperationCanceledException* and *AggregateException*. A PLINQ query consists of parallel tasks, so it is quite possible for both an unhandled exception and cancellation exception to occur on separate tasks of the same query. Therefore, you should be prepared to catch both exceptions. This example uses a separate thread to invoke the cancellation request.

Here is the relevant code.

```
static CancellationTokenSource cs=new CancellationTokenSource();
static void Main(string[] args)
{
    int[] numbers = { 0, 1, 2, 3, 4, 5, 6, 7, 8, 9 };
    (new Thread(new ThreadStart(Cancellation))).Start();
    try
    {
        var result = numbers.AsParallel().WithCancellation(cs.Token)
            .Select(number => PerformSelect(number)).ToList();
    }
    catch (OperationCanceledException ex)
    {
        Console.WriteLine(ex.Message);
    }
    catch (AggregateException ex)
    {
        foreach (var inner in ex.InnerExceptions)
        {
            Console.WriteLine(inner.Message);
        }
    }
}

static void Cancellation()
{
    Thread.Sleep(4000);
    cs.Cancel();
}
```

Reduction

Reduction reduces a collection of elements to a singular value. For example, reduction could return an average value for a series of numbers. Other examples of reduction are calculating a summation, maximum value, or minimum value. In the .NET Framework, reduction is implemented as aggregation. LINQ provides a sequential implementation of aggregation, which runs on a single thread. This limits dependencies and is inherently thread safe. LINQ provides explicit methods for the most common reductions, such as:

- Sum
- Average
- Min

- Max

- Count

For other types of aggregation, you can implement a custom solution by using the *Aggregate* method.

The following is an example of reduction that uses LINQ. The reduction here is *Count*. It returns the count of positive values in a series of numbers.

```
var val=numbers.Where((number)=>number>-1).Count();
```

The next example is a custom aggregation and combines a collection of words as a sentence.

```
string [] words={"this", "is", "a", "string", "concatenation", "."};
string punctuation = ".,@#$%";
string delimiter="";
var sentence= words.Aggregate((element1, element2) =>
{
    delimiter = punctuation.Contains(element2) ? "" : " ";
    return element1+delimiter+element2;
});
```

The *Aggregate* method accepts a delegate as a parameter. The preceding example implements this delegate as a lambda expression. The delegate has two parameters: the partial result, and the next element of the collection. The return value is a partial result. But the parameters to the first *Aggregate* invocation are different. For that first call, the parameters are the first and second elements of the collection, which in this case would be the strings *this* and *is* from the string array. For subsequent iterations, the first parameter would contain the intermediate result.

Reduction in a PLINQ query merges the results from multiple threads. This creates a potential dependency on both the source collection and the result. For this reason, each thread uses thread-local storage, which is non-shared memory, to cache partial results. When operations have completed, the separate partial results are combined into a final result.

Like LINQ, PLINQ also has the standard reductions, such as the *Sum*, *Average*, and *Count* methods. You simply need to add the *AsParallel* clause.

```
var val = numbers.AsParallel().Where((number) => number > -1).Count();
```

You can also perform custom aggregation by using the *Aggregate* method. The signature is different from the same method in LINQ. The following code is the simplest overload of the *ParallelEnumerable.Aggregate* method. The second parameter is the seed and is the first relevant parameter. Thread-local storage for threads used for caching partial results is initialized with the seed. The *updateAccumulatorFunc* function calculates the partial result for a thread. The *combineAccumulatorsFunc* function merges the partial results into a final result. The last parameter is *resultSelector*, which is used to perform a user-defined operation on the final results.

```
public static TResult Aggregate<TSource, TAccumulate, TResult>(
        this ParallelQuery<TSource> source,
        TAccumulate seed,
        Func<TAccumulate, TSource, TAccumulate> updateAccumulatorFunc,
        Func<TAccumulate, TAccumulate, TAccumulate> combineAccumulatorsFunc,
        Func<TAccumulate, TResult> resultSelector
)
```

Next is the first example of a PLINQ query that uses the *Aggregate* method. Reduction is being used to calculate a factorial, which is an individual value. This example calculates the factorial of 5 (*5!*). The answer is *120 (1×2×3×4×5)*. An example in Chapter 3 also calculated a factorial but used a different approach. This example uses the *Enumerable.Range* method to return a collection of integral values ranging from 1 to 5. In the *Aggregate* method, the partial result of each thread is initialized to 1. If initialized to zero, the results would immediately be nullified, because the product of zero and anything else is zero.

```
int value=5;
var factorial=Enumerable.Range(1, value).AsParallel().Aggregate(
    1, (result, number)=>result*number, result=>result);
```

In this tutorial, you will use the *Aggregate* method to calculate the dot product of two matrices. You will then list all three matrices: the two input matrices and one result matrix.

> **Multiply corresponding points in two matrices by using the *Enumerable.Aggregate* method and save the product in a third matrix**

1. Create a console application for C# in Visual Studio 2010. In the *Main* method, define a constant value of four. This is used to set the size of the one-dimensional matrices. In addition, declare and initialize two input matrices.

   ```
   const int len = 4;
   int[] first = new int [len] { 1, 2, 3, 4};
   int[] second = new int[len] { 5, 6, 7, 8};
   ```

2. Starting at zero, create a range of integral values for indexes used with the matrices. Use the *AsParallel* clause to parallelize the *Aggregate* method.

   ```
   var third=Enumerable.Range(0, first.Length).AsParallel()
   ```

3. You define an *integer* array as the first parameter, which is a reference. As such, each thread receives a reference to the *same* array. This is the result matrix and the initial value of each thread. Depending on how the array is used, this might not be thread safe. In this circumstance, the different threads in the calculation will never access the same location in the result array. Therefore, it is thread safe. The next parameter is a delegate. Insert a lambda expression that multiplies the two matrices, two elements at a time. The next parameter should merge the results of the various threads. Because the threads are sharing the same result matrix, a merge is not necessary. The final parameter is an action to be performed on the final result. In this example, there is no action.

```
.Aggregate(new int[len], (result, index) =>
{
    result.SetValue(first[index] * second[index], index);
    return result;
},
(total, subtotal) => total,
(result) => result);
```

4. Display the input and output matrices by using *Console.WriteLine*.

```
foreach (var element in first)
{
    Console.Write(element+" ");
}

Console.WriteLine();

foreach (var element in second)
{
    Console.Write(element+" ");
}

Console.WriteLine();

foreach (var element in third)
{
    Console.Write(element + " ");
}
```

Compile and run the program. Here is the entire application.

```
using System;
using System.Collections.Generic;
using System.Linq;
using System.Text;

namespace Matrix
{
    class Program
    {
        static void Main(string[] args)
        {
            const int len = 4;
            int[] first = new int [len] { 1, 2, 3, 4};
            int[] second = new int[len] { 5, 6, 7, 8};
            var third=Enumerable.Range(0, first.Length).AsParallel().
                Aggregate(new int[len], (result, index)=>
                {
                    result.SetValue(first[index]*second[index], index);
                    return result;
                }, (result)=>result);

            foreach (var element in first)
            {
                Console.Write(element+" ");
            }
```

```
            Console.WriteLine();

            foreach (var element in second)
            {
                Console.Write(element+" ");
            }

            Console.WriteLine();

            foreach (var element in third)
            {
                Console.Write(element + " ");
            }

            Console.WriteLine("Press enter to exit");
            Console.ReadLine();
        }
    }
}
```

The following screen shows the output for the application. It lists the three relevant matrices.

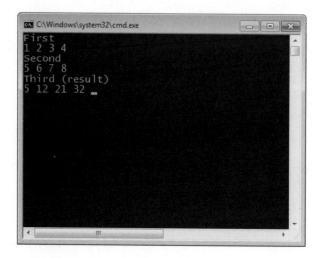

Using MapReduce with PLINQ

MapReduce is a special pattern of reduction used on large computer systems in which data collections can be distributed across a grid of computers. MapReduce allows you to perform an action on this highly dispersed collection of data. You probably do not own a large computer system with hundreds of computer nodes. Fortunately, the MapReduce pattern is also applicable and useful in smaller systems and multicore personal computers. MapReduce transforms a collection first to an ordered key-value pair, which is then reduced (typically based on the key) to a derivative collection.

Here are the basic steps of the MapReduce pattern in PLINQ:

1. Create or define the source, which must be a *ParallelQuery* type.

2. In the map operation, map the input source to an ordered and intermediate collection.

3. Finally, reduce the intermediate collection to the output collection.

PLINQ does not offer a direct implementation of the MapReduce pattern. Fortunately, "Parallel Programming with Microsoft .NET: Design Patterns for Decomposition and Coordination on Multicore Architectures," written by Stephen Toub and available at *http://msdn.microsoft.com/en-us/library/ff963553.aspx,* recommends a possible implementation of the MapReduce pattern in PLINQ. Here is the suggested implementation:

```
public static ParallelQuery<TResult> MapReduce<TSource, TMapped, TKey, TResult>(
this ParallelQuery<TSource> source,
Func<TSource, IEnumerable<TMapped>> map,
Func<TMapped, TKey> keySelector,
Func<IGrouping<TKey, TMapped>, IEnumerable<TResult>
{
return source.SelectMany(map)
.GroupBy(keySelector)
.SelectMany(reduce);
}
```

There are several parameters:

- The source parameter is the source collection.

- The map parameter is a delegate for the operation that maps the input collection to an intermediate collection.

- The *keySelector* parameter is a delegate for the operation that identifies the key. The intermediate collection is grouped on this key.

- The *reduce* parameter is also a delegate. It indicates where the reduction is performed— typically on the range of values associated with each key.

The MapReduce pattern was implemented in the previous chapter by using data parallelism. An example was presented that read Shakespearean sonnets and displayed the word distribution. You can now implement that example by using PLINQ.

The source collection consists of four sonnets.

```
string [] files={    @"C:\shakespeare\Sonnet 1.txt",
                     @"C:\shakespeare\Sonnet 2.txt",
                     @"C:\shakespeare\Sonnet 3.txt",
                     @"C:\shakespeare\Sonnet 4.txt"};
```

Define a PLINQ query with the collection of sonnets as the source. Call the PLINQ implementation of *MapReduce* to create a word count and distribution from these files. The first parameter is a delegate implemented as a lambda expression. In the lambda expression, read

the lines of text in each file, which is then split along delimiters into words. The next parameter identifies each word as a key. The result is an array of *KeyValuePairs* containing the word
(key) and word count.

```
var counts = files.AsParallel().MapReduce(
path => File.ReadLines(path).SelectMany(line => line.Split(delimiters)),
word => word,
group => new[] { new KeyValuePair<string, int>(group.Key, group.Count()) });
```

You can now display the results.

```
foreach (var word in counts)
{
     Console.WriteLine(word.Key + " " + word.Value);
}
```

Compile and run the program. Here is the entire application.

```
using System;
using System.Collections.Generic;
using System.Linq;
using System.Text;
using System.Threading.Tasks;
using System.IO;

namespace MapReduce
{
    static class PLINQ
    {
        public static ParallelQuery<TResult> MapReduce<TSource, TMapped, TKey, TResult>(
            this ParallelQuery<TSource> source,
            Func<TSource, IEnumerable<TMapped>> map,
            Func<TMapped, TKey> keySelector,
            Func<IGrouping<TKey, TMapped>, IEnumerable<TResult>> reduce)
        {
            return source.SelectMany(map)
            .GroupBy(keySelector)
            .SelectMany(reduce);
        }
    }

    class Program
    {
        static void Main(string[] args)
        {
            char [] delimiters={' ', ',', ';', '.'};

            string [] files={    @"C:\shakespeare\Sonnet 1.txt",
                                 @"C:\shakespeare\Sonnet 2.txt",
                                 @"C:\shakespeare\Sonnet 3.txt",
                                 @"C:\shakespeare\Sonnet 4.txt"};

            var counts = files.AsParallel().MapReduce(
                    path => File.ReadLines(path).SelectMany(
```

```
line => line.Split(delimiters)),
                    word => word,
                    group => new[] {
new KeyValuePair<string, int>(group.Key, group.Count()) });

        foreach (var word in counts)
          {
              Console.WriteLine(word.Key + " " + word.Value);
          }

        //Console.WriteLine("Press enter to exit");
        Console.ReadLine();
      }
    }
}
```

The following screen shot shows the partial results from the application.

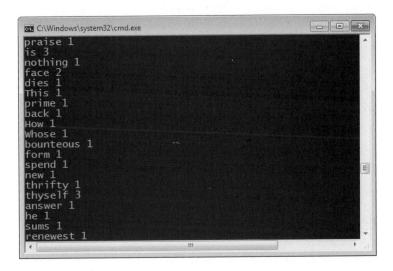

Summary

As an extension of LINQ, PLINQ implements data parallelism while supporting parallel queries across disparate data domains. PLINQ shares many of the same clauses and methods as LINQ. For this reason, if you are familiar with LINQ, you have the underlying knowledge of PLINQ. In most circumstances, just add the *AsParallel* clause to the LINQ query to transform it to PLINQ.

When iterating PLINQ results, use the *ParallelQuery.ForAll* method instead of the *for* and *foreach* methods. Serializing access to the results can negate some of the benefit to parallel processing.

There are several important clauses in PLINQ:

- *ParallelExecutionMode* explicitly sets the PLINQ query to execute in parallel.

- *WithMergeOptions* sets the buffer mode for rendering the results of a PLINQ query.

- *AsSequential* mandates that subsequent LINQ clauses execute sequentially.

- *AsOrdered* orders the results (but the query itself is still executed in parallel).

- *WithDegreeOfParallelism* sets the number of concurrent tasks used in the PLINQ query.

Handle the *AggregateException* exception to catch exceptions raised in a PLINQ query. You can enumerate the *AggregateExceptions.InnerExceptions* attributes to inspect the underlying exceptions raised in one or more parallel tasks assigned to the PLINQ query.

You can cancel a PLINQ query by using the Cancellation model. Create an instance of the *CancellationTokenSource* and pass a cancellation token to the PLINQ query by using the *WithCancellation* method. The PLINQ query can then be canceled with the *CancellationToken .Cancel* method.

Reduction reduces a collection to a value. PLINQ directly supports the most common reductions, such as *Sum*, *Average*, *Max*, *Min*, and *Count*. For a custom reduction operation, use the *ParallelEnumerate.Aggregate* method.

If you want, you can implement the MapReduce pattern for PLINQ. An example implementation is provided at the end of the previous section. You can use that to reduce a source collection to an output collection based on key-value pairs.

Quick Reference

To	Do this
Convert a LINQ query to PLINQ	Add the *AsParallel* clause.
Run a segment of a PLINQ query sequentially	Use the *AsSequential* clause.
Parallelize multiple streams of the PLINQ query	Use *ParallelQuery<TSource>.ForAll* to execute the various streams in parallel.
Set the buffered state for handling the results of a PLINQ query	Use *WithMergeOption.Buffered*, *WithMergeOption.FullyBuffered*, or *WithMergeOption.AutoBuffered*.
Create ordered results	Use the *AsOrdered* clause.
Cancel the iteration of PLINQ results	Use the cancellation model of task parallelism. Signal the cancellation with a *CancellationTokenSource* and handle the *OperationCanceledException* exception.
Perform reduction, such as a count or summation	Use the *ParallelEnumerable.Aggregate* method.

Chapter 5
Concurrent Collections

After completing this chapter, you will be able to

- Understand the benefits of concurrent collections.

- Explain the *IProducerConsumerCollection* interface.

- Use lower-level synchronization, including the *SpinLock* and *SpinWait* structures.

- Use two-phase synchronization.

- Explain and use the *ConcurrentStack* class.

- Explain and use the *ConcurrentQueue* class.

- Explain and use the *ConcurrentBag* class.

- Explain and use the *ConcurrentDictionary* class.

- Explain and use the *BlockingCollection* class.

Microsoft introduced concurrent collections and supporting synchronization primitives in the Microsoft .NET Framework 4. The concurrent collections are thread safe and optimized for concurrent access in a parallel environment. Most importantly, these collections are designed to be scalable in a multicore environment. Concurrent collections are largely lock free, which improves performance when elements are added and removed. If synchronization is required, discrete and lightweight user-mode synchronization is used when possible.

For parallel programming, use the collections in the *System.Collections.Concurrent* namespace in lieu of generic collections in the *System.Collections.Generic* namespace. For example, *ConcurrentQueue<T>* is preferred to *Queue<T>*. Whereas generic collections require user-defined external locks for synchronization, concurrent collections are implicitly thread safe. In some circumstances, external locking is not needed to synchronize access within a concurrent collection in a parallel computing scenario. You can simply use the concurrent collection and rely on the internal mechanisms of the type to assure safe simultaneous access from separate threads.

Performance and scalability are important considerations when using the concurrent collections. The internal implementation of thread safeness in concurrent collections is in general more efficient than generic collections that use external locks, which frequently require locking the entire collection. However, this statement is not universal, and it is dependent on various use scenarios. For example, the *ConcurrentDictionary* performs better than a locked *Dictionary* collection when reading is the most likely operation, and when few updates occur. The reason is that the update operation within a *ConcurrentDictionary* collection requires locking the entire collection, whereas the read operation is lock free. The *Dictionary* collection would need external locks for both reads and updates. However, a *Dictionary* collection is more efficient in read-only scenarios, where no synchronization is required.

This chapter provides an overview—but not a detailed performance analysis—of concurrent collections. For detailed performance information, see "Thread-safe Collections in .NET Framework 4 and Their Performance Characteristics" by Chunyan Song, Emad Omara, and Mike Liddell, available at MSDN at *http://msdn2.microsoft.com.*

It is time to travel back in history. Collections have always had an important role in the .NET Framework. The Microsoft .NET Framework 1.0 included non-generic collections, such as *ArrayList*, *SortedList*, and *Stack*, that were collections of object types. To synchronize access to non-generic collections, you use the *SyncRoot* property as an external lock. Because non-generic collections aggregated object types, they were not type safe. This also caused boxing when value types were added, which affected performance. For these reasons, in the .NET Framework 2.0, Microsoft introduced generic collections that are type safe and provide better performance, such as the *List<T>* and *Queue<T>* collections. Generic collections are templated types. In addition, generic collections do not expose properties to assist with thread synchronization. You must use external locks, and the most common strategy is to lock the entire collection. Of course, locking an entire collection is not especially efficient. The newly introduced concurrent collections address the shortcomings of both non-generic and generic collections and are both type safe and thread safe.

In addition to being type safe and thread safe, concurrent collections have another side benefit. Because external locks are not required, the source code for adding and removing elements in a parallel scenario is simpler for concurrent collections. That is an excellent combination—additional functionality with less code! Here is some sample code to compare coding a generic collection to coding a concurrent collection that requires synchronization. First is the code for a generic collection.

```
lock (genericList)
{
    genericList.Enqueue(number);
}
```

The following code block is functionally the same code, but when using a concurrent collection, you need only one line of code. Using the concurrent collection does not require additional code.

```
concurrentList.Enqueue(number);
```

Concurrent collections are indeed thread safe! However, that does not prevent you from using a concurrent collection in a manner that is not thread safe. For example, it's possible to enumerate a concurrent collection in one thread while another thread is updating the collection at the same time. The enumeration takes a snapshot of the collection, while updates are applied to the original collection. For this reason, the recent updates might not be visible via the enumeration, which can lead to race conditions and other problems. This is not thread safe. You need to be mindful of writing thread safe code even for concurrent collections.

Concurrent collections are available for you to use anywhere but are particularly optimized for parallel programming.

Concepts of Concurrent Collections

In the Framework Class Library (FCL), you can find the concurrent collections in the *System.Collections.Concurrent* namespace. Here are the concurrent collection types:

- *BlockingCollection*
- *ConcurrentBag*
- *ConcurrentDictionary*
- *ConcurrentQueue*
- *ConcurrentStack*

> **Note** You'll learn more about each collection type later in this chapter.

Most of the concurrent collections in the .NET Framework 4 implement the producer-consumer paradigm. (The exception is the *ConcurrentDictionary* class.) In the producer-consumer model, producers add elements to the collection, and consumers remove elements. In a pure producer-consumer scenario, separate threads are dedicated to either adding or removing elements. A single thread would not be responsible for both adding and removing elements. In a mixed producer-consumer scenario, a single thread might be both a producer and a consumer.

BlockingCollection is a wrapper for a producer-consumer collection. The *BlockingCollection* type adds blocking and bounding logistics to the underlying collection.

Producer-Consumers

In the .NET Framework 4, producer-consumer collections implement the *IProducer ConsumerCollection* interface. *ConcurrentQueue* and *ConcurrentStack* implement the *IProducerConsumerCollection* interface for a pure producer-consumer scenario. As such, elements should be added or removed from different threads. For example, with the *ConcurrentQueue* collection, you should have separate threads for queuing and dequeuing elements in the collection.

Mixed producer-consumer collections also implement the *IProducerConsumerCollection* interface, which is optimized for adding and removing elements using the same thread. The *ConcurrentBag* type is an example of a mixed producer-consumer collection. This class maintains a local queue for each thread that accesses the collection. Each thread adds and removes elements by using the private local queue. Add and remove operations on the same local queue are lock free.

Microsoft uses a variety of techniques to make concurrent collections lock free and, when it is available, employs lightweight synchronization. For lightweight synchronization, the concurrent collections use lower-level synchronization constructs, such as the *SpinLock* and *SpinWait* structures. These structures were introduced in the .NET Framework 4. The next section reviews the *SpinLock* and *SpinWait* structures.

Lower-Level Synchronization

When synchronization is required, concurrent collections use lightweight synchronization if possible. This is often less expensive than external locks, such as the *lock* statement.

SpinLock

The *SpinLock* structure is used to synchronize access to a resource.

When there is contention, the *SpinLock* does not block but spins in user mode. Spinning avoids blocking, which requires a kernel-mode lock. Accessing a kernel resource always causes an expensive context switch. After spinning, ideally the contention is removed and execution can continue unimpeded with no transition to kernel mode. In this manner, *SpinLock* is an opportunity for lightweight synchronization without blocking. *SpinLock* is ideal for scenarios involving frequent contention but short waits, where excessive spinning is avoided.

SpinLock is a structure found in the *System.Threading* namespace. Because it is a structure, be careful to avoid unintentional duplicates. When it is used as a parameter in a function, you should pass a *SpinLock* structure by reference (that is, use the *ref* keyword) to avoid creating a copy.

Here is the pattern for using a *SpinLock* structure for synchronization:

1. Declare an instance of a *SpinLock* structure.
2. Define a *try* block.

3. In the *try* block, call *SpinLock.Enter* to enter a section of synchronized code. If another thread has entered but not exited, the current thread will spin. Several threads could be spinning, waiting to enter a section of code.

4. In a *finally* block, call *SpinLock.Exit* to relinquish a section of synchronized code. At this time, one or more threads might be waiting to enter. One of those threads can now enter the serialized section code. Using a *finally* block for *SpinLock.Exit* assures that this method is called, which helps to prevent inadvertent deadlocks.

SpinLock.Enter accepts a single parameter, which is a reference to a Boolean variable. The Boolean variable must be initialized to *false*. The variable is an indicator as to whether the *Enter* method was successful. If successful, the variable is changed to *true*.

Look at the following two-line snippet of code. The *SpinLock* is entered twice in a single thread. Nested locks are a common programming technique. However innocuous this might appear, a *LockRecursionException* is raised. Nested locks can be dangerous and frequently cause program bugs. For this reason, the *SpinLock.Enter* method is non-reentrant.

```
slock.Enter(ref taken1);
slock.Enter(ref taken2);
```

Because it is not reentrant, *SpinLock.Enter* is also more efficient. The method does not have the relevant information required to manage reentrancy.

By default, *SpinLock* tracks thread ownership. Tracking of thread ownership, if present, is set as the first parameter of the *SpinLock* constructor. The *SpinLock.IsThreadOwnerTrackingEnabled* property returns *true* if the tracking is enabled. You can set this parameter of the constructor to *false* and disable tracking. Be careful. With tracking disabled, a reentrant call to *SpinLock.Enter* is allowed. Here is sample code showing a potential deadlock.

```
SpinLock slock = new SpinLock(false);
bool taken1 = false;
bool taken2 = false;
try
{
    slock.Enter(ref taken1);
    slock.Enter(ref taken2);   // Deadlock
    Console.WriteLine("Never reached!");
}
```

You can test a *SpinLock* for availability with the *SpinLock.TryEnter* method. If it is not available, where you would normally block, *TryEnter* would simply return and set the out parameter to *false*. There are two overloads of the method. The first variation will return immediately if the resource is not available. The second version of the *TryEnter* method spins for a specified duration first and then attempts to acquire the resource again. If the resource remains unavailable after spinning, *TryEnter* will then return.

Here is an explanation of some of the members of the *SpinLock* structure:

- **IsHeld** This is a Boolean property and returns *true* if *SpinLock* is held by any thread.
- **IsHeldByCurrentThread** This is a Boolean property and returns *true* if *SpinLock* is held by the current thread.
- **Enter(ref lock lockTaken)** If the *SpinLock* is available, this method gives the current thread ownership of the *SpinLock*. Otherwise, the thread blocks.
- **TryEnter(ref lock lockTaken)** If the *SpinLock* is available, this method gives the current thread ownership of the *SpinLock*. Otherwise, the method returns immediately with *lockTaken* set to *false*.
- **Exit()** This method relinquishes thread ownership of a *SpinLock* structure.

In the following sample code, *slock* is a *SpinLock* structure.

```
bool taken = false;
try
{
    slock.Enter(ref taken);
    DoSomething();
}
finally
{
    if (taken) slock.Exit();
}
```

SpinWait

The *SpinWait* structure is another alternative to heavy synchronization that uses a kernel-level lock. When using a kernel-level lock, such as a monitor or semaphore, an application incurs a costly context switch and other costs related to the kernel-mode transition. With the *SpinWait* structure, you can spin for a short period when there is contention. After spinning, you can attempt to reacquire the resource. If the acquisition is successful then, the overall cost is less than that of the same steps using a kernel-level lock.

SpinWait is a structure in the *System.Threading* namespace. Be careful not to create copies of the *SpinWait* structure. If that occurs, you will have separate entities that are unrelated for the purposes of synchronization.

The *SpinWait* structure is particularly helpful when contention is short. In this scenario, the resource is apt to be available after minimal spinning. Excessive spinning can be expensive and increases CPU utilization. It's important to recognize that this might take away processing cycles from non-spinning threads. Remember, you are spinning because of contention. The quickest way to resolve the contention is to allow the *other* threads to run. Too much spinning can prevent this. As with most things in life, spinning is about balance. Nominal spinning to avoid a context switch to kernel mode is good, but you should avoid spinning more than necessary. For these reasons, the *SpinWait* structure has been designed to "play friendly" with other threads.

- If there is a single processor core, the *SpinWait* structure automatically yields execution at each spin.

- In a multicore core environment, *SpinWait* will occasionally yield the CPU to avoid monopolizing available processor cores. The details of this yield process are outside the scope of this book. Fortunately, the *SpinWait.NextSpinWillYield* property informs you that the next spin will cause execution to yield to another thread.

Here are some of the important members of the *SpinWait* structure:

- **NextSpinWillYield**   This is a Boolean property that returns *true* if the next spin will yield execution.

- **SpinOnce()**   This method performs a spin.

- **SpinUntil(Func<bool> condition)**   This method spins until the specified function predicate returns *true*. The function is called an underdetermined number of times.

Two-Phase Synchronization

SpinWait structures are ideal for implementing the two-phase synchronization model. In the first phase, you try to acquire a shared resource. If the resource is not available, you wait for a short period of time in user mode with lightweight synchronization techniques. After a short wait, attempt to acquire the resource a second time. If the second attempt fails also, then enter the second phase. In this phase, you synchronize with a kernel-level lock and block. At some point in the future, your kernel lock will signal and execution will be continued. You can then acquire the target resource.

The following flowchart diagrams the two-phase synchronization model.

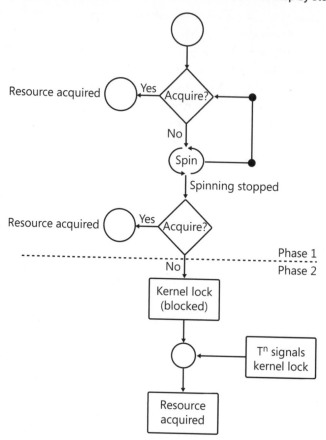

ConcurrentStack

ConcurrentStack is a thread-safe collection optimized for shared access in a parallel or concurrent scenario. No external locks are required for synchronization of the *ConcurrentStack*. Elements are added to the *ConcurrentStack* collection on a last-in-first-out (LIFO) basis. You *push* to add an element and *pop* to remove an element.

The collection implements the *IProducerConsumerCollection* interface and is optimized for pure producer-consumer scenarios. As a pure producer-consumer, ideally the collection should have one dedicated thread for pushing and another for popping elements. Do not push and pop elements on the *ConcurrentStack* collection by using a single thread.

The implementation is lock free. Instead of employing kernel-level locks during contention, spinning and compare-and-swap operations are used to resolve contention.

Here are some of the important members of the *ConcurrentStack* class:

- **Clear**   This removes all elements from the collection.

- **Count**   This is an integer property that returns the count of elements in the collection.

- **IsEmpty**   This is a Boolean property that returns *true* if the collection is empty.

- **Push(T item)**   This method adds an element to the collection.

- **TryPop(out T result)**   This method removes an element from the collection. If it is successful, *true* is returned; otherwise *false* is returned. For example, *false* is returned if the collection is empty.

- **PushRange(T [] items)**   This method adds a range of items to the collection. This is more efficient than adding elements individually. The operation is performed atomically.

- **TryPopRange(T [] items)**   This method removes a range of items to the collection. This is more efficient than removing elements individually. The operation is performed atomically.

Some members of the *ConcurrentStack* class, such as *Count*, *ToArray*, and *GetEnumerator*, use a static snapshot of the concurrent collection, which removes a potential dependency. You can safely use the snapshot and avoid synchronization issues. This can lead to unexpected results as other members work with the current representation of the collection. For example, you could enumerate a *ConcurrentStack* collection while adding members. In this case, the static and dynamic image would be different, and the results might be inconsistent.

In this tutorial, you will use the *ConcurrentStack* collection to track the duration of a method. Implement a log with the *ConcurrentStack* collection where you record the entry and exit times of methods. When dumped, the log is printed in reverse order or basically LIFO. Newer methods are displayed first.

Use the *ConcurrentStack* collection to implement a class to track and log function entry and exit

1. Create a console application for C# in Visual Studio 2010. At the beginning of the program, add *using* statements for the following namespaces:

   - *System.Collections.Concurrent*

   - *System.Threading*

   - *System.Diagnostics*

   - *System.Threading.Tasks*

2. Define *FunctionTracker* as a disposable class. At the top of the class, define several private attributes:

   ❑ Define a static instance of *ConcurrentStack* as the global log.

   ❑ Define a *StackTrace* object to obtain the name of the tracked method.

   ❑ Define a string to hold the function name.

   ❑ Define a *DateTime* object and initialize it to the current time.

```
private static ConcurrentStack<string> log=new ConcurrentStack<string>();
private StackTrace stackTrace = new StackTrace();
private string functionName;
private DateTime startTime=DateTime.Now;
```

3. In the constructor, retrieve and save the name of the calling method with the *StackFrame* object. Add a start entry in the log for the method.

```
public FunctionTracker()
{
    functionName=stackTrace.GetFrame(1).GetMethod().Name;
    log.Push(string.Format("{0} started: {1}", functionName,
        startTime.ToLongTimeString()));
}
```

4. In the *IDisposable.Dispose* method, get the end time of the methods and calculate the duration. Add an exit entry in the log for this information.

```
public void Dispose()
{
    DateTime endTime=DateTime.Now;
    TimeSpan tsDuration = endTime.Subtract(startTime);
    log.Push(string.Format("{0} stopped: {1} [{2}]",
        functionName, endTime.ToLongTimeString(),
            tsDuration.TotalMilliseconds));
}
```

5. Add the *Stop* method, which simply calls the *Dispose* method. The *Stop* method is useful when an object is not being used as a disposable object.

```
public void Stop()
{
    Dispose();
}
```

6. Add two methods to display the log. The *Dump* method removes and displays elements from the log in a *while* loop by using the *TryPop* method. The *Display* method uses an enumerator and a *foreach* loop to display the log without removing any elements.

```
public static void Dump()
{
    string item;
    while (log.TryPop(out item))
    {
```

```
                        Console.WriteLine(item);
            }
       }

       public static void Display()
       {
            foreach (string item in log)
            {
                 Console.WriteLine(item);
            }
       }
  }
```

7. Time to test the application! Create a couple of test functions as shown in the following code. Both use the *FunctionTracker* as a disposable object defined at the beginning of a method. Add both methods to the *Program* class.

```
       public static void FuncA()
       {
           using (new FunctionTracker())
           {
               Thread.Sleep(1000);
           }
       }

       public static void FuncB()
       {
           using (new FunctionTracker())
           {
               Thread.Sleep(2000);
           }
       }
  }
```

8. In the *Main* method, invoke both test functions in parallel. Dump the log to view the results.

```
       using (new FunctionTracker())
       {
           Parallel.Invoke(() => FuncA(), () => FuncB());
       }
       FunctionTracker.Display();
```

9. Build and run the program.

Here is the complete application.

```
using System;
using System.Collections.Generic;
using System.Linq;
using System.Text;
using System.Collections.Concurrent;
using System.Threading;
using System.Diagnostics;
using System.Threading.Tasks;

namespace Example
```

```
    {
        class FunctionTracker: IDisposable
        {
            private static ConcurrentStack<string> log=new ConcurrentStack<string>();
            private StackTrace stackTrace = new StackTrace();
            private string functionName;
            private DateTime startTime=DateTime.Now;

            public FunctionTracker()
            {
                functionName=stackTrace.GetFrame(1).GetMethod().Name;
                log.Push(string.Format("{0} started: {1}", functionName,
                    startTime.ToLongTimeString()));
            }

            public void Dispose()
            {
                DateTime endTime=DateTime.Now;
                TimeSpan tsDuration = endTime.Subtract(startTime);
                log.Push(string.Format("{0} stopped: {1} [{2}]",
                    functionName, endTime.ToLongTimeString(),
                        tsDuration.TotalMilliseconds));
            }

            public void Stop()
            {
                Dispose();
            }

            public static void Dump()
            {
                string item;
                while (log.TryPop(out item))
                {
                    Console.WriteLine(item);
                }
            }

            public static void Display()
            {
                foreach (string item in log)
                {
                    Console.WriteLine(item);
                }
            }
        }
    }

    class Program
    {
        public static void FuncA()
        {
            using (new FunctionTracker())
            {
                Thread.Sleep(1000);
```

```
            }
        }

        public static void FuncB()
        {
            using (new FunctionTracker())
            {
                Thread.Sleep(2000);
            }
        }

        static void Main(string[] args)
        {
            using (new FunctionTracker())
            {
                Parallel.Invoke(() => FuncA(), () => FuncB());
            }
            FunctionTracker.Display();
        }
    }
}
```

This is the output for the application. It dumps the log and lists the start time, exit time, and duration of each tracked method.

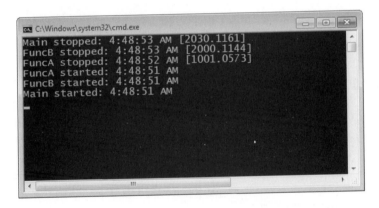

ConcurrentQueue

ConcurrentQueue is a thread-safe collection optimized for shared access in a parallel or concurrent environment. Similar to *ConcurrentStack*, *ConcurrentQueue* is lock free and does not require external locks for synchronization. Elements are added to the *ConcurrentQueue* collection on a first-in-first-out (FIFO) basis. You can queue to add an element and dequeue to remove an element.

Except for using FIFO instead of LIFO access patterns, *ConcurrentQueue* and *ConcurrentStack* are similar. This class also implements the *IProducerConsumerCollection* interface and is optimized for pure producer-consumer scenarios.

Here are some of the important members of the *ConcurrentQueue*:

- **Count**   This property returns the number of elements in the collection, which is an integer.

- **IsEmpty**   This property is a Boolean that returns *true* if the collection is empty.

- **Enqueue (T item)**   This method adds an element to the collection.

- **TryDequeue(out T result)**   This method removes an element from the collection. If it is successful, *true* is returned; otherwise, *false* is returned.

ConcurrentBag

ConcurrentBag is an unordered collection and the final of the three collections in the *System .Collections.Concurrent* namespace that implement the *IProducerConsumerCollection* interface. Unlike the other collections, *ConcurrentBag* is optimized for mixed producer-consumer scenarios, where an element is added and removed using the same thread.

In most circumstances, *ConcurrentBag* is highly efficient, requires minimal synchronization, and is lock free. This is possible because separate local queues are created for each client thread. Each thread adds and removes elements from the local queue, which removes the need for synchronization. However, sometimes the local queue for a thread is empty. In that circumstance, the element must be stolen from the local queue of another thread. This requires synchronization of the shared resource (the local queue) between the two threads.

The following diagram illustrates the behavior of a *ConcurrentBag* collection. In this example, there are two threads, both of which are adding items to the *ConcurrentBag* collection. Each thread has a local queue for this purpose. In the first box, Thread 1 and Thread 2 add items to the *ConcurrentBag* collection. Thread 1 adds two items to its local queue (A and B). Thread 2 adds three items to its local queue (C, D, and E). In the next box, Thread 1 adds an additional item to its local queue. Thread 2 removes an item. Because items are available on the local queue, the item is removed from the local queue of Thread 2. In the next box, Thread 2 removes three additional items. First, Thread 2 removes two items from its local queue. The Thread 2 local queue is now empty. For that reason, it removes the remaining item from the Thread 1 local queue. Finally, in the last box, Thread 1 removes the remaining two items on its local queue.

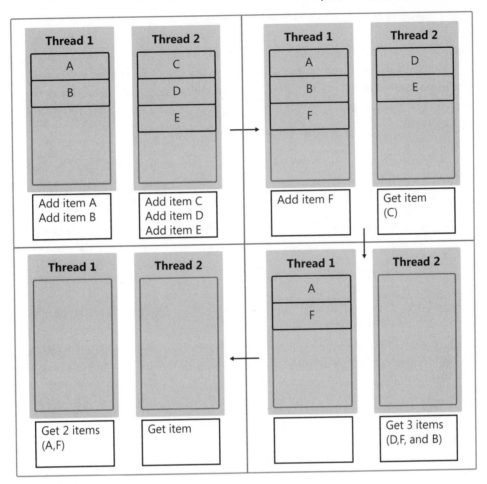

Here are some members of *ConcurrentBag*:

- **Count**   This property returns the number of elements in the collection, which is an integer.

- **IsEmpty**   This is a Boolean that returns *true* if the collection is empty.

- **Add(T item)**   This method adds an element to the collection.

- **TryTake(out T result)**   This method removes an unordered element from the collection. If it is successful, *true* is returned.

- **TryPeek(out T result)**   This method returns but does not remove the next element from the unordered collection. If it is successful, *true* is returned.

ConcurrentBag is useful when sequencing of the collection is not important. You just need a shared collection that is thread safe for adding and removing elements. The best practice is to add and remove elements from the collection by using the same thread. The next tutorial will highlight this. In this tutorial, you simulate a store with customers. The customer list is maintained in a *ConcurrentBag* collection. This example will demonstrate the mixed producer-consumer pattern, where individual elements are added and removed by using the same thread.

Create a customer class to manage a customer list for a store by using a *ConcurrentBag* collection

1. Create a console application for C# in Visual Studio 2010. At the beginning of the program, add *using* statements for the following namespaces:

   ❑ *System.Collections.Concurrent*

   ❑ *System.Threading*

   ❑ *System.Diagnostics*

   ❑ *System.Threading.Tasks*

2. Create a new class called *Person*. At the top of the class, define two fields. Define an instance of the *ConcurrentBag* to hold the customer list. Also, add a string property to hold the customer name.

   ```
   static ConcurrentBag<Person> customerList = new ConcurrentBag<Person>();
   public string Name { get; set; }
   ```

3. In the constructor for the *Person* class, add the current object to the *ConcurrentBag* collection.

   ```
   public Person() {customerList.Add(this);}
   ```

4. Define a method to simulate a customer shopping and then exiting the store. In the method, create an instance of the *Random* class. For shopping, spin the current thread by using the random object. The spin value is *{random<maximum integer}*. After shopping, otherwise known as spinning (spending), the customer leaves the store. For that reason, remove the customer from the customer list by using the *TryTake* method. Remember, *ConcurrentBag* is an unordered list. You are not guaranteed which element is returned. However, *TryTake* should remove elements from the local queue of the current thread first. In our example, the local queue should have a single element, which is the current customer. Test this by comparing the hash code of the current object and the element retrieved from the *TryTake* method. If the two are equal, display a message confirming that the two objects are identical.

```
public void ShopAndExit(){
    Random rand=new Random();
    Thread.SpinWait(rand.Next(int.MaxValue));
    Person cust;
    if (customerList.TryTake(out cust))
    {
        if (cust.GetHashCode() == this. GetHashCode())
        {
            Console.WriteLine("**** {0}=={1} objects are identical ****",
                cust.Name, this.Name);
        }
    }
}
```

5. In the *Main* method, start a *Parallel.For* loop. Iterate the loop four times. Define a lambda expression for the function predicate.

```
Parallel.For(0, 4, (index) =>
```

6. In the lambda expression, create an instance of the *Person* type with a generic name. Next, call the *ShopAndExit* method. Display a message for entering and leaving the store. Also, display the thread identifier. You can then match operations on elements with specific threads.

```
var customer=new Person(){Name="Customer "+
    index.ToString()};
Console.WriteLine("[Thread {0}] {1} entering store.",
    Thread.CurrentThread.ManagedThreadId, customer.Name);
customer.ShopAndExit();
Console.WriteLine("[Thread {0}] {1} leaving store.",
    Thread.CurrentThread.ManagedThreadId, customer.Name);
```

7. Build and run the program.

Here is the complete application.

```
using System;
using System.Collections.Generic;
using System.Linq;
using System.Text;
using System.Collections.Concurrent;
using System.Threading.Tasks;
using System.Threading;

namespace Example
{
    class Person
    {
        static ConcurrentBag<Person> customerList = new ConcurrentBag<Person>();
        public string Name { get; set; }
        public Person() {customerList.Add(this);}
        public void ShopAndExit(){
```

```
            Random rand=new Random();
            Thread.SpinWait(rand.Next(int.MaxValue));
            Person cust;
            if (customerList.TryTake(out cust))
            {
                if (cust.GetHashCode() == this. GetHashCode())
                {
Console.WriteLine("**** {0}=={1} objects are identical ****",
                                  cust.Name, this.Name);
                }
            }
        }
    }

    class Program
    {
        static void Main(string[] args)
        {
            Parallel.For(0, 4, (index) =>
            {
                var customer=new Person(){Name="Customer "+
                    index.ToString()};
                Console.WriteLine("[Thread {0}] {1} entering store.",
                    Thread.CurrentThread.ManagedThreadId, customer.Name);
                customer.ShopAndExit();
                Console.WriteLine("[Thread {0}] {1} leaving store.",
                    Thread.CurrentThread.ManagedThreadId, customer.Name);
            });
        }
    }
}
```

This is the output for the application. Notice that each item is added and removed from the same thread, which is the mixed producer-consumer scenario.

ConcurrentDictionary

ConcurrentDictionary is a thread-safe collection of key-value pairs optimized for parallel programming. Like other concurrent collections, this collection is found in the *System .Collections.Concurrent* namespace. *ConcurrentDictionary* does not implement the *IProducerConsumerCollection* interface and is not a producer-consumer collection.

ConcurrentDictionary has efficient synchronization. The collection is optimized for regular reads and infrequent add and updates. Discrete locking is used internally for updating and adding elements. This is more efficient than using an external lock and locking the entire collection. Reads are the most efficient operation and are lock free.

The capacity of the *ConcurrentDictionary* is settable in the constructor. This is a hint at the capacity and not an absolute. Set the capacity to a value marginally larger than expected.

Here are some of the important members of the *ConcurrentDictionary* type:

- **Count**   This property returns the number of elements in the collection, which is an integer.

- **IsEmpty**   This is a Boolean that returns *true* if the collection is empty.

- **TryAdd(T item)**   This method adds a key-value pair to a collection. If the key exists, the element is not added and *false* is returned.

- **TryUpdate(TKey key, TValue newValue, TValue comparisonValue)**   This method compares the current value to the comparison value. If they are the same, the value is updated to the new value. Otherwise, the method returns *false*.

- **AddOrUpdate(TKey key, TValue, addValue, Func<TKey, TValue, TValue> update Factory>)**   If the key is not present, this method adds the key-value pair to the collection. If the key already exists, the function predicate is called to generate a new value from the existing value.

In the next exercise, you will create an integer array that has duplicate values and add the integer values to a *ConcurrentDictionary*. The integer value is the key. The value is an instance count. You will call *ConcurrentDictionary.AddOrUpdate* to add a new entry or calculate the current instance count.

Create a *ConcurrentDictionary* collection from an integer array, with the integer as the key and the instance count as the value

1. Create a console application for C# in Visual Studio 2010. At the beginning of the program, add *using* statements for the *System.Threading.Tasks* and *System.Collections .Concurrent* namespaces.

2. In the *Main* method, declare an integer array with duplicate values. Also define a *ConcurrentDictionary* with both the key and value as integers.

```
var numbers = new int[] { 1, 2, 4, 2, 3, 1, 2 };
var collection = new ConcurrentDictionary<int, int>();
```

3. Iterate the integer array in parallel by using the *Parallel.ForEach* method.

```
Parallel.ForEach(numbers, (number) =>
```

4. Implement a lambda expression for the *Parallel.ForEach* loop. Each iteration should add the current integer element as a key to the collection. If the key already exists, call a predicate function to increment the value of that key.

```
collection.AddOrUpdate(number, 1, (key, value) =>
    {
        return ++value;
    });
```

5. Iterate and display the key-value pair of the collection.

```
foreach (var entry in collection)
{
    Console.WriteLine("Key: {0} Count: {1}", entry.Key, entry.Value);
}
```

6. Build and run the program.

Here is the complete application.

```
namespace Example
{
    class Program
    {
        static void Main(string[] args)
        {
            var numbers = new int[] { 1, 2, 4, 2, 3, 1, 2 };

            var collection = new ConcurrentDictionary<int, int>();
            Parallel.ForEach(numbers, (number) =>
                {
                    collection.AddOrUpdate(number, 1, (key, value) =>
                        {
                            return ++value;
                        });
                });

            foreach (var entry in collection)
            {
                Console.WriteLine("Key: {0} Count: {1}", entry.Key, entry.Value);
            }
        }
    }
}
```

This is the output for the application.

BlockingCollection

The last collection for this chapter is the *BlockingCollection*. It is a wrapper of a concurrent collection or any class that implements the *IProducerConsumerCollection* interface. *BlockingCollection* adds blocking and bounding semantics to the underlying collection. If a collection is not provided in the *BlockingCollection* constructor, the default underlying collection is *ConcurrentQueue*.

The *TryTake* method is called to remove an element from a producer-consumer collection. The type of collection determines the form that the *TryTake* function is exposed as. For example, *TryTake* is replaced by the *TryDequeue* method in the *ConcurrentQueue* class. The *TryTake* method returns *false* if the collection is empty. If a timeout is specified, the *TryTake* method blocks when the underlying producer-consumer collection is empty and waits for an element to be added to the collection. You can create a dedicated thread for consuming elements to a collection. When no elements are available, the thread would sleep. The next tutorial demonstrates this.

In this tutorial, you will create a *BlockingCollection* and add a dedicated thread to consume elements as they are added to the *BlockingCollection*. You will use a timeout to prevent an infinite wait for a new element. If a timeout occurs, use the cancellation model to cancel further additions to the *BlockingCollection*.

Create a dedicated thread for consuming elements of a *BlockingCollection*

1. Create a console application for C# in Visual Studio 2010. At the beginning of the program, add *using* statements for the following namespaces:

   ❏ *System.Collections.Concurrent*

   ❏ *System.Threading.Tasks*

   ❏ *System.Threading*

2. Define two static variables. First, define a *BlockingCollection* for integer values. Also create a *CancellationTokenSource* variable, which is the implementation of the cancellation model in the Task Parallel Library (TPL).

```
public static BlockingCollection<int> collection = new BlockingCollection<int>();
public static CancellationTokenSource cs = new CancellationTokenSource();
```

3. Add a static method as a handler for when elements are added to the *BlockingCollection*. For our example, just display a message.

```
public static void Handler()
{
    Console.WriteLine("[{0}] Handled and removed",
        DateTime.Now.ToLongTimeString());
}
```

4. In the *Main* method, call *Parallel.Invoke* for two tasks. Each task is implemented as a lambda expression. In a *while* loop, the first task adds elements to the *BlockingCollection* until the operation is canceled. There is an increasingly longer wait between each iteration. Display an appropriate message at each iteration.

```
Parallel.Invoke(new Action[] {()=>
    {
        int value=1000;
        while(!cs.IsCancellationRequested)
        {
            Thread.Sleep(value);
            collection.Add(++value);
            Console.WriteLine("[{0}] Element Added",
                DateTime.Now.ToLongTimeString());
            value += 2000;
        }
    }
```

5. The next task also contains a *while* loop. Each iteration consumers the next element if one is present. Call *TryTake(out T item, int millisecondsTimeout)*, which offers the timeout as a parameter. A reasonable timeout is used to prevent a deadlock. If a timeout occurs, exit the loop and cancel the entire operation.

```
()=>
    {
        int item;
        while(true)
        {
            if(collection.TryTake(out item, 10000))
            {
                Handler();
            }
            else
            {
                // Handle timeout
                Console.WriteLine("Timeout. Program exiting");
                cs.Cancel();
```

```
                                    break;
                                }
                            }
                        }
```

6. Build and run the program.

Here is the complete application.

```
using System;
using System.Collections.Generic;
using System.Linq;
using System.Text;
using System.Collections.Concurrent;
using System.Threading.Tasks;
using System.Threading;

namespace EfficientHandler
{
    class Program
    {

        public static BlockingCollection<int> collection = new
            BlockingCollection<int>();
        public static CancellationTokenSource cs = new CancellationTokenSource();

        public static void Handler()
        {
            Console.WriteLine("[{0}] Handled and removed",
                DateTime.Now.ToLongTimeString());
        }

        static void Main(string[] args)
        {
            Parallel.Invoke(new Action[] {()=>
                {
                    int value=1000;
                    while(!cs.IsCancellationRequested)
                    {
                        Thread.Sleep(value);
                        collection.Add(++value);
                        Console.WriteLine("[{0}] Element Added",
                            DateTime.Now.ToLongTimeString());
                        value += 2000;
                    }
                },
                ()=>
                    {
                        int item;
                        while(true)
                        {
                            if(collection.TryTake(out item, 10000))
                            {
                                Handler();
                            }
                            else
```

```
                                      {
                                          // Handle timeout
                                          Console.WriteLine("Timeout. Program exiting");
                                          cs.Cancel();
                                          break;
                                      }
                                  }
                              }
                          });
                     }
                 }
             }
```

The following graphic shows the output for the application. The task for adding elements might not detect the cancellation immediately. For that reason, there might be an additional add message after the cancellation.

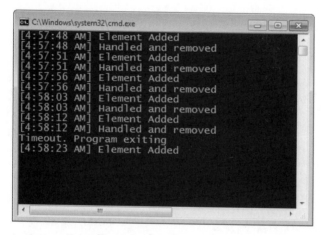

In the previous example, elements were consumed with the *TryTake* method. If the collection is empty, the *TryTake* method blocks. For that reason, a timeout is used to prevent a potentially infinite deadlock of that thread. The following code snippet shows a concise version of the *while* loop for consuming elements in a blocking collection.

```
while(true)
{
    if(!TryTake(out item, 10000)))
    {
break;
}
```

The *BlockingCollection* implements a similar algorithm in the *GetConsumingEnumerable* method, which returns an enumerator. This method returns an enumerator that iterates elements as they are added and blocks if the collection is empty. Like the above code, the enumeration presents a possibility of an infinite deadlock if the collection is permanently empty. For that reason, *CompleteAdding* exists. Invoke this method to notify the *BlockingCollection* that further elements will not be added. You cannot add elements to a *BlockingCollection* after calling the *CompleteAdding* method. If you do, an exception is raised.

Next is a short tutorial on using the *GetConsumingEnumerable* method. You will create an application with three tasks:

- Add elements to a *BlockingCollection*.
- Consume elements by using a *GetConsumingEnumerable* enumerator.
- Mark a *BlockingCollection* as completed.

Implement the *GetConsumingEnumerable* model to add elements to and consume elements from a *BlockingCollection*

1. Create a console application for C# in Visual Studio 2010. At the beginning of the program, add *using* statements for the following namespaces:

   ❑ *System.Collection.Concurrent*

   ❑ *System.Threading.Tasks*

   ❑ *System.Threading*

2. Define a *BlockingCollection* that contains integer values.

   ```
   static BlockingCollection<int> collection=new BlockingCollection<int>();
   ```

3. In the *Main* method, define a *try/catch* block to catch an unhandled exception from parallel tasks.

   ```
   try
   {
   }
   catch(AggregateException ex)
   {
   }
   ```

4. Within the *try* block, define an integer count. This is the value to be added to the *BlockingCollection*. Call the *Parallel.Invoke* method to execute tasks to add elements to the collection, prevent further additions, and display the elements of the collection.

   ```
   int count = 0;
   Parallel.Invoke(new Action[] {
   ```

5. The first task contains an infinite *while* loop. In the *while* loop, add the count to the *BlockingCollection* and increment the count. You should then yield execution for a couple of seconds.

   ```
   ()=> { while(true) {collection.Add(++count); Thread.Sleep(2000);}},
   ```

6. In the next task, read a line from the console. When the user responds, call *CompleteAdding* to finish adding elements to the *BlockingCollection*.

```
()=> { Console.ReadLine(); collection.CompleteAdding(); }
```

7. The final task is a *foreach* loop that uses a *GetConsumingEnumerable* enumerator. In the *foreach* loop, display the values of the collection.

```
()=> {foreach(int value in collection.GetConsumingEnumerable()) Console.
WriteLine(value);}
```

8. In the *catch* block, check for an *InvalidOperationException*. This indicates that an element was added to the collection after *CompleteAdding* was called. Display the appropriate messages.

```
if (ex.InnerException is System.InvalidOperationException)
{
    Console.WriteLine("Adding  complete!");
}
else
{
    Console.WriteLine("Unexpected exception");
}
```

9. Build and run the program.

Here is the complete application.

```
using System;
using System.Collections.Generic;
using System.Linq;
using System.Text;
using System.Collections.Concurrent;
using System.Threading.Tasks;
using System.Threading;

namespace GetConsumingEnumerable
{
    class Program
    {
        private static BlockingCollection<int> collection=new
            BlockingCollection<int>();

        static void Main(string[] args)
        {
            try
            {

                int count = 0;
                Parallel.Invoke(new Action[] {
                ()=> { while(true) {collection.Add(++count);
                    Thread.Sleep(2000);}},
```

```
                    ()=> { Console.ReadLine(); collection.CompleteAdding(); },
                    ()=> {foreach(int value in
                            collection.GetConsumingEnumerable())
                        Console.WriteLine(value);}});
            }
            catch(AggregateException ex)
            {
                if (ex.InnerException is System.InvalidOperationException)
                {
                    Console.WriteLine("Adding  complete!");
                }
                else
                {
                    Console.WriteLine("Another exception");
                }
            }
        }
    }
}
```

The following graphic shows the output for the application.

These examples have demonstrated the blocking capacity of a *BlockingCollection*, but a *BlockingCollection* can also be bounded. There is no limit to the number of elements that can be added to an unbounded collection. You can add elements to a concurrent collection indefinitely if you want. In the *BlockingCollection* constructor, one of the options is to set the bounds of the underlying collection. The bound is the maximum number of elements for the *BlockingCollection*. If the bound is reached, the collection will block on additional adds until elements are removed from the collection. The following source code creates a *BlockingCollection* where the underlying type is *ConcurrentBag* and the bound is 10 elements. For this reason, you are unable to add more than 10 elements to the collection without blocking.

```
var bounded = new BlockingCollection<int>(new ConcurrentBag<int>(), 10);
```

Following is a list of some of the elements of the *BlockingCollection* type:

- **Add(T item)** This adds an item to the blocking collection. If the collection is bound, *Add* will block if the maximum bound is exceeded.

- **CompleteAdding** This notifies the collection that additional items will not be added.

- **Count property** This property returns the number of items in the blocking collection.

- **BoundedCapacity property** This returns the capacity of the current blocking collection.

- **TryTake(out T item)** This method removes an item from the collection. If the collection is empty, it returns *false* and immediately returns.

- **TryTake(out T item, Int32 millisecondsTimeout)** This removes an item from a collection within the designated timeout. If it is successful, it returns *true*.

Summary

The .NET Framework 4 introduces concurrent collections. Concurrent collections are implicitly thread safe and mostly lock free. Unlike generic collections, concurrent collections do not have to use external locks and lock the entire collection, which is inefficient. When there is contention, concurrent collections use spinning and compare-and-swap operations for thread safeness. The goal is to avoid kernel-mode locking, which is more expensive. Concurrent collections are designed to be scalable in a multicore environment.

Except for the *ConcurrentDictionary* type, concurrent collections implement the producer-consumer pattern. A pure producer-consumer collection has dedicated threads for both adding and removing elements. *ConcurrentStack* and *ConcurrentQueue* are optimized for the producer-consumer scenario and are lock free. A mixed producer-consumer is optimized for adding and removing elements using the same thread. *ConcurrentBag* is an example of a mixed producer-consumer and uses limited synchronization. *ConcurrentDictionary* is the only concurrent collection that is not a producer-consumer. It synchronizes adds and updates. However, read operations are lock free.

Low-level synchronization, such as the *SpinLock* and *SpinWait* structures, is used by concurrent collections to minimize synchronization. The *SpinLock* structure is used to spin instead of blocking on contention. You can use the *SpinWait* structure to implement a two-phase synchronization. If there is contention, the first phase spins for synchronization. The second phase, if needed, will block until the resource is available.

BlockingCollection is a wrapper of a collection that implements the *IProducerConsumer Collection* interface. If the underlying type is not specified, it is a *ConcurrentQueue*. *Blocking Collection* adds blocking and bounding semantics to the underlying collection. If the collection is empty, it will block when you try to remove an element. Bounding sets a maximum number of elements for the collection. The collection will block when an attempt is made to add elements beyond the bounded threshold.

Quick Reference

To	Do this
Implement a pure producer-consumer collection	Use a producer-consumer collection, which is optimized for adding and removing elements using different threads. A mixed producer-consumer is optimized for adding and removing elements using the same thread.
Perform lightweight locking	Use the *SpinLock* or *SpinWait* structures. *SpinLock* will spin to avoid an expensive deadlock. You can use *SpinWait* to spin instead of using a hard lock.
Use a thread-safe queue or stack optimized for concurrent access	Use the *ConcurrentQueue* and *ConcurrentStack* collections, respectively.
Use an unordered collection optimized for concurrent access	Use a *ConcurrentBag* collection, which is a mixed producer-consumer. For this type, you should add and remove items from the same thread.
Use a dictionary type optimized for concurrent access	Use *ConcurrentDictionary*.
Use a collection type that can be bounded or blocked	Use the *BlockingCollection* type. You can block when removing items from an empty *BlockingCollection*. If it is bounded, you can block when adding an item beyond the bounded capacity.

Chapter 6
Customization

After completing this chapter, you will be able to

- Implement a custom producer-consumer class.

- Describe the benefits of partitioning a data domain.

- Explain chunking and its role in parallel programming.

- Describe the *Partitioner<TSource>* and *OrderablePartitioner<TSource>* classes.

- Implement a custom partitioner.

- Explain the role of a task scheduler.

- Implement a custom task scheduler.

The previous chapters introduced several classes in the Task Parallel Library (TPL) that are pivotal to parallel programming. These classes are ideal for most—but not every—circumstance. Therefore, the TPL is extensible, so you can extend various classes to meet the specific requirements of your application. This chapter explains how to customize some of the major classes in the TPL.

The generalized implementation of parallel computing in the Microsoft .NET Framework 4 is adequate for most scenarios involving concurrent programming. However, it is nearly impossible to craft a perfect solution for every scenario. Fortunately, so you can use it in unanticipated situations, the TPL is extensible, as mentioned previously. Of course, customization should not be your *first* choice; instead, you should review the capabilities of the TPL thoroughly before undertaking the challenge of extending one of the classes. In the rare circumstance where customization is required, you'll probably find this chapter invaluable.

Identifying Opportunities for Customization

As you might recall from Chapter 5, "Concurrent Collections," you implement *IProducer ConsumerCollection* to support a producer-consumer collection. In the producer-consumer model, a producer object adds to the collection and a consumer object removes elements. A pure producer-consumer is optimized for add and remove operations occurring on different threads. Mixed producer-consumers should have the producer and consumer objects run on the same thread. Producer-consumer collections include *ConcurrentQueue*, *ConcurrentStack*, and *ConcurrentBag* collections, which you'll find in the .NET Framework class library in the *System.Collections.Concurrent* namespace. You can find a more detailed explanation of producer-consumer classes in Chapter 5.

The following list provides some examples of where customization can provide benefits:

- **Custom Producer-Consumer Collections**   Although the TPL provides some consumer-producer collections, you can also create a custom consumer-producer. An "auditable collection" is an example of a situation for which a custom producer-consumer collection might be useful. In this scenario, you would create and maintain an audit trail for each element added to the collection. When a consumer removes an element, the element is logically (but not physically) removed from the collection. By leaving the object physically in place, you can create an audit trail of all activity.

- **Load Balancing with Custom Partitioners**   The TPL partitions a data domain to balance workload across available processor cores. Load balancing is how parallel computing achieves much of its performance improvement. Short tasks incur more relative overhead from context switches, synchronization, and parallelization; in fact, that overhead might outweigh the benefits of parallelization. In such circumstances, you might want to group multiple parallel operations into a single task, a concept called *chunking*. The chunk size is the extent of the grouping within a partition. *Range partitioning* is a concept that is helpful when you can determine the number of tasks in advance. With range partitioning, you set the chunk size of each partition as a parameter. Based on your knowledge of the application and the problem domain, you might want to implement a custom partitioner to achieve better load balancing.

- **Custom Task Schedulers**   The TPL schedules tasks via a task scheduler. The default scheduler uses the .NET Framework 4 thread pool to queue and eventually schedule tasks. When there is unique behavior to implement, you can create a custom task scheduler and set your own scheduling polices. A prime example would be a logging scheduler—a scheduler instrumented to trace various phases of task scheduling. For ultimate flexibility, you could enable or disable the tracing through a configuration file.

When you are extending the TPL, performance benchmarking is critical! It is the confirmation that your extensions are having a positive impact on the performance of your application. There are several "moving parts" in a parallel application, which makes it sometimes difficult to anticipate every action and reaction. The only true affirmation of expected performance improvement is benchmarking. There are several new debugging windows in Microsoft Visual Studio 2010, such as the Parallel Tasks and Parallel Stacks windows. Many of the new debugging windows help with the benchmarking of a concurrent application. You'll learn about these in much more detail in Chapter 7, "Reports and Debugging."

Custom Producer-Consumer Collections

A class that implements the producer-consumer pattern is a façade for adding and removing elements from a collection where there is a separate producer and consumer thread. Of course, this must be done in a thread-safe manner with minimal synchronization.

To create a custom producer-consumer type, you implement the *IProducerConsumer Collection<T>*interface. Producer-consumer collections are enumerable; therefore, the *IProducerConsumerCollection<T>* interface inherits from the *IEnumerable<T>*, *IEnumerable*, and *ICollection* interfaces. In addition, producer-consumer classes should be optimized for concurrent access.

In the producer-consumer pattern, a producer object adds elements to the collection, and a consumer object removes elements. If you want, you can implement the producer and consumer collection in a single object that handles both addition and removal. There are plenty of opportunities for custom producer-consumer collections. For example, you could create a custom producer-consumer collection when implementing a stock analysis application. The producer would be the stock feed, which would create objects for individual stocks. The consumers would be broker objects, which analyze (consume) the individual stock data. As another example, in an accounting application, producers generate accounting transactions, and could include various system modules, such as the Accounts Receivable, Accounts Payable, and Payroll modules. The consumers are the various report generators, including the general ledger journal, payroll report, or accounts receivable aging analysis.

If you plan to implement a custom producer-consumer, you should know what some of the important members of the *IProducerConsumerCollection* interface are:

- **GetEnumerator**   This method returns an enumerator that can be used to iterate the collection.

  ```
  IEnumerator GetEnumerator()
  ```

- **TryAdd**   This method tries to add an item to the collection.

  ```
  bool TryAdd(T item)
  ```

- **TryTake**   This method tries to return the next value as an out parameter. You should also remove that item from the collection.

  ```
  bool TryTake(out T item)
  ```

- **IsSynchronized**   This is a Boolean property that returns *true* if the collection is thread safe.

  ```
  bool IsSynchronized { get; }
  ```

- **Count**   This property returns the number of elements in the collection.

  ```
  int Count { get; }
  ```

In the following procedure, you will create a custom producer-consumer that aggregates identical values. When adding a duplicate value, the class does not preserve duplicated values in the collection. Instead, it keeps a single value with an accompanying instance count. For example, this collection {0, 1, 2, 3, 1, 1, 3} would become {{0,1}, {1,3}, {2,1}, {3,2}}. Implementing a custom consumer-producer collection is not overly complicated, but it does require several members. To reduce complexity, this sample code uses macro locking, but you can always implement more discrete locking in real-world situations.

Create a custom consumer-producer collection that aggregates identical values

1. Create a console application for Microsoft Visual C# in Visual Studio 2010. Add *using* statements for the *System.Threading, System.Threading.Tasks, System.Collections,* and *System.Collections.Concurrent* namespaces.

2. Define a custom producer-consumer class that inherits and implements the *IProducer ConsumerCollection* interface. Define a *Dictionary<TKey, TValue>* collection at the beginning of the class that will hold values and instance counts.

```
class ConcurrentAggregate<T>: IProducerConsumerCollection<T>
{
        Dictionary<T, int> collection =new Dictionary<T,int>();
}
```

3. Implement an *Add* method to add new elements to the collection. In the method, attempt to get the value of the provided item. If you are successful, add 1 to the item value by using the *Dictionary<TKey, TValue>.Add* method. Otherwise, set the key value to 1.

```
public void Add(T item)
{
    int count;
    if (collection.TryGetValue(item, out count))
    {
        collection[item] = count + 1;
    }
    else
    {
        collection.Add(item, 1);
    }
}
```

4. Add the *Remove* method to remove an element from the collection. Retrieve and decrement the value of the item. If the value is zero, remove the item from the collection. You can use the *Dictionary<TKey, TValue>.Remove* method.

```
public bool Remove(T item)
{

    int count;
    if (collection.TryGetValue(item, out count))
    {
        --count;
        if (count > 0)
        {
            collection[item] = count;
            return true;
        }
        else
```

```
            {
                return collection.Remove(item);
            }
        }
        return false;
    }
```

5. Return the instance count of the specified key with the *GetInstanceCount* method.

```
public int GetInstanceCount(T key)
{
    lock (this)
    {
        return collection[key];
    }
}
```

6. You must implement the *GetEnumerator* method twice. Both times the method returns an enumerator to the collection. First, convert the collection to an enumerable type and then return the enumerator.

```
public IEnumerator<T> GetEnumerator()
{
    return ToArray().AsEnumerable().GetEnumerator();
}

IEnumerator IEnumerable.GetEnumerator()
{
    return ToArray().AsEnumerable().GetEnumerator();
}
```

7. You need to implement a couple of methods from the *IProducerConsumerCollection* interface. The *TryAdd* method simply defers to the already implemented *Add* method. The *TryTake* method returns the first element as an *out* parameter. The first element is then removed from the collection.

```
public bool TryAdd(T item)
{
    lock (this)
    {
        Add(item);
    }

    return true;
}

public bool TryTake(out T item)
{
    lock (this)
    {
        item = collection.First().Key;
        collection.Remove(item);
        return true;
    }
}
```

8. The next three methods you will implement return either the entire collection or a subset as an array. The *ToArray* method iterates the collection and builds an array of key values, which it subsequently returns. The *CopyTo* method uses the *ToArray* method to copy the underlying collection to an array provided as a parameter.

```
public T[] ToArray()
{
    List<T> temp=new List<T>();
    foreach (var item in collection)
    {
        temp.Add(item.Key);
    }
    return temp.ToArray();
}

public void CopyTo(T[] array, int index)
{
    lock (this)
    {
        ToArray().CopyTo(array, index);
    }
}

public void CopyTo(Array array, int index)
{
    lock (this)
    {
        ToArray().CopyTo(array, index);
    }
}
```

9. Implement the *IsSynchronized, Count,* and *SyncRoot* properties as expected. The *IsSynchronized* property returns *true* if the object is synchronized and implicitly thread safe. *Count* returns the number of elements in the underlying collection. The *SyncRoot* property returns a synchronization object that is usable for synchronizing the underlying collection in a concurrent environment. You have now completed a custom producer-consumer. Time for the champagne!

```
public bool IsSynchronized { get { return false; } }
public int Count { get { return collection.Count(); } }
public Object SyncRoot { get { throw new NotSupportedException(); } }
```

10. In the *Main* method, create an instance of your custom producer-consumer. Also, declare an array of integer values. Iterate the collection of numbers, adding the values to the producer-consumer collection.

```
var list = new ConcurrentAggregate<int>();
var numbers = new int[] { 4, 2, 1, 3, 3, 3, 2, 4, 1, 5 };
Parallel.ForEach(numbers, (number) =>
{
    list.Add(number);
});
```

11. In a separate loop, iterate the consumer-producer collection, displaying the values and instance count.

```
foreach (var item in list)
{
    Console.WriteLine("Item {0} Instances {1}",
        item, list.GetInstanceCount(item));
}
```

12. Build and run the application.

Here's the complete code for the application.

```
using System;
using System.Collections.Generic;
using System.Linq;
using System.Text;
using System.Collections;
using System.Collections.Concurrent;
using System.Threading;
using System.Threading.Tasks;

namespace CustomProducerConsumer
{
    class ConcurrentAggregate<T>: IProducerConsumerCollection<T>
    {
        Dictionary<T, int> collection =new Dictionary<T,int>();

        public void Add(T item)
        {
            int count;
            if (collection.TryGetValue(item, out count))
            {
                collection[item] = count + 1;
            }
            else
            {
                collection.Add(item, 1);
            }
        }

        public bool Remove(T item)
        {

            int count;
            if (collection.TryGetValue(item, out count))
            {
                --count;
                if (count > 0)
                {
                    collection[item] = count;
                    return true;
                }
                else
                {
```

```
                return collection.Remove(item);
        }
    }
    return false;
}

public int GetInstanceCount(T key)
{
    lock (this)
    {
        return collection[key];
    }
}

public IEnumerator<T> GetEnumerator()
{
    return ToArray().AsEnumerable().GetEnumerator();
}

IEnumerator IEnumerable.GetEnumerator()
{
    return ToArray().AsEnumerable().GetEnumerator();
}

public bool TryAdd(T item)
{
    lock (this)
    {
        Add(item);
    }

    return true;
}

public bool TryTake(out T item)
{
    lock (this)
    {
        item = collection.First().Key;
        collection.Remove(item);
        return true;
    }
}

public T[] ToArray()
{
    List<T> temp=new List<T>();
    foreach (var item in collection)
    {
        temp.Add(item.Key);
```

```
            }
            return temp.ToArray();
        }

        public void CopyTo(T[] array, int index)
        {
            lock (this)
            {
                ToArray().CopyTo(array, index);
            }
        }

        public void CopyTo(Array array, int index)
        {
            lock (this)
            {
                ToArray().CopyTo(array, index);
            }
        }

        public bool IsSynchronized { get { return false; } }
        public int Count { get { return collection.Count(); } }
        public Object SyncRoot { get { throw new NotSupportedException(); } }
    }


    class Program
    {
        static void Main(string[] args)
        {
            var list = new ConcurrentAggregate<int>();
            var numbers = new int[] { 4, 2, 1, 3, 3, 3, 2, 4, 1, 5 };
            Parallel.ForEach(numbers, (number) =>
            {
                list.TryAdd(number);
            });

            foreach (var item in list)
            {
                Console.WriteLine("Item {0} Instances {1}",
                    item, list.GetInstanceCount(item));
            }
            Console.WriteLine("Press enter to exit");
            Console.ReadLine();
        }
    }
```

When you run this application, you'll see the output shown in the following graphic, which lists each value along with the corresponding instance count.

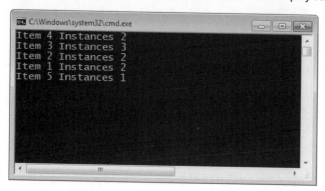

Task Partitioners

You can improve load balancing (and thereby performance) in some applications by implementing a custom partitioner. The default partitioner might not be ideal in all circumstances. For example, when operations are of disparate length, a chunk size of one creates disproportionate work and uneven load balancing. In these and other similar scenarios, your knowledge of the problem domain and the software application can hint at a better scheduling scheme.

Speedup does not exist in isolation from contrary factors. One contrary factor is overhead for parallelization and synchronization. The relative importance of the overhead is inversely related to the duration of the parallel operation. As the length of the parallel operation increases, the impact of overhead diminishes. Longer tasks mean less synchronization, scheduling, and thread-context-switching costs. However, there might not be enough long tasks to keep the processors busy. You must find the ideal balance between parallelization and overhead. Continual load balancing is the objective, in which you keep the processor cores busy and achieve maximum speedup.

The following code displays an array in a parallel loop.

```
Parallel.ForEach(numbers, (value) => Normalize(value));
```

When the *Normalize* operation in the above code has a short duration, single chunking might not be effective. The overhead from parallelizing the loop might translate into minimal speedup. Changing the partitioning to assign more work to each task could improve the *parallelization-to-overhead* ratio and increase the relative performance. You accomplish this by increasing the chunk size. You can create a custom partitioner to increase the chunk size.

For custom partitioning, *Parallel.For* and *Parallel.ForEach* accept *Partitioner<TSource>* and *OrderablePartitioner<TSource>* as parameters. Both classes are enumerable and are found in the *System.Collections.Concurrent* namespace. In addition, *OrderablePartitioner* supports ordered partitioning—more about that later.

The *Partitioner.Create* method creates a custom partitioner that supports chunking. Here's an example of using a custom partitioner with a *Parallel.ForEach* method.

```
Parallel.ForEach(Partitioner.Create(0, numbers.Count()), (keypair) => Normalize(keypair));
```

Partitioner.Create generates a *Tuple<int, int>*. The tuple represents the range of items that the task should handle. You can interpret the tuple as *Tuple<start, end>*. In the parallel operation, you use the tuple to iterate the proper range of elements in the collection, as shown in the following example.

```
public static void Normalize(Tuple<int, int> range)
{
    for (int start = range.Item1; start < range.Item2; ++start)
    {
        // Normalization
    }
}
```

You can set the chunk size directly by using range partitioning and a custom partitioner. The following example uses range partitioning. This code iterates the collection from zero until the last element is reached. In this case, the chunk size for each task or partition is two.

```
Parallel.ForEach(Partitioner.Create(0, numbers.Count(), 2), (range) => Normalize(range));
```

In the next step-by-step procedure, you will create a collection of methods that are then enumerated and invoked as tasks. Because the number of methods is known in advance, you can use range partitioning. The code invokes two methods per task. Each method displays the current task identifier and method number to confirm that range partitioning is indeed being performed.

Enumerate and execute an array of methods, displaying the results to correlate the methods to specific tasks

1. Create a console application for C# in Visual Studio 2010. Add *using* statements for the *System.Threading, System.Threading.Tasks,* and *System.Collections.Concurrent* namespaces.

2. In the *Program* class, define a static integer variable, which is initialized to zero. This variable is used to identify the current method.

   ```
   static int count = 0;
   ```

3. Define a static method called *DoSomething*. In *DoSomething*, increment the method count in a thread-safe manner. Display the current method index and task identifier. Use the *Thread.SpinWait* method to simulate a compute-bound task.

   ```
   static void DoSomething()
   {
       int localCount = Interlocked.Increment(ref count);
   ```

```
        Console.WriteLine("Task {0} : Task {1}",
            Task.CurrentId, localCount);
        Thread.SpinWait(int.MaxValue / 10);
}
```

4. In the *Main* method, define an array of *Action* delegates initialized to *DoSomething* methods.

```
var methods = new Action[] {   DoSomething, DoSomething,
                               DoSomething, DoSomething,
                               DoSomething, DoSomething,
                               DoSomething, DoSomething};
```

5. In a *Parallel.ForEach* loop, invoke the methods in the collection. Create a custom partition with the *Partitioner.Create* method. Set range partitioning and a chunk size of two. The parallel operation is a lambda expression. In the lambda expression, iterate the collection based on the range provided and invoke the corresponding method.

```
Parallel.ForEach(Partitioner.Create(0, methods.Length, 2), range=>
{
    for (int index = range.Item1; index < range.Item2; ++index)
    {
        methods[index]();
    }
});
```

6. Build and run the application.

Here's the complete code for the application.

```
using System;
using System.Collections.Generic;
using System.Linq;
using System.Text;
using System.Threading;
using System.Threading.Tasks;
using System.Collections.Concurrent;

namespace RangePartitioning
{
    class Program
    {
        static int count = 0;

        static void DoSomething()
        {
            int localCount = Interlocked.Increment(ref count);
            Console.WriteLine("Task {0} : Method {1} Started.",
                Task.CurrentId, localCount);
            Thread.SpinWait(int.MaxValue / 10);
        }

        static void Main(string[] args)
        {
```

```
var methods = new Action[] {   DoSomething, DoSomething,
                                 DoSomething, DoSomething,
                                 DoSomething, DoSomething,
                                 DoSomething, DoSomething };

        Parallel.ForEach(Partitioner.Create(0, methods.Length, 2), range=>
        {
            for (int index = range.Item1; index < range.Item2; ++index)
            {
                methods[index]();
            }
        });
    }
  }
}
```

The following image shows the application's output. Each task executes two methods, as defined by the range partitioning value. For example, Task 1 executes Method 1 and Method 6.

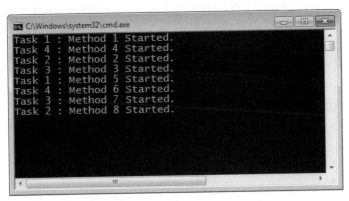

One of the problems with setting a specific chunk size with range partitioning is that you lose a degree of flexibility. One alternative is to query the number of processors at run time and set the partitioning accordingly. However, to save time and effort, you can just use the default implementation provided in the TPL.

Instead of using range partitioning, the TPL *Partitioner.Create* method can set the chunk size at run time automatically. In the next exercise, you will rely on *Partitioner.Create* to set the best chunk size. You'll create an array of integers, enumerate them in a *Parallel.ForEach* loop, and display the number of items handled in each partition to confirm the chunk size selected by *Partitioner.Create*.

Use a custom partitioner created by the TPL to enumerate an array of integers in a *Parallel.ForEach* loop

1. Create a new C# console application in Visual Studio 2010. Add *using* statements for the *System.Threading*, *System.Threading.Tasks*, and *System.Collections.Concurrent* namespaces.

2. In the *Program* class, define a static integer counter named *partition*, and initialize it to zero. This variable will count partitions.

```
static int partition= 0;
```

3. In the *Main* method, create an array of values numbered from 0 to 50.

```
var numbers = Enumerable.Range(0,50).ToArray();
```

4. Iterate the numbers by using a *Parallel.ForEach* method. Create a custom partition to help. The custom partitioner will set the correct chunk size at run time. Define the task as a lambda expression. The current range is the first parameter of the lambda expression. The next two parameters are the loop state, which is not used, and the current index value.

```
Parallel.ForEach(Partitioner.Create(0, numbers.Length),
        (range, notused, partition ) =>
```

5. In the lambda expression, increment the partition count in a thread-safe manner. Record the current partition in a string buffer.

```
int _partition=Interlocked.Increment(ref partition);
string buffer = string.Format("Partition {0,3}: ", _partition);
```

6. In a standard *for* loop, iterate the range of elements for this partition. Add the current value from the collection to the string buffer. To simulate compute-bound work, call the *Thread.SpinWait* method.

```
for (int index = range.Item1; index < range.Item2; ++index){     Thread.SpinWait(4000);
    buffer+=string.Format(" {0,3}", numbers[index]);}
```

7. After the *for* loop, display the buffer.

```
Console.WriteLine(buffer);
```

8. Build and run the application.

Here is the complete application.

```
using System;
using System.Collections.Generic;
using System.Linq;
using System.Text;
using System.Threading;
using System.Threading.Tasks;
using System.Collections.Concurrent;

namespace BasicExample
{
    class Program
    {
        static int partition= 0;
```

```
static void Main(string[] args)
{
    var numbers = Enumerable.Range(0,50).ToArray();

    Parallel.ForEach(Partitioner.Create(0, numbers.Length),
        (range, notused, partition ) =>
    {
        string buffer = string.Format("Partition {0,3}: ", partition);
        for (int index = range.Item1; index < range.Item2; ++index)
        {
            Thread.SpinWait(4000);
            buffer+=string.Format(" {0,3}", numbers[index]);
        }
        Console.WriteLine(buffer);
    });

    Console.WriteLine("Press enter to exit");
    Console.ReadLine();
}
}
}
```

The following images show the output from the application. The chunk size is two, which is the number of elements displayed with each partition.

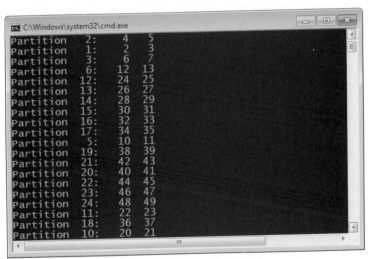

The *Parallel.Create* method sets the appropriate chunk size *dynamically* at run time. Revisit your application, change the number of elements in the array to 200, and then rerun the application. *Parallel.Create* will automatically change the chunk size to eight at run time as the application begins to scale. Of course, the actual result depends on your hardware architecture and number of available processor cores.

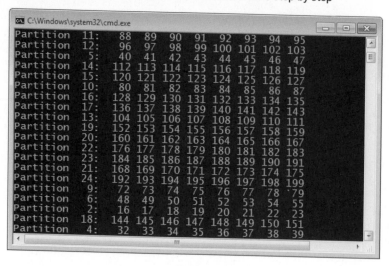

Advanced Custom Partitioners

At times, you might want to implement an entirely new partitioner, because no two problems are alike. You'll find plenty of opportunities for creativity. For example, you might want to implement a different chunk size for each partition. In the previous section, you set the chunk size either to a fixed value at compile time or dynamically at run time, but in both cases, the chunk size was consistent for all partitions. You could, however, set the chunk size on a per-partition basis, based on the available workload. To do that, you would have to create a custom partitioner.

Custom partitioners start by inheriting the *Partitioner<TSource>* or *Orderable-Partitioner<TSource>* class and implementing the required methods and properties. Both are abstract classes in the *System.Collection.Concurrent* namespace. Because *OrderablePartitioner<TSource>* inherits from *Partitioner<TSource>*, the implementations are similar. In addition to partitioning, *OrderablePartitioner* enforces indexing.

Using *Partitioner<TSource>*

To create a custom partitioner, you would first create a new class derived from *Partitioner <TSource>*. Because that's an abstract class, you must *GetPartitions*. If the *SupportDynamic Partitions* property returns *true*, you should also implement *GetDynamicPartitions*:

- **GetPartitions**   You call this method to return an array of partitions. Each partition is individually enumerable and has a range of items that the partition will handle.

  ```
  IList<IEnumerator<TSource>> GetPartitions(int partitionCount)
  ```

- **GetDynamicPartitions**   Unlike *GetPartitions*, which returns a collection of partitions, *GetDynamicPartitions* returns individual partitions on demand. The method returns an enumerable. You can use the enumerator to iterate partitions with the *MoveNext* method or another technique, such as a *foreach* method.

```
IEnumerable<TSource> GetDynamicPartitions()
```

- **SupportsDynamicPartitions**   Some methods, such as *Parallel.ForEach*, require implementation of *GetDynamicPartitions*. This property confirms that *GetDynamicPartitions* is implemented. If it is, *true* is returned.

```
bool SupportsDynamicPartitions { get; }
```

Follow these rules when creating a custom partitioner:

- Enumerate the entire input collection.

- Do not skip elements.

- Do not duplicate elements.

- If the collection is orderable, ensure that indexes should be unique and non-negative.

In this next example, you will create a custom partitioner in which the chunk size is incremented in each partition. For example, if there are four partitions and the chunk size for the first partition is one, the second would increase to a chunk size of two, partition three would have a chunk size of three, and so on.

Create a custom partitioner that assigns an increasingly large chunk size to each partition

1. Create a new C# console application in Visual Studio 2010. Add *using* statements for the *System.Threading, System.Threading.Tasks, System.Collections,* and *System.Collections.Concurrent* namespaces.

2. Define a class that inherits the *Partitioner<TSource>* type. This is your custom partitioner. At the beginning of the class, declare a collection to store the input data.

```
IList<TSource> list;
```

3. Create a constructor to assign the input data to the list collection.

```
public CustomPartitioner(IList<TSource> input)
{
    list = input;
}
```

4. Create an enumerable object as a nested class, and have it inherit the *IEnumerable <TSource>* interface. This class will manage the enumerator for the outer class.

```
class EnumerableWrapper : IEnumerable<TSource>
```

5. Add three fields to the enumerable class:

   ❑ A collection to cache the data collection from the outer class

   ❑ An index variable to track the current element

   ❑ Another variable to track the number of partitions

```
IList<TSource> list = null;
int index = -1;
int partitionSize = 0;
```

6. You can now implement the *IEnumerable.GetEnumerator* method. Use the popular iterator pattern to reduce the amount of code required. (You can review the iterator pattern at *msdn.microsoft.com;* the "Design Pattern in .NET: Iterator" article is a good resource.) As partitions are requested, increment the partition size. Set the range of the partition as a factor of the partition size. Use the *yield* statement to add each element to the partition. If the collection has been fully enumerated, break the enumeration. Keep track of the current index.

```
public IEnumerator<KeyValuePair<long, TSource>> GetEnumerator()
{
    int localPartition = Interlocked.Increment(ref partitionSize);
    int localIndex = Interlocked.Increment(ref index);
    int begin = localIndex;
    int end = begin + localPartition;
    int i = 0;
    for (i = begin; i < end; ++i)
    {
        if (i >= list.Count)
        {
            localIndex = i;
            yield break;
        }
        yield return list[i];
    }
    Interlocked.Decrement(ref index);
}
```

7. Implement *IEnumerable.GetEnumerator*, which defers to the *GetEnumerator* method. The nested enumerable class is now complete.

```
IEnumerator IEnumerable.GetEnumerator()
{
    return ((IEnumerable<TSource>)this).GetEnumerator();
}
```

8. Your custom partitioner supports dynamic partitions. For that reason, implement the *GetDynamicPartitions* method. In the method, return an instance of the nested enumerable class, which is used to enumerate partitions. Also, implement the *SupportsDynamicPartitions* property to confirm that dynamic partitions are supported.

```
public override IEnumerable<TSource> GetDynamicPartitions()
{
    return new EnumerableWrapper();
}
public override bool SupportsDynamicPartitions { get { return true; } }
```

9. Complete the custom partitioner with the *GetPartitions* method. Throw an exception if the partition count is invalid. Create an unordered collection to hold the requested partitions. In a loop, add partitions to the collections. At the end, return the collection of partitions.

```
public override IList<IEnumerator<TSource>> GetPartitions(int partitionCount)
{
    if (partitionCount < 1)
        throw new ArgumentOutOfRangeException("partitionCount");
    var obj = new List<IEnumerator<TSource>>();
    var enumerable = GetDynamicPartitions();
    for (int i = 0; i < partitionCount; ++i)
    {
        obj.Add(enumerable.GetEnumerator());
    };
    return obj;
}
```

10. In the *Main* method, test your custom partitioner. Create a collection of numbers. Initialize the custom partitioner with the *numbers* collection. In a *Parallel.ForEach* loop, use the custom partitioner. In the task, do some work and display the current task ID and item from the *numbers* collection.

```
static void Main(string[] args)
{
    int [] numbers = new int[] { 1, 2, 3, 5, 7, 8, 4, 5, 6, 7, 8, 9, 10 };
    var samplePartitioner = new CustomPartitioner<int>(numbers);
    Parallel.ForEach(samplePartitioner, (item) =>
    {
        Thread.SpinWait(20000);
        Console.WriteLine("Task {0} Item {1}", Task.CurrentId, item);
    });
}
```

11. Build and run the program.

Here is the complete code for the application.

```
using System;
using System.Collections.Generic;
using System.Linq;
using System.Text;
using System.Collections.Concurrent;
using System.Threading;
using System.Collections;
using System.Threading.Tasks;
```

```
namespace PartitionerNamespace
{

    class CustomPartitioner<TSource>: Partitioner<TSource>
    {
        IList<TSource> list;

        public CustomPartitioner(IList<TSource> input)
        {
            list = input;
        }

        class EnumerableWrapper : IEnumerable<TSource>
        {
            IList<TSource> list = null;
            int index = -1;
            int partitionSize = 0;

            public EnumerableWrapper(IList<TSource> _list)
            {
                list = _list;
            }

            public IEnumerator<TSource> GetEnumerator()
            {
                int localPartition = Interlocked.Increment(ref partitionSize);
                int localIndex = Interlocked.Increment(ref index);
                int begin = localIndex;
                int end = begin + localPartition;
                int i = 0;
                for (i = begin; i < end; ++i)
                {
                    if (i >= list.Count)
                    {
                        localIndex = i;
                        yield break;
                    }
                    yield return list[i];
                }
                Interlocked.Decrement(ref index);
            }

            IEnumerator IEnumerable.GetEnumerator()
            {
                return ((IEnumerable<TSource>)this).GetEnumerator();
            }
        }

        public override IEnumerable<TSource> GetDynamicPartitions()
        {
            return new EnumerableWrapper(list);
        }

        public override bool SupportsDynamicPartitions { get { return true; } }
```

```
    public override IList<IEnumerator<TSource>> GetPartitions(int partitionCount)
    {
        if (partitionCount < 1)
            throw new ArgumentOutOfRangeException("partitionCount");
        var obj = new List<IEnumerator<TSource>>();
        var enumerable = GetDynamicPartitions();
        for (int i = 0; i < partitionCount; ++i)
        {
            obj.Add(enumerable.GetEnumerator());
        };
        return obj;
    }
}

class Program
{

    static void Main(string[] args)
    {
        int [] numbers = new int[] { 1, 2, 3, 5, 7, 8, 4, 5, 6, 7, 8, 9, 10 };
        var samplePartitioner = new CustomPartitioner<int>(numbers);
        Parallel.ForEach(samplePartitioner, (item) =>
        {
            Thread.SpinWait(10000);
            Console.WriteLine("Task {0} Item {1}", Task.CurrentId, item);
        });

        Console.WriteLine("Press enter to exit");
        Console.ReadLine();
    }
}
}
```

The following image shows the output for the application. Note that each task handles an increasing number of items; this behavior is defined in the partition.

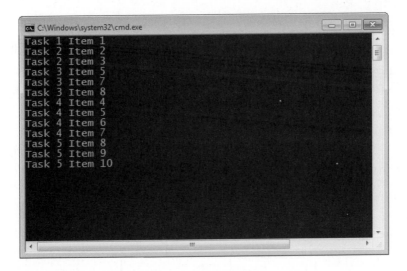

Using *OrderablePartitioner<TSource>*

You would implement the *OrderablePartitioner<TSource>* class instead of *Partition<TSource>* when you need to support indexing. As mentioned previously, *OrderablePartitioner<TSource>* is derived from *Partition<TSource>* and has similar methods. The primary difference is that the methods have an extra parameter to accommodate an index.

The following list describes the important members of the *OrderablePartitioner<TSource>* type. *GetOrderablePartitions* is abstract and is the only method that must be implemented.

- **GetOrderablePartitions**   This method returns a static list of partitions. Each partitioner is an enumerator and represents a collection of elements to be handled in the partition. As mentioned, this method is abstract and must be implemented in the derived class.

  ```
  IList<IEnumerator<KeyValuePair<long, TSource>>> GetOrderablePartitions(int
  partitionCount)
  ```

- **GetOrderableDynamicPartitions**   This method returns each partition on demand. Call it repeatedly to get more than one partition.

  ```
  IEnumerable<KeyValuePair<long, TSource>> GetOrderableDynamicPartitions()
  ```

- **SupportsDynamicPartitions**   Some methods, such as *Parallel.ForEach*, require dynamic partitions. This property confirms the implementation of that method. Return *true* if the *GetOrderableDynamicPartitions* method is implemented.

  ```
  bool SupportsDynamicPartitions { get; }
  ```

OrderablePartitioner has special properties, which are normally set in the constructor. Here are the properties:

- **KeysNormalized**   Keys must be distinct. If this property is *true*, indexes must be distinct and contiguous.

- **KeysOrderedAcrossPartitions**   If this property is *true*, elements are in order across partitions. The first partition has the initial elements, and the last partition has the final elements.

- **KeysOrderedInEachPartition**   If this property is *true*, elements are ordered within a partition.

In the previous tutorial, you implemented a custom partitioner by using *Partitioner<TSource>* and assigned chunks of increasing sizes to partitions. That example can be updated to use an *OrderablePartitioner*. Here is the *IEnumerable.GetEnumerator* method of the new example. As you can see in the comments, there are two minor changes. The biggest change is converting *<TSource>* to *KeyPair<long, TSource>*. The additional generic type parameter is the index of the current element.

```
// In the following line, <TSource> changed to KeyValuePair<long, TSource>
        public IEnumerator<KeyValuePair<long, TSource>> GetEnumerator()
        {
                int localPartition=Interlocked.Increment(ref partitionSize);
                int localIndex = Interlocked.Increment(ref index);
                int begin = localIndex;
                int end = begin + localPartition;
                int i = 0;
                for (i = begin; i < end; ++i)
                {
                    if (i >= list.Count)
                    {
                        localIndex = i;
                        yield break;
                    }
                    yield return new KeyValuePair<long, TSource>(i, list[i]);
                }
                Interlocked.Decrement(ref index);
        }
```

Here is the full implementation of the class.

```
using System;
using System.Collections.Generic;
using System.Linq;
using System.Text;
using System.Collections.Concurrent;
using System.Threading;
using System.Collections;
using System.Threading.Tasks;

namespace PartitionerNamespace
{

    class CustomPartitionerer<TSource> : OrderablePartitioner<TSource>
    {
        IList<TSource> list;

        public CustomPartitionerer(IList<TSource> input): base(true, false, true)
        {
            list = input;
        }

        class EnumerableWrapper : IEnumerable<KeyValuePair<long, TSource>>
        {
            IList<TSource> list = null;
            int index = -1;
            int partitionSize = 0;

            public EnumerableWrapper(IList<TSource> _list)
            {
                list = _list;
            }
```

```csharp
                public IEnumerator<KeyValuePair<long, TSource>> GetEnumerator()
                {
                        int localPartition=Interlocked.Increment(ref partitionSize);
                        int localIndex = Interlocked.Increment(ref index);
                        int begin = localIndex;
                        int end = begin + localPartition;
                        int i = 0;
                        for (i = begin; i < end; ++i)
                        {
                            if (i >= list.Count)
                            {
                                localIndex = i;
                                yield break;
                            }
                            yield return new KeyValuePair<long, TSource>(i, list[i]);
                        }
                        Interlocked.Decrement(ref index);
                }

                IEnumerator IEnumerable.GetEnumerator()
                {
                    return ((IEnumerable<TSource>)this).GetEnumerator();
                }

            }

        public override IEnumerable<KeyValuePair<long, TSource>>
GetOrderableDynamicPartitions()
            {
                return new EnumerableWrapper(list);
            }

        public override bool SupportsDynamicPartitions { get { return true; } }

        public override IList<IEnumerator<KeyValuePair<long, TSource>>>
GetOrderablePartitions(int partitionCount)
            {
                if (partitionCount < 1)
                    throw new ArgumentOutOfRangeException("partitionCount");
                var obj = new ConcurrentBag<IEnumerator<KeyValuePair<long, TSource>>>();
                var enumerable = GetOrderableDynamicPartitions();
                for (int i = 0; i < partitionCount; ++i)
                {
                    obj.Add(enumerable.GetEnumerator());
                }
                return obj.ToList();
            }

        }


    class Program
    {

        static void Main(string[] args)
```

```
    {
        int[] numbers = new int[] { 1, 2, 3, 5, 7, 8, 4, 5, 6, 7, 8, 9, 10 };
        CustomPartitionerer<int> samplePartitioner =
          new CustomPartitionerer<int>(numbers);
        Parallel.ForEach(samplePartitioner, (item, state, index) =>
        {
            Thread.SpinWait(10000);
            Console.WriteLine("Task {0} Item {1}", Task.CurrentId,
                item);
        });

        Console.WriteLine("Press enter to exit");
        Console.ReadLine();
    }
  }
}
```

Custom Schedulers

Task schedulers are responsible for scheduling and executing tasks on open threads. The .NET Framework 4 thread pool is the default scheduler. Although this section is about custom task schedulers, you should reserve custom schedulers for those rare occasions when the default scheduler is not sufficient. Until then, this section will at least be entertaining. All task schedulers implement the *TaskScheduler* class, which you'll find in the *System.Threading.Tasks* namespace.

As mentioned, the default scheduler is ideal for most parallel operations. The .NET Framework 4 thread pool employs several techniques to improve performance and reduce possible contention. The default scheduler maintains both a global queue and local queues as part of the strategy to reduce contention—and thereby the need for synchronization. Maintaining multiple queues removes the global queue as a single source of contention. Top tasks are placed on the global queue, and subtasks are placed on local queues. Multiple threads can access the global queue, which requires coordination. Local queues are typically accessed from one thread, which removes the need for synchronization in most circumstances. However, local queues are work-stealing queues. If a thread's local queue is empty, that thread can steal work from another local queue. Stealing a task from a non-affinity local queue does require minimum synchronization. Long-running tasks can adversely affect the performance of the .NET Framework 4 thread pool.

The Context Scheduler

The TPL actually includes two schedulers. The default scheduler uses the .NET Framework 4 thread pool. The other scheduler included in the TPL is the Synchronization Context scheduler. This scheduler runs tasks on the *originating* thread, not on a separate thread. This is particularly useful for tasks that access user interface controls. As you probably know, user interface controls are accessible only from the user interface thread that created the control—and that restriction also applies to tasks running on a different thread. Look at the following code, which attempts to update a text box control from a task.

```
Parallel.ForEach(numbers, (item) =>
{
    Thread.Sleep(1000);
    txtNumber.Text = item.ToString();
});
```

If only it were that easy. Unfortunately, the preceding code is unsuccessful, and the error shown in the following image occurs. This is the expected exception that occurs when you attempt to access a control from an unrelated thread.

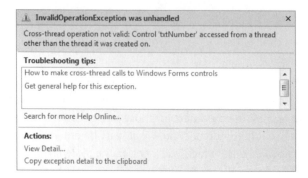

In contrast, the following code works perfectly! The only difference is that it adds a call to the *TaskScheduler.FromCurrentSynchronizationContext* method, which returns a synchronization context scheduler, updating a *ParallelOptions* object so that it references the new scheduler. The code then passes that *ParallelOptions* object to one of the *Parallel.ForEach* method over-loads. Because the context for the scheduler is the user interface thread, the code executes successfully and updates the text box without errors.

```
options.TaskScheduler = TaskScheduler.FromCurrentSynchronizationContext();
    foreach(item in numbers)
    {
        Thread.Sleep(1000);
        txtNumber.Text = item.ToString();
    };
```

The Task Scheduler

As mentioned, the default task scheduler—the .NET Framework 4 thread pool—functions best with short, discrete tasks. To execute a series of long-running operations in parallel, you might want to implement a custom scheduler. Here are some other situations in which a cus-tom scheduler might be helpful:

- You could use a custom scheduler when you want to execute tasks on threads with specific thread priority—for example, to lower the thread priority to keep the user interface more responsive when performing concurrent tasks.

- You could implement a task scheduler that supports ordered tasks. You might want to strictly enforce FIFO or LIFO execution.

The first step when implementing a custom scheduler is to inherit the *TaskScheduler* class. *TaskScheduler* is a partially implemented class. As such, you can defer to the base class implementation by using the *base* keyword. In addition, you inherit the cancellation model, exception management, and other standard behavior from the base class implementation, which is great, because it saves a lot of work; you don't have to implement all the plumbing a task scheduler requires to build a custom task scheduler.

You must override these methods in your custom scheduler:

- *GetScheduledTasks*   This method returns an enumerable list of tasks that are pending execution on the scheduler.

  ```
  IEnumerable<Task> GetScheduledTasks()
  ```

- *QueueTask*   This method is called to give the scheduler the next task to be queued. Add the task to the collection of tasks waiting to execute.

  ```
  void QueueTask(Task task)
  ```

- *TryExecuteTaskInline*   This method executes the task inline on the current thread. This avoids having to use another thread. You must decide whether to execute already queued tasks. Return *false* if the task is not executed in this specific call.

  ```
  bool TryExecuteTaskInline(Task task, bool taskWasPreviouslyQueued)
  ```

These members are optional:

- *TryDequeue*   This method removes the provided task from the task queue. If it is successful, return *true*.

  ```
  bool TryDequeue(Task task)
  ```

- *TryExecuteTask*   This tries to execute the provided task. If it is successful, return *true*. Return *false* if you do not execute the task. You should not execute the same task twice.

  ```
  bool TryExecuteTask(Task task)
  ```

Using a Custom Task Scheduler

There are several ways to plug in a custom scheduler. One option is to create an instance of the *ParallelOptions* class and set the scheduler with the *TaskScheduler* property. You saw this technique demonstrated earlier. Overloads of both the *Parallel.ForEach* and *Parallel.For* methods accept *ParallelOptions* as a parameter. The following example code sets a custom scheduler by using *ParallelOptions*.

```
var numbers = Enumerable.Range(0, 100);
ParallelOptions options = new ParallelOptions();
options.TaskScheduler = new CustomScheduler();
Parallel.ForEach(numbers, options, item => DoSomething());
```

You can also assign a task scheduler directly to a task by using the *Task.Start* method. An overload of the *Task.Start* method accepts *TaskScheduler* as a parameter, as shown here.

```
Task t = new Task(() => DoSomething());
t.Start(new CustomScheduler());
```

You can also designate a custom scheduler in the *TaskFactory.StartNew* method. Several overloads of *TaskFactory.StartNew* accept a *TaskScheduler* as a parameter. Unfortunately, there is no simple overload with parameters for just the task and the custom scheduler. Here's an example that assigns a custom scheduler by using the *TaskFactory.StartNew* method.

```
TaskFactory.StartNew(()=>DoSomething(),cts.Token , TaskCreationOptions.None,
new CustomScheduler());
```

Finally, you can create the custom scheduler in the constructor of a *TaskFactory*.

```
var tf=new TaskFactory(new CustomScheduler());d
tf.StartNew(()=>DoSomething());
```

Creating a Custom Scheduler

In the following exercise, you will create a custom scheduler. Your scheduler will wrap each task with a setup and cleanup method. By using this feature, you can assign global setup and cleanup methods to tasks executed on the scheduler. Task schedulers are difficult to keep simple, so to keep this example task scheduler relatively simple, you will not make the task scheduler disposable, implement error handling, or check for exceptions, all of which you should do in real-world code.

Create a custom task scheduler that supports setup and cleanup methods

1. Create a new C# console application in Visual Studio 2010. Add *using* statements for the *System.Threading, System.Threading.Tasks,* and *System.Collections.Concurrent* namespaces.

2. Start by defining a custom task scheduler that inherits from the *TaskScheduler* class. At the beginning of the class, define a list collection to track queued tasks. Also define two *Action<Task>* delegates that will handle the setup and cleanup code.

```
List<Task> tasks = new List<Task>();
Action<Task> Setup;
Action<Task> Cleanup;
```

3. In the custom scheduler constructor, initialize the setup and cleanup methods. Both should default to null.

```
public CustomScheduler(Action<Task> _Setup=null,
    Action<Task> _Cleanup=null)
{
    Setup = _Setup;
    Cleanup = _Cleanup;
}
```

4. It's time to override specific *TaskScheduler* methods. First, implement the *QueueTask* method. Add the given task to the task collection in a thread-safe manner. Create a new thread. Within the thread, call the *Setup*, *TryExecuteTask*, and *Cleanup* methods. Make the new thread a background thread and then start the thread.

```
protected override void QueueTask(Task currentTask)
{
    lock (this)
    {
        tasks.Add(currentTask);
    }
    Thread t = new Thread(new ThreadStart(() =>
    {
if(Setup!=null) Setup(currentTask);
TryExecuteTask(currentTask);
if(Cleanup!=null) Cleanup(currentTask);
    }));
    t.IsBackground = true;
    t.Start();
}
```

5. Override the *TryDequeue* method. Remove the provided task from the task collection in a thread-safe manner.

```
protected override bool TryDequeue(Task task)
{
    lock (this)
    {
        tasks.Remove(task);
    }
    return true;
}
```

6. Add the *GetScheduledTasks* method to return the collection of queued tasks waiting to execute.

```
protected override IEnumerable<Task> GetScheduledTasks()
{
    return tasks.ToArray();
}
```

7. For simplicity, the *TryExecuteTaskInline* method is not implemented. Override this method and return *false*. You have completed your first custom scheduler!

```
protected override bool TryExecuteTaskInline(Task task,
bool taskWasPreviouslyQueued)
{
    return false;
}
```

8. In the *Main* method, test the custom scheduler. Create a range of integer values from 0 to 10. Create an instance of the *ParallelOptions* type. Assign *ParallelOptions* *.TaskScheduler* an instance of the custom scheduler. In the constructor, provide a setup and cleanup method as parameters. In each method, display the task identifier.

```
var numbers = Enumerable.Range(0, 10);
ParallelOptions options = new ParallelOptions();
options.TaskScheduler = new CustomScheduler((task) =>
{
    Console.WriteLine("Before Task {0,2}", task.Id);
}, (task) =>
{
    Console.WriteLine("After  Task {0,2}", task.Id);
});
```

9. Next, iterate the collection of numbers with a *Parallel.ForEach* method with the *ParallelOptions* object as a parameter. This will provide a reference for the custom scheduler to the *Parallel.ForEach* method. The actual parallel operation is a lambda expression. In the lambda, display the current value. Add a couple of tabs to more easily distinguish this from other output.

```
Parallel.ForEach(numbers, options, (number) =>
{
    Console.WriteLine("\t\tValue = {0}", number);
});
```

10. Build and run the program.

Here's the complete code for the example application.

```
using System;
using System.Collections.Generic;
using System.Linq;
using System.Text;
using System.Threading;
using System.Threading.Tasks;
using System.Collections.Concurrent;

namespace Scheduler
{
    public class CustomScheduler : TaskScheduler
    {
        List<Task> tasks = new List<Task>();
        Action<Task> setup;
```

```
    Action<Task> cleanup;

    public CustomScheduler(Action<Task> _setup=null,
        Action<Task> _cleanup=null)
    {
        setup = _setup;
        cleanup = _cleanup;
    }

    protected override void QueueTask(Task currentTask)
    {
        lock (this)
        {
            tasks.Add(currentTask);
        }
        Thread t = new Thread(new ThreadStart(() =>
        {
            setup(currentTask);
            TryExecuteTask(currentTask);
            cleanup(currentTask);
        }));
        t.Start();
    }

    protected override bool TryDequeue(Task task)
    {
        lock (this)
        {
            tasks.Remove(task);
        }
        return true;
    }

    protected override IEnumerable<Task> GetScheduledTasks()
    {
        return tasks.ToArray();
    }

    protected override bool TryExecuteTaskInline(Task task,
        bool taskWasPreviouslyQueued)
    {
        return false;
    }
}
class Program
{
    static void Main(string[] args)
    {
        var numbers = Enumerable.Range(0, 10);
        ParallelOptions options = new ParallelOptions();
        options.TaskScheduler = new CustomScheduler((task) =>
        {
            Console.WriteLine("Before Task {0,2}", task.Id);
        }, (task) =>
        {
            Console.WriteLine("After  Task {0,2}", task.Id);
```

```
        });

        Parallel.ForEach(numbers, options, (number) =>
        {
            Console.WriteLine("\t\tValue = {0}", number);
        });
    }
}
}
```

The following image shows the output for the application. You can see the messages from both the setup and cleanup methods.

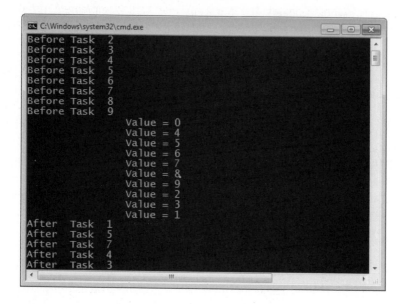

Summary

If you have unique requirements, you can customize the three major components of parallel programming in the .NET environment.

- Producer-consumer collections

- Task partitioners

- Task schedulers

Customizing the TPL is fun and often useful. This chapter provides several practical examples where customization might be beneficial, such as creating a task scheduler that executes lower-priority tasks. However, customization should be reserved for unique situations where the default features of the TPL are not best utilized. In most scenarios, the TPL is ideal and is preferred to a custom solution.

Producer-consumer collections support the producer-consumer pattern, where producer objects add objects and consumer objects remove objects from the underlying collection. To create a custom producer-consumer, you implement key members of the *IProducerConsumerCollection* interface. The *GetEnumerator* method, the *TryAdd* method, the *TryTake* method, the *IsSynchronize* property, and the *Count* property are the essential methods and properties to implement.

Partitioners partition or group parallel operations into tasks for efficient load balancing. You can create custom partitioners by simply calling the *Partitioner.Create* method. You can also create entirely new partitioners by inheriting the *Partitioner<TSource>* or *OrderablePartitioner<TSource>* classes. The important members to implement include the *GetPartitions* method, the *GetDynamicPartitions* method, and the *SupportsDynamicPartitions* property.

The task scheduler queues and later executes tasks. The default task scheduler is the .NET Framework 4 thread pool, which employs a mixture of a global queue and local queues. The global queue is for top tasks, and the local queues hold nested tasks. This model improves performance by reducing the need for synchronization. You can create custom task schedulers by inheriting the *TaskScheduler* class. The important methods to implement are the *GetScheduledTasks*, *QueueTask*, *TryExecuteTaskInline*, *TryDequeue*, and *TryExecuteTask* methods.

Quick Reference

To	Do this
Create a custom producer-consumer type	Implement the *IProducerConsumerCollection* interface.
Create a partitioner	Invoke the *Partitioner.Create* method, which returns a partitioner.
Use a second strategy to create a custom partitioner	Implement the *Partitioner<TSource>* or *OrderablePartitioner<TSource>* abstract class. *OrderablePartitioner<TSource>* supports custom partitioning and indexed or ordered access within each partition.
Create a custom scheduler to replace the default scheduler (.NET Framework 4 thread pool)	Implement the *TaskScheduler* class.
Schedule tasks on a specific thread context	Use the *TaskScheduler.FromCurrentSynchronizationContext* method. For example, you can execute tasks specifically on the user interface thread to access user interface controls.

Chapter 7
Reports and Debugging

After completing this chapter, you will be able to

- Perform live debugging of a managed application.

- Create and open managed dumps.

- Perform post-mortem analysis by using dumps.

- Use the Parallel Tasks window.

- Understand both views of the Parallel Stacks window.

- Configure projects for the Concurrency Visualizer.

- Understand the various views of the Concurrency Visualizer.

- Analyze real-world problems with the Concurrency Visualizer.

Parallel applications are in general more complex than sequential versions of the same application. Threads, tasks, synchronization, and other aspects of parallel programming add extra levels of complexity. For this and other reasons, parallel applications are uniquely challenging to implement and maintain. The Task Parallel Library (TPL) abstracts some of this complexity. When something goes wrong, however, it is sometimes necessary to understand the semantics of parallel programming. Visual Studio 2010 offers several new features that can help you debug parallel code. You can discover the source of deadlocks, isolate load imbalances, explore synchronization bottlenecks, and investigate other problems that occur in a parallel application.

Maximum processor utilization, scalability, and effective load balancing in a multicore environment are some of the goals of a parallel application. You'll see how to take advantage of the various windows and reports discussed in this chapter to verify these important milestones. You should set and then evaluate these benchmarks on a regular basis to assure success.

A discussion of debugging and maintaining parallel applications can be long and arduous. An entire book could be written just on managed debugging alone. For example, John Robbins is the author of *two* complete books on the subject; the latest is *Debugging Microsoft .NET 2.0 Applications* (Microsoft Press, 2006). This chapter can provide only an overview of general debugging techniques. Walkthroughs are also provided to help you understand the important topics introduced in this chapter.

Debugging with Visual Studio 2010

Visual Studio provides an intuitive interface for debugging both managed and native applications. The Visual Studio debugger is a separate component within the Visual Studio integrated development environment (IDE). Visual Studio 2010 introduces many new debugging features, such as the ability to create and save managed dumps. In addition, you can now use Visual Studio to perform managed post-mortem analysis on a dump.

Live Debugging

You can perform real-time debugging of a running application. This is considered *live debugging*, which you can start in several different ways:

- You can start debugging from an active project. Open the Visual Studio project for your managed application. This should be a runnable application, such as a Console or Windows Forms application. Select Debug from the menu, and then select Start Debugging. (The shortcut key is F5.) Assuming that your program compiles successfully, the application will start with the debugger attached.

- You can attach the debugger to a running application by using Visual Studio. From the menu, select Debugging, and then select Attach To Process. The dialog box shown in the following image appears. Select the application you want to debug from the list, and then click the Attach button. If you have a corresponding project available, you might want to open it first. This would help with source-level debugging.

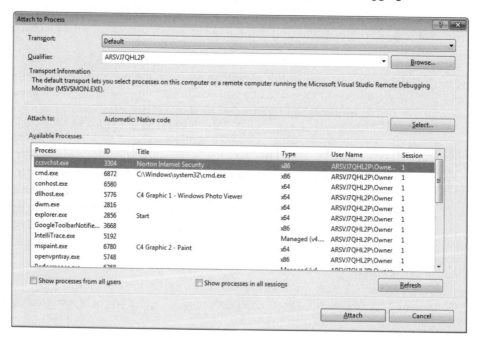

- The last option is known as *Just-In-Time debugging*. When an application crashes, a dialog box appears that presents you with several choices (see the following image). One of the options is to attach the debugger and begin debugging the application in a Visual Studio session. From the crash dialog box, select the Continue button to begin Just-In-Time debugging. Visual Studio installs itself as the default Just-In-Time debugger at installation.

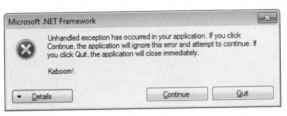

Most of the user interface for debugging, such as the various debugging windows, is not available for use unless the application is running but interrupted. It is hard to debug a moving target. However, there are a variety of techniques to interrupt an application, most normally breakpoints. You can insert a breakpoint into a running application from the Debug menu in Visual Studio.

There are several types of breakpoints:

- **Location**   This sets a breakpoint on a specific source statement.

- **Condition**   This honors the breakpoint when a Boolean condition is *true*. For example, you can honor the breakpoint if a variable contains a specific value.

- **Hit Count**   This sets a breakpoint on a specific instance, such as every third instance or when a variable exceeds a certain value.

- **Filter**   This type filters a breakpoint on a thread, process, or machine. This is useful when there are several threads executing through the same source code. In this circumstance, it might be useful to break on a specific thread.

- **When Hit**   This executes a macro or displays a trace message when the breakpoint is hit. A When Hit breakpoint is also known as a *Tracepoint* and looks different than other breakpoints: It appears as a diamond, not as a red circle. By default, when they are hit, When Hit breakpoints do not break! When one of these breakpoints is hit, the trace is displayed or the macro is executed. You can choose to break at the breakpoint by selecting that option in the Tracepoint dialog box. If this option is chosen, the breakpoint changes to the common red circle for breakpoints and execution is interrupted when the breakpoint is hit.

Most developers set a location breakpoint by using the F9 function key. Simply place the insertion point at the target location in your source code and click F9. The F9 shortcut key acts as a toggle to turn a breakpoint on or off. You can also convert an existing breakpoint to another type by using the context menu. Right-click the breakpoint in the source window or in the Breakpoints window to change the type, as shown in the following image.

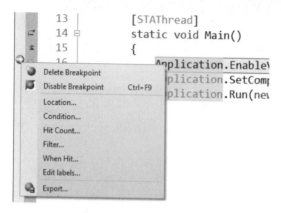

Performing Post-Mortem Analysis

Post-mortem analysis involves debugging an application *after* execution has completed—a task that is most often accomplished with dumps. Managed debugging of dumps is an important new feature of Visual Studio 2010 and includes creating and opening managed dumps, which is extremely important in a production environment in which live debugging is not an option. Instead of debugging, you can create a dump of the application. Dumps require updated symbols; symbol management is beyond the scope of this chapter, but you can find several online resources for guidance.

To create a dump, you first interrupt the running application. One method is to choose Debug from the menu and then select Break All. After interrupting the application, choose Save Dump As from the Debug menu. The Save Dump As dialog box appears. Enter the name, and select the type of dump you want to create. You can create dumps both with or without heap information. The default is mini dumps with heap information. To create dumps of applications already running, start with Tools | Attach To Process in Visual Studio, which might include identifying a remote machine. You can then create the dump.

You can also open managed dumps in Visual Studio. If possible, open the related project first. The dump file does not have to be created in Visual Studio—it might have been created from another application, such as Windows Task Manager, WinDbg, or ADPlus. After opening a dump, Visual Studio displays the Minidump File Summary, as shown in the next image. This window presents summary information pertaining to the dump, including when the dump was created, the list of loaded modules, and the originating operating system. To start debugging with the dump, select the Debug With Mixed or Debug With Native Only button (the green triangles in the Actions section). You can then begin your analysis by using the various debug windows.

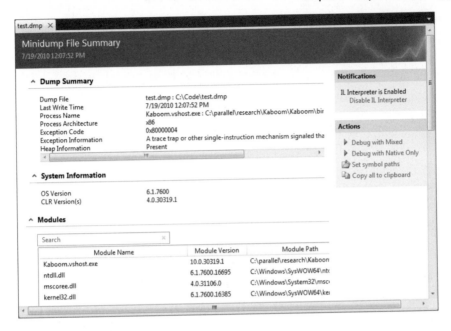

Debugging Threads

Threads play a major role in parallel applications. For debugging purposes, you'll find thread information in the Threads window. As with most debugging windows, select Debug | Windows to open the Threads window. You'll often want to use the Call Stack and the Threads windows together; if you open one of these windows, you should probably open the other. Selections in the Threads window, such as the current thread, can affect the results shown in the Call Stack window.

The following image shows the Threads window.

	ID	Managed ID	Category	Name	Location	Priority
Example 1.vshost.exe (id = 2092) : C:\parallel\Chapter 7\Example 1\Example 1\bin\Debug\Example 1.vshost.exe						
	5188	0	Worker Thread	<No Name>	<not available>	Highest
	196	3	Worker Thread	<No Name>	<not available>	Normal
	3784	6	Worker Thread	vshost.RunParkingWindow	[Managed to Native Transition]	Normal
	6940	7	Worker Thread	.NET SystemEvents	[Managed to Native Transition]	Normal
	4816	8	Main Thread	Main Thread	Reporting_Example.Program.Main	Normal
	2576	10	Worker Thread	Worker Thread	Reporting_Example.XClass.ME	Normal
	6668	13	Worker Thread	Worker Thread	Reporting_Example.XClass.MK	Normal
	6604	11	Worker Thread	Worker Thread	Reporting_Example.XClass.MM	Normal
⇨	7080	9	Worker Thread	Worker Thread	Reporting_Example.XClass.MJ	Normal
	6556	12	Worker Thread	Worker Thread	Reporting_Example.XClass.MJ	Normal
	7032	14	Worker Thread	<No Name>	<not available>	Normal
	6056	15	Worker Thread	<No Name>	<not available>	Normal
	6852	16	Worker Thread	<No Name>	<not available>	Normal

The threads in the preceding windows are from the sample application for this chapter. The application itself is trivial. It was created solely to demonstrate various aspects of the debug windows. You'll find the code for the sample application listed at the end of this chapter. As shown in the Threads window, this sample application hosts a variety of threads.

There are several columns in the Threads window; the first two columns are untitled.

- **First column (no heading)**   This is for flags. Flagging a thread allows you to group, highlight, or filter threads.

- **Second column (no heading)**   This is the active threads column. A yellow arrow indicates the current thread. If a white arrow appears in this column, it indicates a thread that has been interrupted by the debugger.

- **ID**   The ID is the operation system identifier for the thread.

- **Managed ID**   This is the common language runtime (CLR) identifier for the thread.

- **Category**   The Category is the type of thread, such as the Main or Worker thread.

- **Name**   This contains the name assigned to the thread, if any. You should always name threads, because it makes debugging easier.

- **Location**   This is the entry point method for the thread. When you point to a row in this column, the call stack for that thread is displayed (see the following figure).

- **Priority**   The last column is the thread priority.

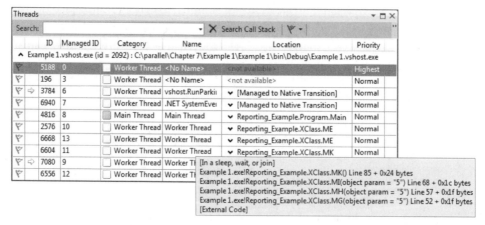

The columns are easy to change and organize. Click a column heading to sort on that column. You can also drag column headers to reorder the location of columns and add columns by using the Columns arrow at the right end of the Columns label.

A right-click context menu is available for the threads in the Threads window. Two of the commands on the context menu are Switch To Thread and Freeze. Switching to a thread makes the chosen thread the current thread. You can also double-click a thread in the Threads window to perform the switch. In either case, the yellow arrow will move to that thread row. The Freeze command suspends a thread. You can use this command to isolate threads that are running the same source code.

What are all of these threads doing? You can discover that by pointing to the Location column for a particular thread to present the Call Stack window. You'll find a persistent view of this information in the Call Stack window. When you change the current thread in the Threads window, the content of the Call Stack window updates to reflect the new selection. The following image shows both the Threads window and Call Stack window.

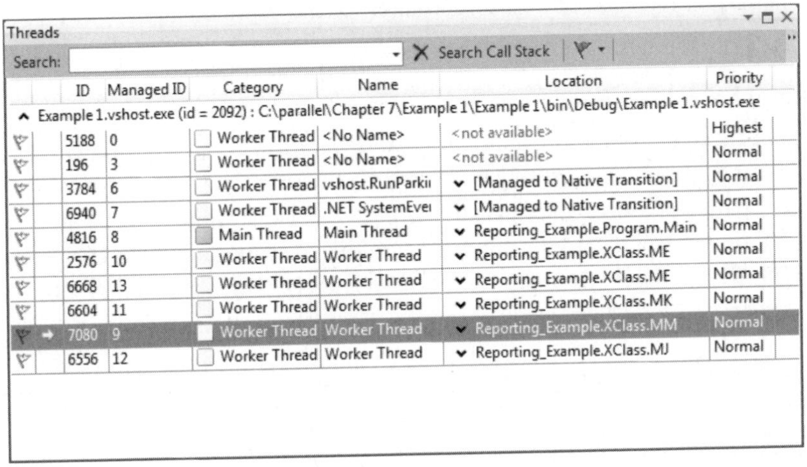

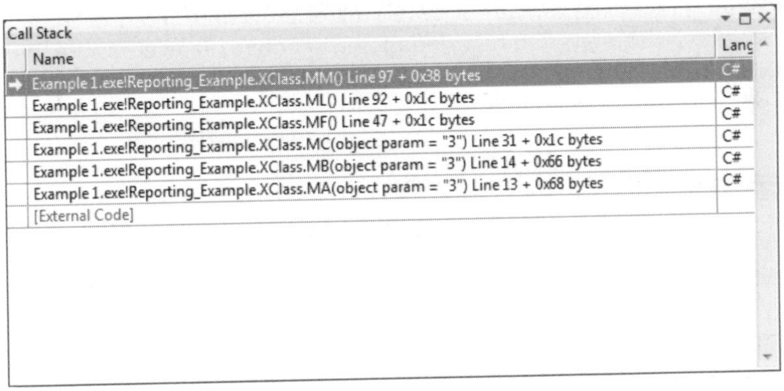

By default, external code might not be shown in the Call Stack window because it tends to clutter the window. To view external code, right-click to open the context menu in the Call Stack window. Select Show External Code to immediately view the external code, as shown in the next image.

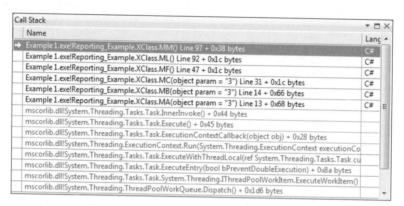

Examine the bottom half of the preceding Call Stack window. You'll see clear evidence of a task being created, queued, and finally invoked on a thread in the .NET Framework 4 thread pool. This is evidence of a parallel application. In the Call Stack window, you can expand the Name column to view parameters and other information pertaining to the method. For example, this is the detailed information for the *ExecuteWithThreadLocal* method. You can see that the Task ID and an entry point method are the parameters.

```
mscorlib.dll!System.Threading.Tasks.Task.ExecuteWithThreadLocal(ref
System.Threading.Tasks.Task currentTaskSlot = Id = 4,
Status = Running, Method = "Void MA(System.Object)") + 0x160 bytes
```

You might think that there must be a more direct way to obtain this information. Of course there is! Visual Studio 2010 offers two new debugging windows, Parallel Tasks and Parallel Stacks, for viewing tasks more directly.

Using the Parallel Tasks Window

Tasks, tasks, and more tasks! Parallel programs are built upon tasks. In the TPL, tasks are wrappers for parallel operations that are later queued and scheduled on threads in the .NET Framework 4 thread pool, which is the default scheduler. As such, tasks are the central ingredient of a parallel program; tasks replace threads as the basic unit of execution. Tasks are part of the additional complexity found in parallel code. For these reasons, debugging a parallel application often begins with debugging tasks.

Visual Studio 2010 introduces the Parallel Tasks window for monitoring and debugging tasks. The Parallel Tasks window is similar to the Threads window in its look and feel and functionality. For those familiar with the Threads window, transitioning to the Parallel Tasks window should be simple. The next image shows the Parallel Tasks window.

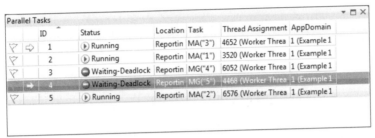

The Parallel Tasks window displays several columns. Some of these columns are identical to those in the Threads window:

- **First column (no heading)**   You can flag a task in the first column. Flagging is used to group, highlight, or filter tasks.

- **Second column (no heading)**   This is the active task column. A yellow arrow indicates the current task. If a white arrow appears in this column, it indicates the task that has been interrupted by the debugger.

- **ID**   The ID is the task identifier.

- **Status**   Status is the execution state of the task, such as running, waiting, or deadlocked. The appropriate icon is displayed at the left end of the column.

- **Location**   This column shows the location of the task in the call stack. If you point to an entry in this column, the entire call stack for the task is displayed. The entry point method for the task is displayed at the bottom of the call stack (see the next image).

- **Task**   This is the entry point method and argument for the task.

- **Thread Assignment**   Tasks run on threads. This column displays the name and thread identifier of that thread.

- **AppDomain**   This identifies the application domain for the task.

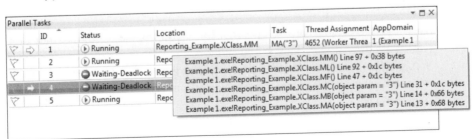

Click a column heading to sort on that column, or drag a column heading to change the column order. You can use the context menu to select additional columns, such as the Task and AppDomain columns. You can also group tasks on a particular column. Choose Group By *ColumnName* from the context menu. In the following image, the tasks are grouped by status.

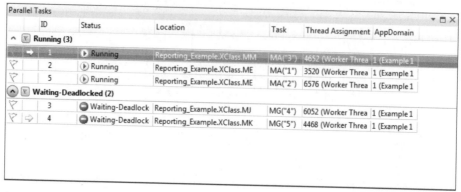

Developers often struggle to resolve deadlock conditions. Here, the Parallel Tasks window comes to the rescue! In this example, both Task 2 and Task 3 are deadlocked on something. What is the reason for the deadlock? In the next exercise, you will discover the answer to that question. The exercise assumes that you have created an application from the sample code at the end of the chapter. Results vary from machine to machine. This is to be expected, because not all machines are identical.

Use the Parallel Tasks window to find the source of a deadlock

1. If you have not done so already, create a console application for Microsoft Visual C# in Visual Studio 2010. Replace the code in the application with the source code at the end of this chapter.

2. Build the application and start debugging. A breakpoint instruction is programmatically embedded in the application. The program will automatically break at the hardcoded breakpoint.

3. From the Debug menu, choose Windows. Open the Parallel Tasks window. Use the context menu, as shown earlier, to group tasks on the Status column.

4. Now that the columns are grouped by status, you can easily observe that Task 2 and Task 3 are deadlocked. Point to the status column for Task 2. As shown in the following image, a tooltip is displayed that indicates that Task 2 is waiting for a *System.Object* owned by thread *7992*. Upon examining the call stack, you see that Task 3 is running on that thread.

Note The task and thread numbers might vary on your machine.

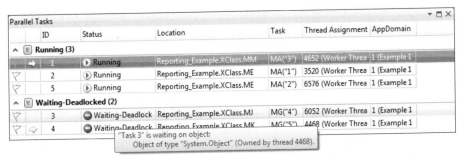

5. Point to the status for Task 3. Once again, you'll see a tooltip. Task 3 is also blocked and waiting for a *System.Object*. This object is owned by thread *4780*.

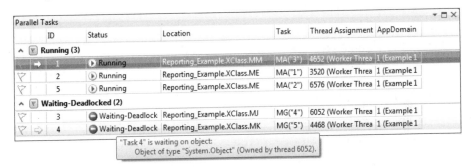

6. Evidence points to a deadlock because Task 2 and Task 3 are both blocked and waiting for each other. You can examine the source code to confirm this. In the Parallel Tasks window, open the context menu for Task 3. Select Switch To Task. This will jump to the actual source code for that task (see the next image). The final statement executed for the current stack frame is highlighted, which is the *Monitor.Enter* method on the *s2* object as a parameter. This is where the task deadlocked. You should note that the task has already acquired a lock for the *s1* object.

```
public void MJ()
{
    Monitor.Enter(s1);
    Thread.SpinWait(int.MaxValue / 20);
    Monitor.Enter(s2);
    Monitor.Exit(s2);
    Monitor.Exit(s1);
}
```

7. Repeat the steps for Task 2 to view the source code (see the following image). You should see that this task has stopped on a *Monitor.Enter* method for the *s1* object, which is the same object that Task 3 already owns. *Aha!* This confirms that Task 2 and Task 3 are hopelessly deadlocked on each other. Admittedly this example is somewhat contrived. However, it demonstrates many of the features of the new Parallel Tasks window.

```
public void MK()
{
    Monitor.Enter(s2);
    Thread.SpinWait(int.MaxValue / 10);
    Monitor.Enter(s1);
    Monitor.Exit(s1);
    Monitor.Exit(s2);
}
```

Using the Parallel Stacks Window

The Parallel Stacks window displays a call stack from the perspective of parallel execution. Similar to the Threads and Call Stack windows, the Parallel Tasks and Parallel Stacks windows are frequently used together.

There are two views of the Parallel Stacks window: Threads view and Tasks view. In the TPL, a task is the encapsulation of a parallel operation. This is the reason developers focus on tasks when developing a parallel application—threads are largely abstracted. However, when things go wrong, information on threads is often helpful. For example, knowing which threads share the same call stack can be useful. For this reason, the Parallel Stacks window has both a Threads view and a Tasks view. You can select the desired view in the drop-down list at the top of the Parallel Stacks window.

The Threads View

The Threads view of the Parallel Stacks window shows the call path of threads through concurrent code. Each thread represents a separate path of execution. Call stacks are represented as nodes or boxes in the window. Each node lists methods of the call stack. The current stack frame is highlighted with a yellow arrow, and a white arrow (if any) indicates the stack frame in which execution was interrupted by the debugger. The current path through the application is shown with a bold blue arrow line. The status of a thread is shown above the call stack in the terminating node. On the left side of the window, you can use the Zoom slider control to scale the window.

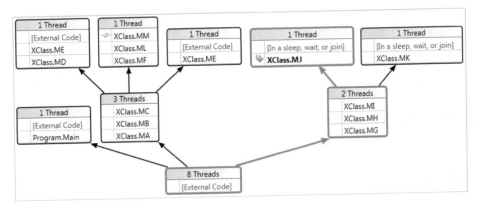

There are a few method icons:

- **Yellow arrow**   The active stack frame for the current thread

- **Green arrow**   The active stack frame for a noncurrent thread

- **Cloths thread icon (two squiggly lines)**   The active stack frame for a noncurrent call stack

You can switch the current stack frame by double-clicking one of the noncurrent frames. This changes the context for many things, such as the local variables.

Some threads can follow the same path and share a common call stack. When that occurs, that node is shared by multiple threads, as annotated in the node header. In the diagram at the beginning of this section, two threads share the {MG, MH, MI} class stack. If you want to identify the specific threads, you can point to the header. A tooltip appears that displays the thread identifier and type for each thread, as shown in the next image.

The preceding diagram depicts two threads sharing a call stack. Afterward, the threads deviate. One thread calls the XClass.MJ method, while the other calls XClass.MK. You can point to the header for the nodes to identify the specific threads.

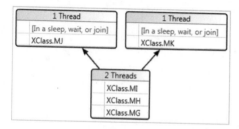

Obviously, pointing can be helpful in a variety of ways. For example, when you point to a method in the call stack, the tooltip displays the stack frame for each of the concurrent threads. In addition to the thread identifier, the display includes parameters and source line information. The stack frame for the current thread appears in bold (when multiple threads are running through this particular call stack, as shown here).

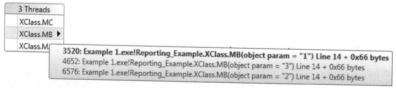

The Threads view has a toolbar that offers various commands.

From left to right, here's an explanation of the toolbar buttons:

- **View drop-down list**   Toggles between the Threads view and the Tasks view
- **Stack frames**   Shows stack frames for threads flagged in the Threads window
- **Method view**   Shows the callers and callees of the current method
- **Auto Scroll To Current Stack Frame**   Scrolls to bring the current stack frame into the visible window
- **Toggle Zoom Control**   Toggles the Zoom slider control between visible and non-visible

You can right-click any method in the call stack to open a context menu, as shown in the following image.

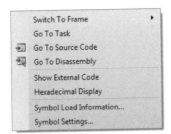

The context menu commands are as follows:

- **Switch to Frame**   Selects the current method as the active stack frame
- **Go To Task**   In the Tasks view, shows the task for this method
- **Go To Source Code**   Jumps to the source code for a particular method
- **Go To Disassembly**   Opens the disassembly for a particular method
- **Show External Code**   Displays external code that is not in your code
- **Hexadecimal Display**   Switches between hexadecimal and decimal numbers
- **Symbol Load Information**   Displays the status of symbols for this method
- **Symbol Settings**   Allows you to configure symbol information

The Bird's Eye View is a super cool feature. You can pan a reduced version of the graph within a miniature window. This is useful if you have a large diagram and want to quickly view a non-visible area. The Bird's Eye View button is at the intersection of the right and bottom toolbars. When you click the button, an insert appears that contains the diagram. The shaded area is your view. Click and drag within the Bird's Eye view to reposition the diagram. If the diagram is entirely visible, neither the scrollbars nor the Bird's Eye View button appear.

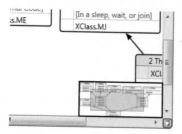

The Tasks View

The Tasks view shows the call stack of tasks and is the other view available in the Parallel Stacks window. In general, this view presents the application from the perspective of tasks and removes other extraneous information. It shows the call path of tasks, where each node is an individual call stack. The current path is highlighted with a bold blue arrow. All this should sound familiar at this point, because for ease of use, the Threads and Tasks views are similar.

Here is the Tasks view.

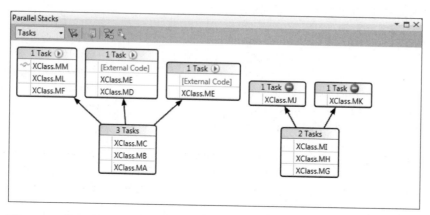

The preceding diagram shows five tasks. Two threads execute on the same call stack, which is {MI, MH, MG}. One of the tasks then calls MJ. The other task calls MK. Three threads share the {MC, MB, MA} call stack before separating paths. If you point to a node header, you will display a tooltip with information on each task in the call stack. If you point to the header with three tasks, here's what is displayed:

Within a node, you can point to a specific method. A tooltip appears that provides the frame number, the full symbol name, the parameters, and source line information, as shown next.

The active stack frame of the current task is highlighted with a yellow arrow. In general, the same arrows and other icons are available as in the Threads view—but they apply to tasks rather than threads.

The end node of each call path includes the task status in the header, shown as an icon. In the following end node, the red circle with a dash indicates a deadlock. As in other examples, you can point to the task header for more detail, as shown here.

Using the Concurrency Visualizer

Performance analysis of a parallel application is more challenging than performance analysis of a sequential application. A parallel application has more moving parts, such as tasks, threads, the thread pool, and synchronization. Therefore, Microsoft created the Concurrency Visualizer as an advanced profiler and included this powerful tool in Visual Studio 2010. The Concurrency Visualizer provides a wide assortment of charts and reports to help you visualize and analyze the performance of your parallel application.

The Concurrency Visualizer is feature rich. This section contains only an overview of this comprehensive tool, but you can find detailed articles and videos on this subject on MSDN. For example, see "Concurrent Visualization Techniques in the VS2010 Profiler," by Phil Pennington.

The Concurrency Visualizer is an Event Tracing for Windows (ETW) consumer and receives kernel-level data from low-level tracing in the operating system. ETW provides several benefits. It's implemented as part of the operating system kernel and not the user-mode application. Because it is non-invasive, ETW has minimal impact on your application. ETW is a systemwide resource and provides a single tracing model that all developers can depend on. As an ETW subscriber, the Concurrency Visualizer has certain restrictions:

- Visual Studio must have administrative privileges to launch the Concurrency Visualizer.

- By default, 64-bit applications cannot view a complete stack trace in the Concurrency Visualizer. You must set the Disable Paging Executive flag in the registry. Run the following command from the command line to update the registry appropriately.

```
REG ADD "HKLM\System\CurrentControlSet\Control\Session Manager\Memory
  Management" -v DisablePagingExecutive -d 0x1 -t REG_DWORD -f
```

After updating the registry key, you must reboot the system before attempting to use the Concurrency Visualizer.

■ ETW can consume considerable storage, which might cause data loss and an error when you are using the Concurrency Visualizer. Increase the ETW buffer size to resolve this problem.

To start the Concurrency Visualizer, select Launch Performance Wizard from the Analyze menu to begin profiling. In the Performance Wizard dialog box, shown here, you select the Concurrency option and the Visualize The Behavior Of A Multithreaded Application check box.

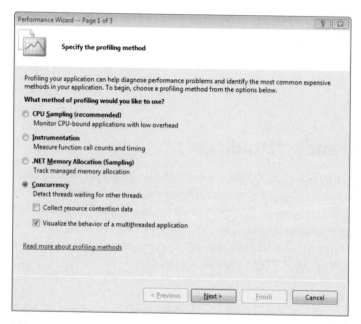

Then proceed to the next screen. In this screen, you select the project you intend to profile. If you want to start an executable, you can choose the An Executable (.EXE File) option. When you choose this, you'll see a different dialog box in which you can browse to the target executable.

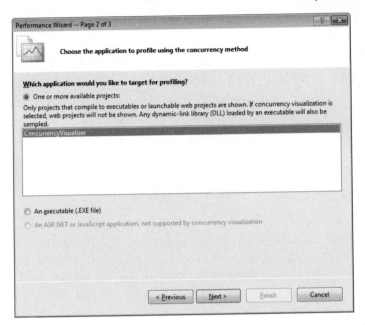

The next window is essentially a confirmation screen. Here you click the Finish button to accept the current settings and begin profiling. Clicking the Previous button allows you to revisit settings and make changes.

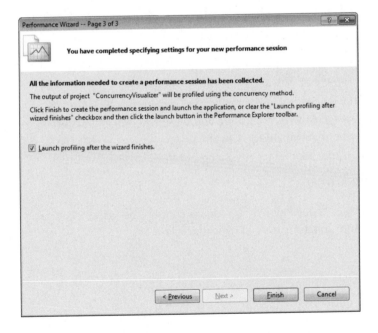

Your application starts, and trace data is collected as the application runs. Select the *Stop Profiling* link to stop performance profiling. The data analysis begins when the profiling stops. Be patient, because the analysis might take some time. When the analysis completes, the Concurrency Visualizer presents three views: CPU Utilization, Threads, and Cores.

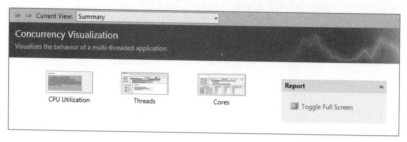

The Performance Explorer opens automatically and provides an overview of the profiling sessions. You can run multiple profiling sessions and save them to individual files with a .psess extension. Each session appears in the Performance Explorer window, shown here.

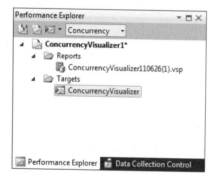

From the command line, you can collect data for the Concurrency Visualizer by using the Visual Studio Profiler. This allows you to automate the process, which is especially helpful on production machines where Visual Studio is not installed.

CPU Utilization View

CPU Utilization view displays utilization of the logical cores in the system. Logical cores include virtual cores from solutions such as hyperthreading.

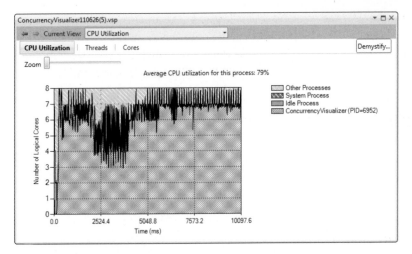

In the preceding graphic, the y-axis represents the logical cores, and the x-axis is the timeline, shown in milliseconds. There is a Zoom slider control above the graph. Drag right to enlarge the graph. You can also drag the mouse horizontally across the graph to zoom in to a portion of the graph.

Each color on the graph indicates a type of process and its relative CPU utilization. The legend explains the purpose of each color.

- Green indicates the CPU utilization of the current application.

- Yellow shows CPU utilization for other applications.

- Red is the percentage of CPU utilization accorded to the system.

- Gray shows idle processor cores.

If in doubt, you can point to an area of the graph to see a tooltip that provides information on that portion of the graph. For example, if you point to the green portion of the graph, the name and process identifier for the current process displays.

CPU Utilization view is good for exposing a variety of problems, including low CPU utilization, which could be an indicator of deadlocks or over-synchronization. You can even spot excessive CPU utilization from other applications competing for processor resources.

The Threads View

The Threads view provides the most information of the three views. There are several regions to the Threads view, as depicted in the following graphic.

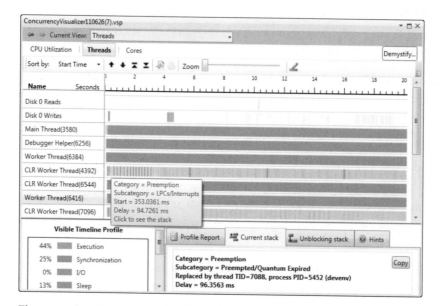

The central region is a graph, where the x-axis is a timeline in milliseconds. The y-axis presents mixed information. The top two rows are disk-read and disk-write activity. The remaining rows are threads. These rows are labeled with a brief description and the thread identifier. The various color segments in the bar graph indicate execution status. For example, green indicates a running thread. The Visible Timeline Profile has an explanation of each category. It also shows the percentage of time spent in each of these categories.

The execution categories are:

- **Execution** The thread is running unimpeded.

- **Synchronization** The thread is blocked for synchronization. The Concurrency Visualizer will attempt to identify the source of the synchronization.

- **I/O** The thread is blocking on an input/output event.

- **Sleep** The thread voluntarily yields the CPU. *Thread.Sleep* is the most common method for yielding the CPU.

- **Memory Management** The thread is incurring blocking events related to memory-related activities, such as page faults.

- **Preemption** The thread is preempted by another thread. For example, this would occur when a higher-priority thread starts running.

- **UI Processing**   The user interface has a message pump, which handles messages for the main window. For a responsive user interface, the message pump is typically idle while waiting to respond to the next user interface message. This category indicates the amount of work the user interface thread is performing in response to user interface requests.

You can sort the threads in the graph on these categories. The sort button appears above and to the left of the graph.

A segment is a contiguous region in one category of execution. You can point to a segment for additional information. You'll see different information depending on the category. As shown in the following graphic for preemption, the replacing thread, the delay, and other information is displayed in the tooltip.

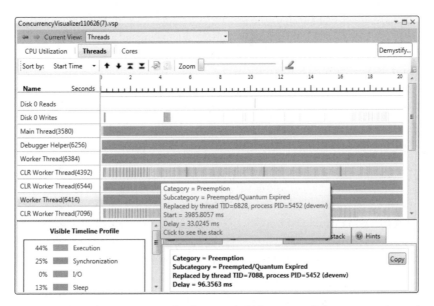

You can also select segments in the graph. When you click a segment to select it, the selection enlarges for emphasis. In addition, some regions of the graph are in the context of the selected segment, such as the Current stack and Unblocking stack results.

As with CPU Utilization view, you can enlarge the entire graph by using the Zoom slider control or by dragging horizontally to zoom in to a particular span.

You can also hide threads to focus on specific threads. Using the row labels, select the threads you want to hide. Open the context menu for the selection, and choose Hide. The graph for these is hidden threads and does not contribute to the analysis performed for graph or reports. The calculations in the Threads view are adjusted to reflect only the visible threads.

The Report Section

The report section, shown here, appears at the bottom of the graph in the Threads view.

The first tab is the Profile Report. The Profile Report can present different reports based on the category selected in the Visible Timeline Profile. The default report is the Per-Thread Summary report. Select Execution in the Visible Timeline Profile to see the Execution Profile report. Select the Synchronization category for the Synchronization Blocking Profile report, and so on. The Sleep Blocking Profile is shown in the next image. This report displays a sampling showing when methods are in a sleep state. The Inclusive Blocking column includes sampling for both the selected method and its calling methods. The Exclusive Blocking column shows the sampling for that method alone. In the following report, the last method contributes the entire sampling, because the Inclusive Blocking and Exclusive Blocking columns are identical.

The Current Stack tab shows the call stack of the selected segment in the Threads View graph. If you select a different segment, the call stack is updated to reflect that. The Current Stack report might display addition information; the category of the selected segment sets the context for this information. For example, the report for a preemption segment, as shown here, explains the type of synchronization and length of delay.

The Unblocking Stack tab is helpful in finding a deadlock. When the category of the segment is Synchronization, switch to the Unblocking Stack tab to view the call stack of the competing thread that controls the synchronization.

The Cores View

The last view of the Concurrency Visualizer—and probably the simplest—is the Cores view, which maps thread activity onto processor cores, as shown here.

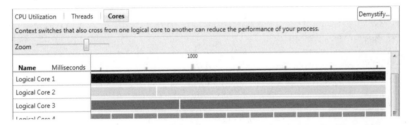

The graph shows a timeline of the application applied to each processor. The y-axis shows the processors, and the x-axis shows the timeline, in microseconds. In this graph, each thread displays in a unique color. Gaps represent idle time on that processor core. If you point to a particular segment, the thread identifier will appear.

Below the graph is a report on the number of context switches per thread. Excessive context switches can adversely affect performance. Several factors can contribute to this problem, including short tasks, improper chunking, and so on. The focus of the report is cross-core context switching. From a performance perspective, cross-core context switching is especially expensive relative to a normal context switch. Cross-core switching happens when a thread resumes on a different processor after a context switch. You lose performance optimization because the original processor cache related to the thread is unavailable.

Unlike the other views, the Cores view does not have any context menus.

In this tutorial, you will use each of the three views and the major features of the Concurrency Visualizer. Three scenarios are presented to cover different aspects of the Concurrency Visualizer. Expect similar but not identical results, because different hardware and other variations in the environment can alter the outcome.

Enumerate a collection of numbers both sequentially and in parallel, and compare the results with the Cores view

1. Create a console application for C# in Visual Studio 2010. Add *using* statements for the *System.Threading* and *System.Threading.Tasks* namespaces. In the *Main* method, ask for user acknowledgement before exiting the application. If user acknowledgment is not provided, the application will conclude prematurely.

```
using System;
using System.Collections.Generic;
using System.Linq;
using System.Text;
using System.Threading;
using System.Threading.Tasks;


namespace VisualizerTutorial
{
    class Program
    {
        static void Main(string[] args)
        {
            Console.WriteLine("Press enter to exit");
            Console.ReadLine();
        }
    }
}
```

In the Program class, create a method that represents compute bound work.

```
static void DoSomething()
{
    Thread.SpinWait(int.MaxValue / 10);
}
```

Define a method that iterates a collection of numbers from 0 to 1000. Iterate the collection sequentially using a foreach method. Perform compute bound work in the loop operation. In the Main method, start a thread with the previous function as the entry point.

```
static void ParallelLoop()
{
```

```
    var numbers = Enumerable.Range(0, 1000);
    foreach (var number in numbers)
    {
        DoSomething();
    }
}
static void Main(string[] args)
{
    new Thread(new ThreadStart(ParallelLoop)).Start();
    Console.WriteLine("Press enter to exit");
    Console.ReadLine();
}
```

2. Start the Currency Visualizer from the Analyze menu, and then select Launch Perfor-
    mance Wizard. Stop profiling the application after 5 to 10 seconds. Open the Cores
    view in the Concurrency Visualizer. The graph will show load imbalance. Notice the light
    utilization of most processor cores. The diagram also shows that one thread is running
    across all the cores, which is not terribly efficient, either. This will cause cross-core con-
    text switching.

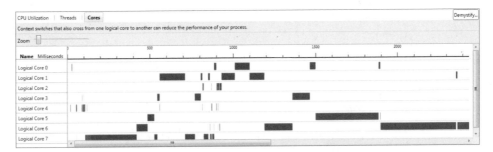

3. Now change your application to iterate the numbers collection by using a
    Parallel.ForEach method for parallel programming.

```
static void ParallelLoop()
{
    var numbers = Enumerable.Range(0, 1000);
    Parallel.ForEach(numbers, (number) =>
    {
        Thread.SpinWait(int.MaxValue / 10);
    });
}
```

4. Rerun the Concurrency Visualizer and open the Cores view. This looks much better! Every processor core shows continuous activity. In addition, each core is running a different thread, which is more efficient than what was shown in the previous results.

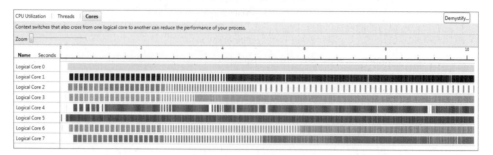

5. Switch to CPU Utilization view. You'll see that the application has high CPU utilization and periodically peaks at 100% utilization. Your application is likely not executing alone on your local machine; it probably shares the system with other running applications. Those applications can also impact CPU utilization. You can test this. Remember, the yellow portion of the graph is other processes, and utilization of the current process is green.

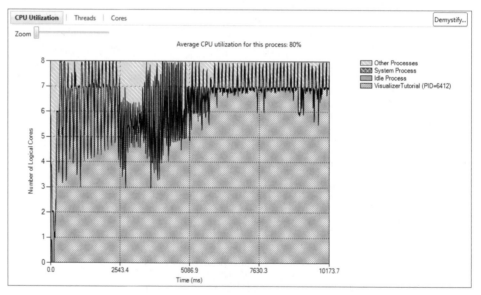

6. Start another instance of Visual Studio 2010. Keep the other session of Visual Studio open. You are going to build a console application just to burn CPU cycles. Create a console application for C# in Visual Studio 2010. Add a *using* statement for the *System.Threading* namespace.

7. In the *Main* method, create a background thread that spins in an infinite loop. Set thread priority to above normal.

```
Thread t1 = new Thread(new ThreadStart(() => {
    while (true) Thread.SpinWait(int.MaxValue); }));
t1.IsBackground = true;
t1.Priority=ThreadPriority.AboveNormal;
```

8. Similarly, create a second thread. Start both threads.

```
Thread t2 = new Thread(new ThreadStart(() => {
    while (true) Thread.SpinWait(int.MaxValue); }));
t2.IsBackground = true;
t2.Priority = ThreadPriority.AboveNormal;

t1.Start();
t2.Start();
```

9. Read from the console to prevent the application from exiting. Display an appropriate message. Build and run the application. The application will spin endlessly, consuming CPU cycles.

10. Start profiling the original application for the Concurrency Visualizer. With both applications running, the system will be noticeably less responsive. After five seconds, stop profiling. The Concurrency Visualizer will open. Revisit the CPU Utilization view. There is a noticeable variance in the graph. As expected, the amount of CPU utilization for other applications is much greater than before. This is because those applications are competing for processor resources.

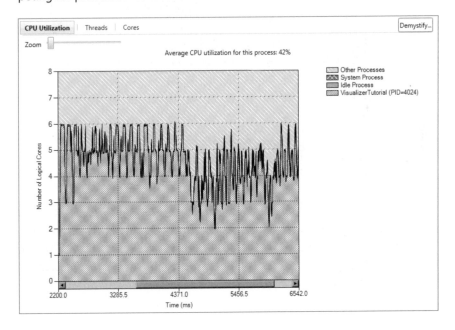

11. The Concurrency Visualizer will attempt to analyze synchronization events to provide instructive information. In this part of the tutorial, you will create two threads that compete for a lock. This can be shown in the Threads view. In the *Main* method, define a new object. The object is used for synchronization.

```
object sync = new object();
```

12. Create and start two identical threads. In each thread, lock on the synchronization object, and then sleep for a couple of seconds. This creates a race condition, and the second thread to reach the lock will block. That thread will remain blocked for around two seconds.

```
new Thread(new ThreadStart(() =>
{
    lock (sync)
    {
        Thread.Sleep(2000);
    }

})).Start();

new Thread(new ThreadStart(() =>
{
    lock (sync)
    {
        Thread.Sleep(2000);
    }

})).Start();
```

13. Rebuild the application and start profiling for the Concurrency Visualizer. Stop the profiling after 5 to 10 seconds. Open the Threads view. Find the two dependent threads in the graph. One of the threads starts with a synchronization segment. Select and point to that segment. The tooltip should confirm that the thread was blocked for nearly 2 seconds. A connector line appears. This vertical bar joins both threads participating in the synchronization.

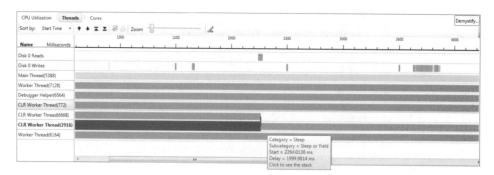

14. At the bottom of the Threads view, select the Current Stack tab to view the call stack of the selected thread. Double-click the last (bottom) method of the call stack. You will jump in the source code to the location of the synchronization, which is the lock statement. Next, select the Unblocking Stack tab to view the call stack of the other thread. Again, scroll to the bottom of the call stack. Double-click the last method. You will jump to the location in source code where the lock was released.

Congratulations! You now know where the lock originated and was released. Here is the complete application.

```
using System;
using System.Collections.Generic;
using System.Linq;
using System.Text;
using System.Threading;
using System.Threading.Tasks;

namespace VisualizerTutorial
{
    class Program
    {
        static void DoSomething()
        {
            Thread.SpinWait(int.MaxValue / 10);
        }

        static void ParallelLoop()
        {
            var numbers = Enumerable.Range(0, 1000);
            Parallel.ForEach(numbers, (number) =>
            {
                DoSomething();
            });
        }
        static void Main(string[] args)
        {
            new Thread(new ThreadStart(ParallelLoop)).Start();

            object sync = new object();
            new Thread(new ThreadStart(() =>
            {
                lock (sync)
                {
                    Thread.Sleep(2000);
                }

            })).Start();

            new Thread(new ThreadStart(() =>
```

```
        {
            lock (sync)
            {
                Thread.Sleep(2000);
            }

        })).Start();
        Console.WriteLine("Press enter to exit");
        Console.ReadLine();
    }
  }
}
```

The Sample Application

This is the source code for the application used earlier in this chapter.

```
using System;
using System.Collections.Generic;
using System.Linq;
using System.Text;
using System.Threading;
using System.Threading.Tasks;
using System.Diagnostics;

namespace Reporting_Example
{
    class XClass
    {
        public void MA(object param) { MB(param); }
        public void MB(object param) { MC(param); }

        object s1 = new object();
        object s2 = new object();

        public void MC(object param)
        {
            if (param == "1")
            {
                MD();
            }
            if (param == "2")
            {
                ME();
            }
            if (param == "3")
            {
                MF();
            }
        }

        public void MD()
        {
```

```csharp
        ME();
    }

    public void ME()
    {
        while (true) Thread.SpinWait(int.MaxValue / 20);
    }

    public void MF()
    {
        ML();
    }

    public void MG(object param)
    {
        MH(param);
    }

    public void MH(object param)
    {
        MI(param);
    }

    public void MI(object param)
    {
        if (param == "4")
        {
            MJ();
        }
        else
        {
            MK();
        }
    }

    public void MJ()
    {
        Monitor.Enter(s1);
        Thread.SpinWait(int.MaxValue / 20);
        Monitor.Enter(s2);
    }

    public void MK()
    {
        Monitor.Enter(s2);
        Thread.SpinWait(int.MaxValue / 10);
        Monitor.Enter(s1);
    }

    public void ML()
    {
        MM();
    }

    public void MM()
```

```
                {
                    while (true) { Thread.SpinWait(int.MaxValue / 3); Debugger.Break(); };
                }

            }

            class Program
            {
                static XClass obj = null;

                static void Main(string[] args)
                {
                    obj = new XClass();

                    Task.Factory.StartNew(obj.MA, "1");
                    Task.Factory.StartNew(obj.MA, "2");
                    Task.Factory.StartNew(obj.MA, "3");

                    Task.Factory.StartNew(obj.MG, "4");
                    Task.Factory.StartNew(obj.MG, "5");

                    Console.WriteLine("Press enter to exit");
                    Console.ReadLine();
                }
            }
        }
```

Summary

Visual Studio 2010 has been enhanced to assist in maintaining and debugging parallel applications. The enhancements include the introduction of new debugging windows and reports. Parallel programs are generally more sophisticated and complex than sequential programs. The Task Parallel Library (TPL) has done an excellent job of abstracting developers from the hardcore details and nuances of developing a parallel application. However, when something goes wrong, you need a new assortment of tools for debugging multicore applications. A suite of these tools is now available in Visual Studio 2010.

You can now create and open managed dumps for post-mortem analysis. This is especially beneficial for production debugging in which a full debugger might not be installed on the target machine. Dumps are also convenient for remote debugging. For these reasons, the integration of managed dumps into Visual Studio 2010 is helpful to all developers of managed applications, including programmers of parallel applications.

The Threads and Call Stack windows are not new to Visual Studio but are nonetheless useful when you are debugging a parallel application. The Threads window lists the active threads with details such as thread identifier, status of the thread, category of thread, and thread name. In the Threads window, you can flag a thread, freeze a thread, and switch context to a particular thread. The Call Stack window shows the call stack of the current thread.

The Parallel Tasks and Parallel Stacks windows are new in Visual Studio 2010. The Parallel Tasks window provides detailed information on each task. Task identifier, status of the task, location of the task, entry point method, and additional information are some of the details available. As in the Threads window, in the Parallel Tasks window you can flag a task or freeze the underlying thread. You can also jump to the source code for that task. There are two views of the Parallel Stacks window. The Threads view shows the call stacks for active threads. The Tasks view shows the call stacks from the perspective of active tasks. You can point to nodes in the Parallel Stacks window to get valuable information on either tasks or threads.

The Concurrency Visualizer works with the Visual Studio Profiler to provide detailed graphs and reports on the performance of a parallel application. The CPU Utilization view shows utilization of logical cores for the current process, system processes, all other processes, and idle time. The Threads view plots each thread along a timeline. Each thread is separated into segments based on different categories, such as execution, synchronization, I/O, sleep, and so on. The top rows of the Threads view are reserved for Disk Reads and Disk Writes. Finally, the Cores view maps thread execution to processor cores.

Quick Reference

To	Do this
View the current tasks of an application	Open the Parallel Tasks window by clicking the Debug menu and selecting Parallel Tasks Window.
Show additional detail about a particular item in a parallel debugging window	Point to the item.
Display the call stack from the perspective of parallel execution	Open the Parallel Stacks window by clicking the Debug menu and selecting the Parallel Stacks Window.
Scroll to a specific quadrant of a large Parallel Stacks window view	Use the Bird's Eye View button (in the lower-right corner) and pan the view (the shaded area).
Profile a parallel application	Start the Concurrency Visualizer by opening the Analyze menu and then select Launch Performance Wizard. In the Performance Wizard dialog box, choose the Concurrency option.
Create a report to display CPU utilization over a specific timeframe	In the Concurrency Visualizer, open the CPU Utilization view.
In a deadlock, identify the controlling thread	Open the Threads view of the Concurrency Visualizer. Select a deadlocked segment. In the report section (at the bottom), view the Unblocking Stack report.

Index

Donis Marshall

Donis Marshall has more than 20 years of experience using Microsoft technologies to design and build enterprise software for leading companies in several industries. As a Microsoft MVP, he is recognized as an exceptional technical community leader who actively shares his real-world expertise with others. Experienced in training developers and engineers with Microsoft products, Donis is the author of *Programming Microsoft Visual C# 2008*, *Solid Code*, and *Programming Microsoft Visual C# 2005*.